PROBLEMS AND EXERCISES FOR INTERMEDIATE MICROECONOMICS

Frank Westhoff
Amherst College

To accompany INTERMEDIATE MICROECONOMICS AND ITS APPLICATION

Sixth Edition

Walter Nicholson
Amherst College

THE DRYDEN PRESS
Chicago New York San Francisco
Philadelphia Montreal Toronto
London Sydney Tokyo

Cover Image: (Check)

Address for Editorial Correspondence
The Dryden Press, 301 Commerce Street, Suite 3700, Fort Worth, TX 76102

Address for Orders
The Dryden Press, 6277 Sea Harbor Drive, Orlando, FL 32887
1-800-782-4479, or 1-800-433-0001 (in Florida)

ISBN: 0-03-074811-9

Printed in the United States of America

3 4 5 6 7 8 9 0 1 2 095 9 8 7 6 5 4 3 2 1

The Dryden Press
Harcourt Brace College Publishers

TABLE OF CONTENTS

INTRODUCTION

This Study Guide will help you understand the material presented in *Intermediate Microeconomics and Its Application*, 6/e, by Walter Nicholson. It contains three elements to help you grasp the concepts presented in the textbook: walking tour summaries, multiple-choice questions, and running glossaries. Each walking tour summary and running glossary omits key words and replaces them with blanks. After studying a chapter, you should write the missing key words in the blanks in the left-hand margin. Also, you should answer the multiple-choice questions in the same manner. The answers appear at the end of each chapter.

I designed the Study Guide to keep you actively involved. You cannot simply skim through the following pages paying little attention to the material. You must continuously fill in the blanks. We hope that by being an active participant, rather than a passive spectator, you will learn the material faster and more thoroughly.

Frank Westhoff

PART 1

INTRODUCTION

CHAPTER 1

ECONOMIC MODELS

WALKING TOUR SUMMARIES

DEFINING ECONOMICS

1. ___________ ___________ exists because there are not enough productive resources available to satisfy all human wants. There is not enough land, labor, and capital to produce all the food, clothing, automobiles, furniture, etc. that we
2. ___________ human beings would like to consume. ___________ studies the allocation of scarce resources among alternative end uses. Economists strive to understand how decisions to use land, labor, and capital in alternative productive processes
3. ___________ are made. ___________ is the study of the economic choices individuals and firms make.

WHY ECONOMISTS USE THEORETICAL MODELS

Real-world economies are very complex. Every day thousands of firms and millions of households make thousands of millions of decisions. These decisions affect the allocation of scarce resources among alternative productive processes. It is impossible to describe all these decisions in complete detail; so, economists make

4. ___________ ___________ assumptions to formulate models.

SUPPLY AND DEMAND: THE DEVELOPMENT OF AN ECONOMIC MODEL

In *The Wealth of Nations* Adam Smith first observed
that the pattern of market-determined prices provided a
powerful "invisible hand" to direct resources into activities
5. ___________ where they are _________ valuable. Smith's explanation of
how prices are determined proved only partially correct,
however. Smith argued that a good's cost of production
determines its price. David Ricardo recognized that Smith's
view of price determination was incomplete. He introduced
6. ___________ the law of ___________ marginal returns. As more and
more of a good is produced the additional cost associated
7. ___________ with the production of one more unit ___________. Both
Smith and Ricardo only considered production when
explaining prices.

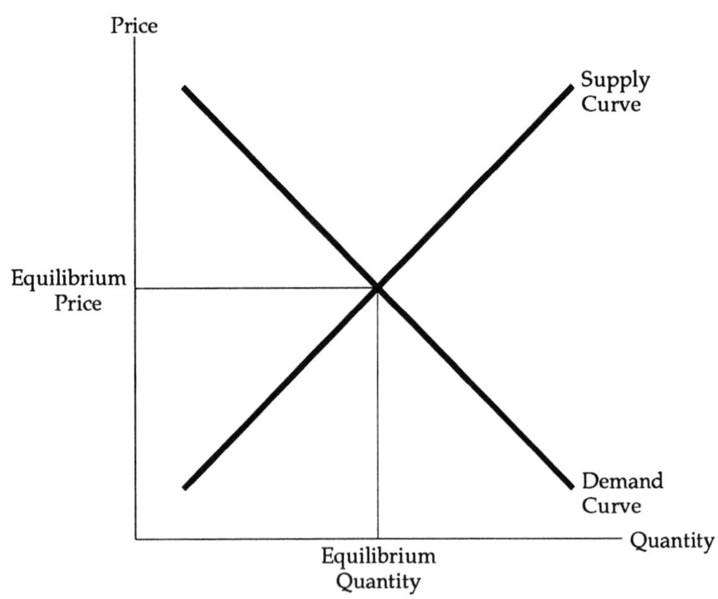

Figure 1.1: *Demand and Supply Curves*

Alfred Marshall extended Ricardo's notion of margin-
8. ___________ alism to include not only production, but also ___________.
He recognized that the ___________ unit consumed and
9. ___________ produced determines a good's value. As we consume more
and more of a good, we are not willing to pay as much for
10. ___________ the ___________ unit. That is, *marginal usefulness*
11. ___________ ______________ and the demand curve slopes
12. ___________ ___________. On the other hand, as firms produce more

and more of a good the change in total cost required to
13. __________ produce one additional unit __________. That is,
marginal cost increases and the supply curve slopes
14. __________ __________ . The demand and supply curves together
determine a good's exchange value. The intersection of the
15. __________ demand and supply curves illustrates the __________
16. __________ price. This is a __________ equilibrium model because it
depicts the determination of a single good's price.

MODELS OF MANY MARKETS

17. __________ A __________ equilibrium model describes the
interrelationship of the markets for all goods. The *production possibility curve* illustrates all the combinations of goods that can be produced from a fixed amount of resources. The
18. __________ production possibility curve slopes __________ reflecting
the opportunity cost of each good. The production possibility curve illustrates how much of one good must be sacrificed to produce more of another good.

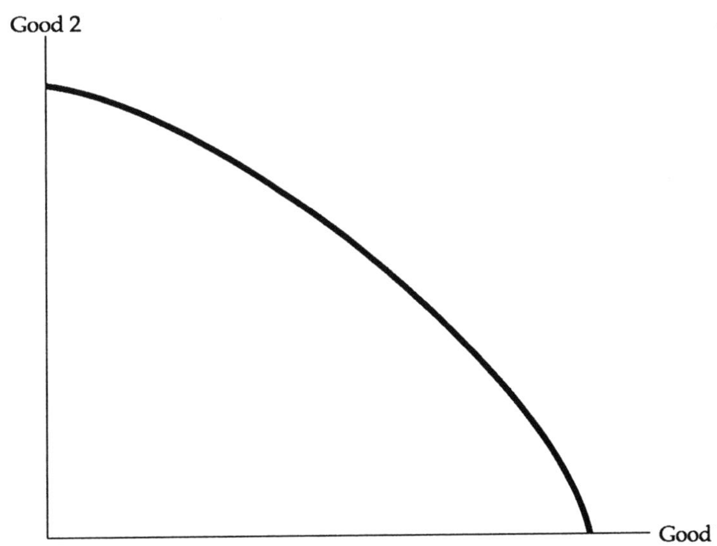

Figure 1.2: *Production Possibilities Curve*

HOW ECONOMISTS VERIFY THEORETICAL MODELS

Since models must make simplifying assumptions, they obviously ignore some aspects of the real world.
19. __________ Although by their nature models will __________ describe
all the complexities of the real world, economists strive to

develop models which capture the essence of the economic process. The following question then arises: How well does a model capture the crucial elements of the process it

20. ___________ purports to describe? We use two tests. The ___________ test of the assumptions tries to judge how closely the model's simplifying assumptions conform to reality. It is often difficult if not impossible to assess this, however. Furthermore, many economists object to this approach by contending that simplifying assumptions are necessarily

21. ___________ unrealistic. They advocate the use of the ___________ method: How well does a model explain and predict real-world events?

POSITIVE VERSUS NORMATIVE ECONOMICS

22. ___________ ___________ economics analyzes how and why resources are actually allocated in the economy.

23. ___________ ___________ analysis studies whether or not resources are allocated correctly.

MULTIPLE-CHOICE QUESTIONS

24. _____ Scarcity exists because
   a. the price of goods is too low.
   b. the price of goods is too high.
   c. there are not enough productive resources to satisfy all human wants.
   d. corporations seek to maximize profits.
   e. a and c.

25. _____ Economists study how
   a. scarce resources are allocated among alternative end uses.
   b. decisions to use land, labor, and capital in productive processes are made.
   c. firms make decisions.
   d. none of the above.
   e. a, b, and c.

26. _____ Productive processes do not include the
   a. growing of wheat.
   b. weaving of cloth.
   c. eating of food.
   d. production of missiles.
   e. a, b, and d.

27. _____ Scarcity exists in

a. less developed nations.
b. socialist nations.
c. capitalist nations.
d. industrialized nations.
e. all the above.

28. _____ In formulating models economists

a. make simplifying assumptions.
b. capture all the complexities of the real world.
c. prove how lazy they are.
d. ignore no aspects of the real world.
e. a and c.

29. _____ Direct tests to verify a model involve

a. seeing how well the model explains and predicts real-world events.
b. performing laboratory experiments.
c. seeing how closely the model's assumptions conform to reality.
d. replicating previously performed experiments.
e. all the above.

30. _____ Indirect tests to verify a model involve

a. seeing how well the model explains and predicts real-world events.
b. performing laboratory experiments.
c. seeing how closely the model's assumptions conform to reality.
d. replicating previously performed experiments.
e. a and b.

31. _____ Positive economics

a. studies how resources should be allocated.
b. studies only those aspects of economics about which all economists agree.
c. studies only those aspects of economics about which economists disagree.
d. describes how and why resources are allocated.
e. a and c.

32. _____ Normative economics

a. studies how resources should be allocated.
b. studies only those aspects of economics about which all economists agree.
c. studies only those aspects of economics about which economists disagree.
d. describes how and why resources are allocated.
e. a and c.

RUNNING GLOSSARY

33. ___________ ___________: the study of the economic choices individuals and firms make.

34. ___________ Models: simple theoretical descriptions that capture the ___________ of how the economy works.

35. ___________ Supply-demand model: a model describing how a good's price is determined by the behavior of the ___________ who buy the good and the firms that sell it.

36. ___________ Law of ___________ returns: hypothesis that the cost associated with producing one more unit of a good rises as more of that good is produced.

37. ___________ Equilibrium price: the price at which both buyers and sellers are in agreement about the ___________ of the good being sold.

38. ___________ Partial equilibrium model: an economic model of a ___________ market.

39. ___________ ___________ equilibrium model: an economic model of a complete system of markets.

40. ___________ Production possibility frontier: a graph showing all possible ___________ of goods that can be produced with a fixed amount of resources.

41. ___________ ___________ cost: the amount of one good that cannot be produced if more of another good is produced.

42. ____________ Direct approach: verifies an economic model by examining the validity of the ____________ on which the model is based.

43. ____________ ____________ approach: verifies an economic model by examining how accurately it predicts and explains real-world events.

44. ____________ ____________ economic analysis: theories that explain how resources actually are used in an economy.

ANSWERS

1. Scarcity
2. Economics
3. Microeconomics
4. simplifying
5. most
6. diminishing
7. increases
8. consumption
9. last
10. next
11. decreases
12. downward
13. increases
14. upward
15. equilibrium
16. partial
17. general
18. downward
19. never
20. direct
21. indirect
22. Positive
23. Normative
24. c
25. e
26. c
27. e
28. a
29. c
30. a
31. d
32. a
33. Microeconomics
34. essence
35. individuals
36. diminishing
37. quantity
38. single
39. General
40. combinations
41. Opportunity
42. assumptions
43. Indirect
44. Positive

CHAPTER 2

GRAPHICAL AND MATHEMATICAL TOOLS USED IN ECONOMICS

WALKING TOUR SUMMARIES

FUNCTIONS OF ONE VARIABLE: Y = f(X)

1. ____________ Y is a *function* of X. The value of Y depends on the value of X. Y is the __________ variable, X is the independent variable.

GRAPHING FUNCTIONS OF ONE VARIABLE

Linear Functions

2. ____________
3. ____________
4. ____________
5. ____________

The graph of a *linear function* is a __________ line. The *Y-intercept* is the value Y takes on when X is __________ . The *X-intercept* is the value X takes on when __________ is zero. The slope is the ratio of the change in Y to the __________ in X:

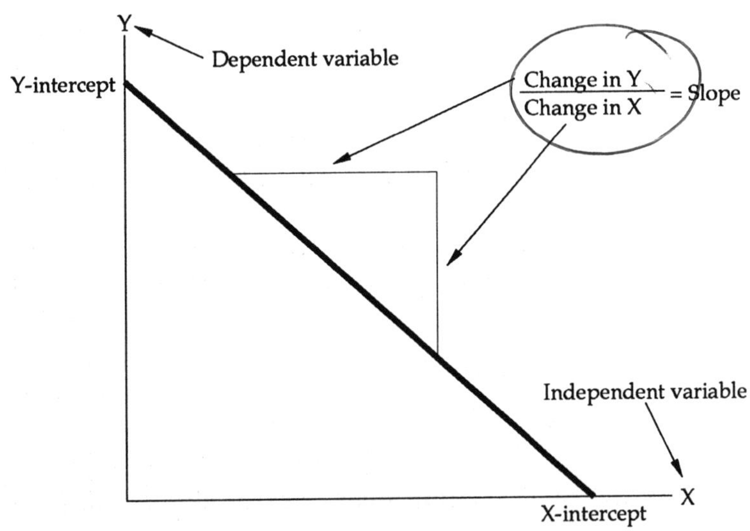

Figure 2.1: *Linear Function*

6. ____________ When the Y-intercept of a linear function changes, the graph of the function shifts up or down in a ________ fashion.

7. ____________ When the slope changes, the graph of the function rotates about its ________ intercept.

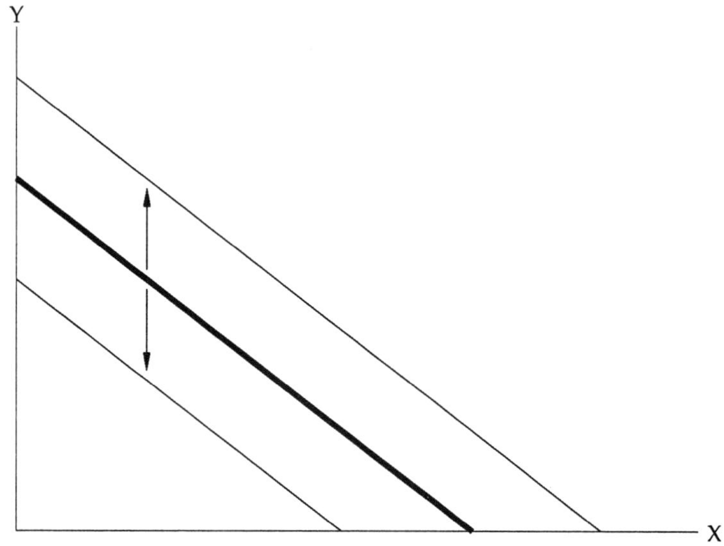

Figure 2.2: *Changes in the Y-intercept*

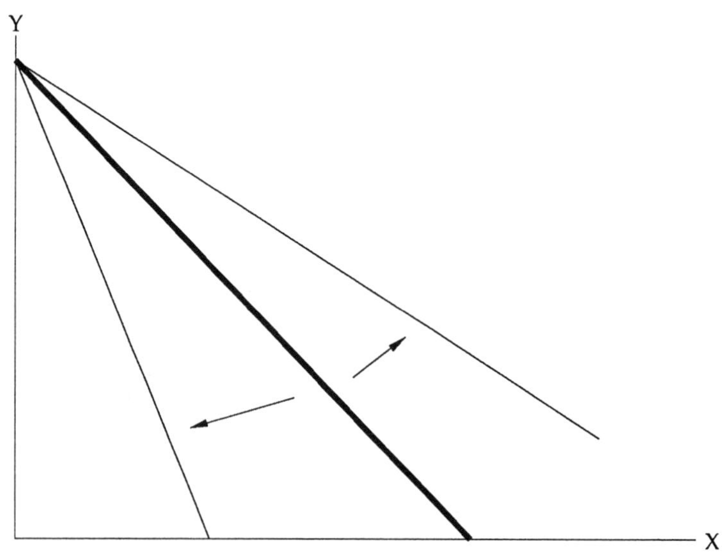

Figure 2.3: *Changes in the Slope*

Nonlinear Functions

8. ____________ The graph of a *nonlinear function* is a ________ line. The slope of a nonlinear function at a particular point is the

9. ____________ slope of the straight line, which is ________ to the function at that point:

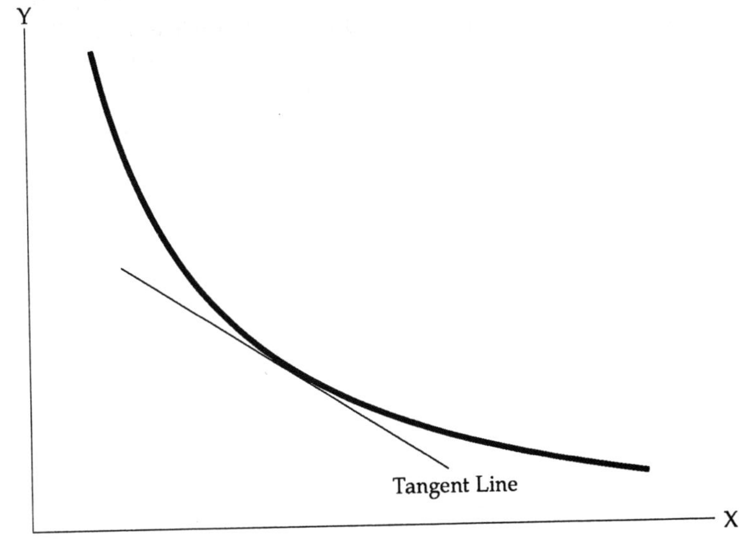

Figure 2.4: *Tangent Line for a Nonlinear Function*

10. ____________ The slope of a function equals ________ whenever the function reaches its maximum or minimum value.

FUNCTIONS OF TWO OR MORE VARIABLES: Y = f(X,Z)

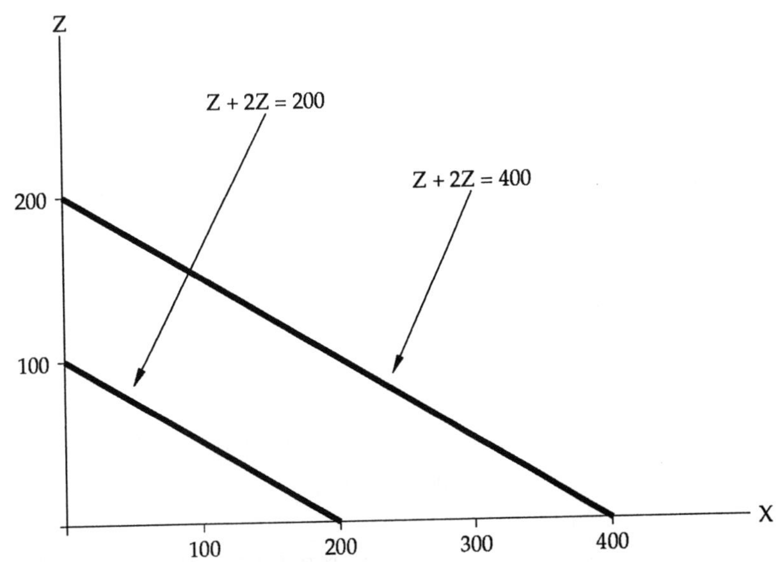

Figure 2.5: *Contour Lines for* $Y = X + 2Z$

Y is a function of X and Z. The value of Y depends on
11. ____________ the value of X and the value of Z. Y is the ________
12. ____________ variable; X and Z are the independent variables. ________
lines are used to graph functions of two or more variables. To draw a contour line first choose a constant value of Y. Then plot all the combinations of X and Z where f(X,Z) equal that constant on a graph. Repeat this procedure for several constant values of Y.

SIMULTANEOUS EQUATIONS

The most simple example of simultaneous equations is when two variables are related by two different linear equations. The solution can be illustrated by plotting the
13. ____________ two equations on the same graph. The point of ________
is the solution; that is, the point of intersection is the X and Y, which simultaneously meet the conditions of both equations. Figure 2.6 illustrates the solution for the equations Y=1.5X and Y=200-0.5X:

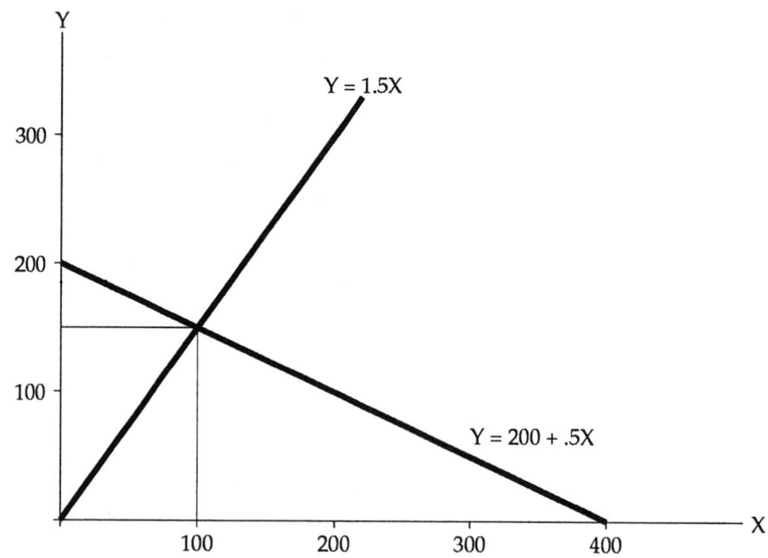

Figure 2.6: *Simultaneous Equations*

SPECIAL FEATURES OF MATHEMATICS IN ECONOMICS

First, most variables used in economics cannot take on negative values: for example, prices and quantities can be positive or zero, but never negative. Second, economists sometimes reverse the axes in a graph by putting the

14. ____________ ____________ variable on the vertical rather than horizontal axis: for example, with a supply or demand curve the

15. ____________ independent variable, ____________, is placed on the vertical

16. ____________ axis and the dependent variable, ____________, is placed on the horizontal axis.

MULTIPLE-CHOICE QUESTIONS

17. _______ If Y is a function of X then the
    a. values of X and Y are unrelated.
    b. values of X and Y are determined simultaneously.
    c. value of Y is determined by the value of X.
    d. value of X is determined by the value of Y.
    e. sum of X and Y is constant.

18. _______ If Y is a function of X then
    a. Y is called the dependent variable.
    b. X is called the dependent variable.
    c. Y is called the independent variable.
    d. X is called the independent variable.
    e. a and d.

19. _______ The graph of a linear function must be
    a. upward sloping.
    b. downward sloping.
    c. straight.
    d. curved.
    e. none of the above.

20. _______ The X-intercept of a linear function is
    a. the value X equals when Y equals 0.
    b. the value Y equals when X equals 0.
    c. where the function's graph intersects the X-axis.
    d. where the function's graph intersects the Y-axis.
    e. a and c.

21. _______ The Y-intercept of a linear function is
    a. the value X equals when Y equals 0.
    b. the value Y equals when X equals 0.
    c. where the function's graph intersects the X-axis.
    d. where the function's graph intersects the 45 degree line.
    e. b and d.

22. _______ The slope of a linear function equals

a. the X-intercept divided by the Y-intercept.
b. the Y-intercept divided by the X-intercept.
c. the change in X divided by the change in Y.
d. the change in Y divided by the change in X.
e. a and c.

23. _______ When the Y-intercept of a linear function changes with no change in slope the graph must

a. shift in a parallel fashion.
b. rotate about the X-intercept.
c. rotate about the Y-intercept.
d. shift toward the origin.
e. a and d.

24. _______ When the slope of a linear function changes with no change in the Y-intercept the graph must

a. shift in a parallel fashion.
b. rotate about the X-intercept.
c. rotate about the Y-intercept.
d. shift toward the origin.
e. a and b.

25. _______ The graph of a nonlinear function must be

a. upward sloping.
b. downward sloping.
c. straight.
d. curved.
e. none of the above.

26. _______ The slope of a nonlinear function at a particular point is the slope of the

a. secant line at that point.
b. straight line connecting the point and the origin.
c. straight line connecting the point and the X-intercept.
d. tangent line at that point.

27. _______ If Y is a function of X and Z then

a. the value of Y is determined by the values of X and Z.
b. X and Z are the dependent variables.
c. Y is the dependent variable.
d. X and Z are the independent variables.
e. a, c, and d.

28. ______ Contour lines are

a. always straight lines.
b. always curved lines.
c. always upward sloping.
d. always downward sloping.
e. used to graph functions of two or more variables.

29. ______ The points that lie on the same contour line must keep the value of the function

a. equal to zero.
b. constant.
c. positive.
d. negative.
e. equal to or greater than zero.

30. ______ Graphically the solution to a system of two equations is depicted by

a. the midpoint of their X-intercepts.
b. the midpoint of their Y-intercepts.
c. the intersection of the two equations.
d. none of the above.
e. a and b.

RUNNING GLOSSARY

31. ____________ ____________: the basic elements of algebra, usually called X, Y, etc., that may be given any numerical value in an equation.

32. ____________ Functional notation: a way of denoting the fact that the value of one variable (Y) ____________ on the value of another variable (X) or a set of variables.

33. ____________ Independent variable: a variable that is ____________ by the action of other variables and may be assigned any value.

34. ____________ ____________ variable: a variable whose value is determined by another variable or set of variables.

35. ____________ Linear function: an equation that is represented by a ____________ line graph.

36. ____________ Y-intercept: the value of Y when X equals ____________.

37. ____________ X-intercept: the value of ____________ when Y equals zero.

38. ____________ ____________ function: an equation that includes terms in X squared and (possibly) X.

39. ____________ Simultaneous equations: a set of equations with more than one variable that must be solved ____________ for a particular solution.

40. ____________ ____________: the use of small numbers at the bottom of variables to identify them as separate variables.

41. ____________ Contour lines: lines in two dimensions that show the sets of values of the independent variables that yield the ____________ value for the dependent variable.

ANSWERS

1. dependent
2. straight
3. zero
4. Y
5. change
6. parallel
7. Y
8. curved
9. tangent
10. zero
11. dependent
12. Contour
13. intersection
14. independent
15. price
16. quantity
17. c
18. e
19. c
20. e
21. b
22. d
23. a
24. c
25. d
26. d
27. e
28. e
29. b
30. c
31. Variables
32. depends
33. unaffected
34. Dependent
35. straight
36. zero
37. X
38. Quadratic
39. together
40. Subscripts
41. same

PART 1

INTRODUCTION

WALKING TOUR PROBLEMS

LINEAR EQUATION REVIEW

1. Consider the equation: $Y = 6 - 3X$

   a. Graph the line.

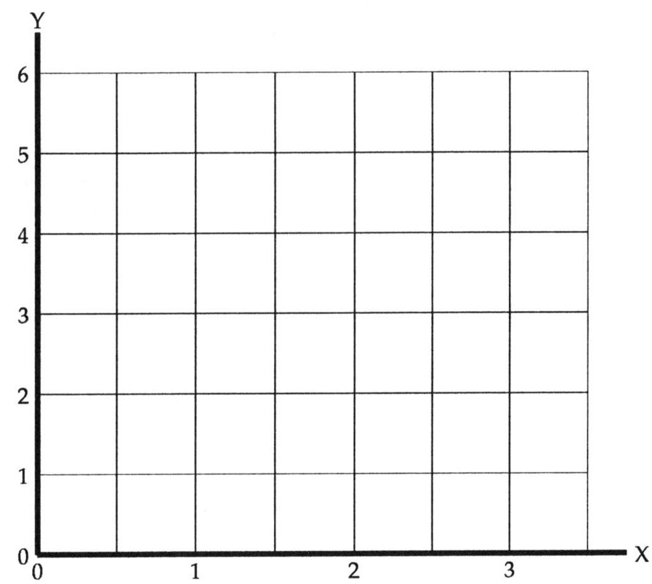

   b. What is the X-intercept?

1. ____________

2. ____________

The line described by the above equation crosses the X-axis at its X-intercept. Since Y is ____________ all along the X-axis, the X-intercept is what X equals whenever ____________ is 0.

$$0 = 6 - 3X$$
$$3X = 6$$
$$X = 2$$

The answer is 2.

c. What is the Y-intercept?

The line described by the above equation crosses the
3. __________ Y-axis at its Y-intercept. Since __________ is 0 all
4. __________ along the Y-axis, the Y-intercept is what __________
equals whenever X is 0.

$$Y = 6 - 2(0)$$
$$Y = 6$$

The answer is 6.0.

d. What is the slope?

5. __________ The __________ of a straight line is the ratio of the
change in Y to the change in X as one moves between
any two points on the line. To calculate the slope
first choose two points lying on the line. Then
determine how much Y changes between the two
6. __________ points and how much X changes. Last, __________
the change in Y by the change in X. We have already
found two points on the line, the two intercepts. The
7. __________ X-intercept is __________; hence, the point (2,0) is
on the line. The Y-intercept is 6; hence, the point
8. __________ (__________) is on the line also. Moving from the
X-intercept to the Y-intercept, X decreases by
9. __________ __________ (from 2 to 0) and Y increases by
10. __________ __________ (from 0 to 6). The slope is (6/–2) = -3.

The answer is –3.

2. Consider the equation: $8X + 4Y = 32$

a. Graph the line.

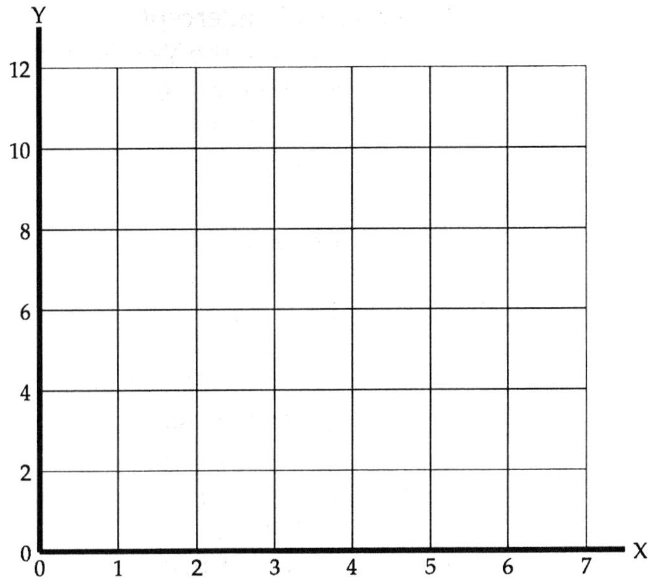

b. What is the X-intercept?

The line described by the above equation crosses the

11. ____________ ______-axis at its X-intercept. Y is zero all along the

12. ____________ ______-axis, the X-intercept is what X equals

13. ____________ whenever Y is __________.

$$8X + 4(0) = 32$$
$$8X = 32$$
$$X = 4$$

The answer is 4.

c. What is the Y-intercept?

The line described by the above equation crosses the

14. ____________ Y axis at the _____-intercept. X equals zero all along

15. ____________ the _____-axis, the Y-intercept is what Y equals

16. ____________ whenever ______ is zero.

$$8(0) + 4Y = 32$$
$$4Y = 32$$
$$Y = 8$$

The answer is 8.

d. What is the slope?

17. ____________ The slope of a straight line is the ____________ of the change in Y to the change in X as one moves between any two points on the line. To calculate the slope first choose two points lying on the line. Then determine how much Y changes between the two points and how much X changes. Last, divide the change in Y by the change in X. We have already found two points on the line, the two intercepts. The X-intercept is 4;
18. ____________ hence, the point (____________) is on the line. The Y-
19. ____________ intercept is ____________; hence, the point (0,8) is on the line also. Moving from the X-intercept to the Y-
20. ____________ intercept, X decreases by ____________ (from 4 to 0) and Y increases by 8 (from 0 to 8). The slope is $(8/-4) = -2$.

The answer is –2.

3. The equation is $4X + 12Y = -36$

21. ____________ a. What is the X-intercept?

22. ____________ b. What is the Y-intercept?

23. ____________ c. What is the slope?

4. The equation is $20X - 5Y = 100$

24. ____________ a. What is the X-intercept?

25. ____________ b. What is the Y-intercept?

26. ____________ c. What is the slope?

5. The equation is $Y = 25 - 5X$

27. ____________ a. What is the X-intercept?

28. ____________ b. What is the Y-intercept?

29. ____________ c. What is the slope?

CONTOUR LINE REVIEW

1. Consider the contour line XZ = 20 and the point X=5 and Z=3.

   a. Graph the contour line.

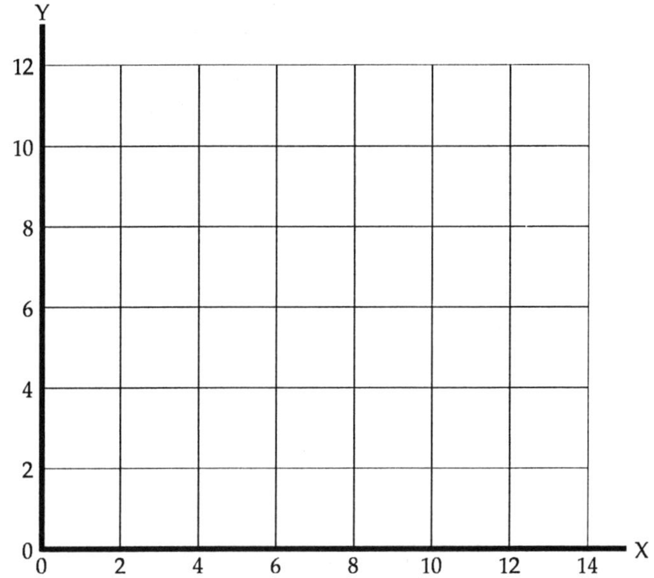

   b. Is the point below, above, or on the contour line?

   At the point X=5 and Z=3, the function XZ = (5)(3) =
30. ____________ ____________. Since 15 is less than 20, the point is
31. ____________ ____________ the contour line.

   The answer is below.

2. Consider the contour line XZ = 100 and the point X=20 and Z=6.

   a. Graph the contour line.

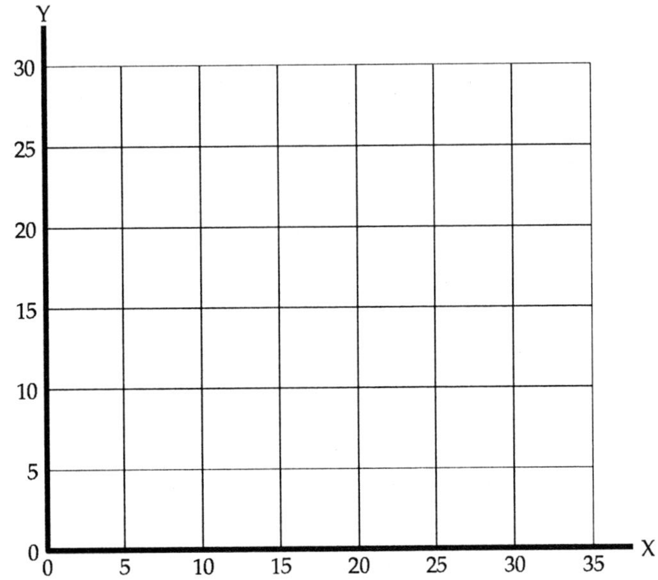

   b. Is the point below, above, or on the contour line?

      At the point X=20 and Z=6, the function XZ = (20)(6)
32. ____________ = 120. Since 120 is greater than ____________, the point is above the contour line.

      The answer is above.

3. Consider the contour line XZ = 160 and the point X=4 and Z=40. Is the point below, above, or on the contour
33. ____________ line?

4. Consider the contour line XZ = 10 and the point X=3 and
34. ____________ Z=4. Is the point below, above, or on the contour line?

5. Consider the contour line XZ = 50 and the point X=3 and
35. ____________ Z=20. Is the point below, above, or on the contour line?

ANSWERS

1. zero
2. Y
3. X
4. Y
5. slope
6. divide
7. 2
8. 0,6
9. 2
10. 6
11. X
12. X
13. zero
14. Y
15. Y
16. X
17. ratio
18. 4,0
19. 8
20. 4
21. –9
22. –3
23. –1/3
24. 5
25. –20
26. 4
27. 5
28. 25
29. –5
30. 15
31. below
32. 100
33. on
34. above
35. above

PART 2

CHOICE AND DEMAND

CHAPTER 3

THE ECONOMIC THEORY OF CHOICE

WALKING TOUR SUMMARIES

DEFINITION OF UTILITY

Economists define *utility* as the satisfaction an individual receives from the various activities he pursues. We shall focus our attention on two particular activities: the consumption of good X and the consumption of good Y. We represent the utility of an individual by the following function:

Utility = U(X, Y; other things).

The utility an individual receives depends on the quantity of
good X consumed, the quantity of good Y consumed, and
1. ___________ "other things." By using the ___________ paribus
assumption that "other things" do not change we can
simplify the utility function:

Utility = U(X, Y).

Economists use an individual's utility function to describe
2. ___________ how the individual ranks various ___________ of goods. In
our case a bundle of goods consists of a specific amount of
good X and a specific amount of good Y. If the individual
prefers a particular bundle of goods, bundle A, to a second
bundle of goods, bundle B, then the utility he derives from
3. ___________ A will ___________ the utility derived from B. If the
individual finds bundles A and B equally attractive, then the
4. ___________ utility of A will ___________ the utility of B. Last, if he
prefers bundle B to bundle A, the utility of B will
5. ___________ ___________ the utility of A.

ASSUMPTIONS ABOUT UTILITY

Consistency of Preferences

When considering any two bundles A and B, we assume that an individual will either prefer A to B, or prefer B to A, or will find them equally attractive. If this condition is met, we say that preferences are *complete.* Second, we assume that preferences are *transitive.* Consider three bundles A, B, and C. If an individual prefers A to B and
6. ____________ also prefers B to C, then he ____________ A to C.

More Is Better

An individual always prefers to consume more of a good.

MARGINAL RATE OF SUBSTITUTION (MRS)

7. ____________ An individual's *marginal rate of* ____________ of good
X for Y equals the amount of good Y the individual is willing to give up in order to get one additional unit of good X; it represents the ratio by which the individual is willing to substitute the goods. An individual's marginal rate of substitution depends upon the bundle of goods he is now consuming. As the individual consumer substitutes more and more X for Y, his marginal rate of substitution
8. ____________ ____________. We call this phenomenon *diminishing*
marginal rate of substitution.

INDIFFERENCE CURVES

9. ____________ To construct an ____________ *curve* for an individual
first choose a particular level of utility. The indifference curve illustrates all the different bundles that will provide the individual with the specified level of utility. That is, an indifference curve illustrates all the combinations of good X and good Y that will provide the individual with a particular level of utility. An indifference curve is a
10. ____________ ____________ line of the utility function. Whenever two
11. ____________ bundles lie on the ____________ indifference curve, the
individual finds them equally attractive. The individual prefers a bundle on the indifference curve to any bundle
12. ____________ lying ____________ the curve. He prefers any bundle lying
13. ____________ above to a bundle ____________ the indifference curve.

INDIFFERENCE CURVES AND THE MARGINAL RATE OF SUBSTITUTION

14. __________ The __________ of an individual's indifference curve shows how the individual can substitute the goods while remaining at the same level of utility. This slope equals the ratio by which the individual is willing to substitute good X for good Y, his marginal rate of substitution. The slope of an individual's indifference curve and his marginal rate of substitution represent the same thing.

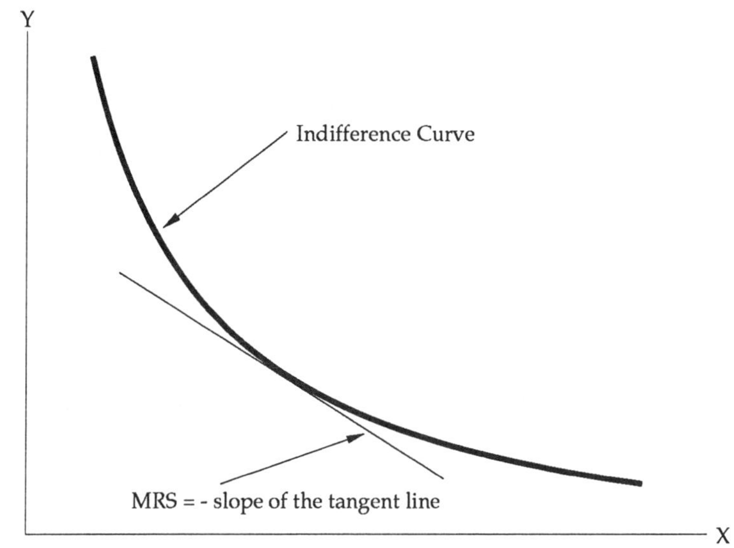

Figure 3.1: *Indifference Curve*

THE BUDGET CONSTRAINT

An individual's *budget constraint* illustrates all the bundles that the individual can afford with his fixed amount
15. __________ of __________. That is, an individual's budget constraint illustrates all the combinations of good X and good Y that the individual can afford. An individual cannot afford
16. __________ bundles that lie __________ his budget constraint. The
17. __________ __________-intercept of the budget constraint represents how much of good Y the individual could buy if he spent all his income on good Y. The Y-intercept just equals his income divided by the price of good Y, I/P_Y. Similarly, the
18. __________ __________-intercept equals I/P_X. The slope of the

19. ____________ budget constraint is the ____________ of the price ratio, $-(P_X/P_Y)$.

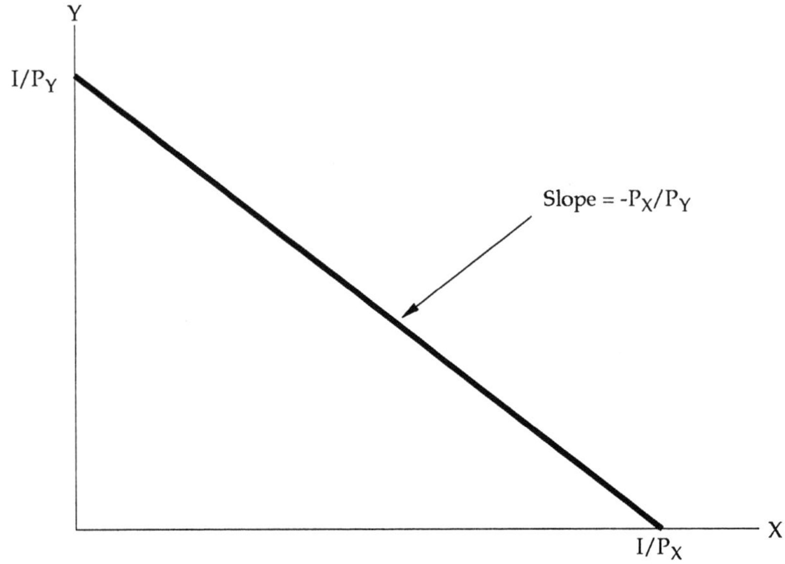

Figure 3.2: *Budget Constraint*

UTILITY MAXIMIZATION

Of all the bundles of goods an individual can afford, he will choose that bundle which provides him with the
20. ____________ ____________ utility. On the graph the individual will choose that bundle on his budget constraint which maximizes his utility. The individual's indifference curve passing through the utility maximizing bundle will be
21. ____________ ____________ to the budget constraint. In this situation any bundle that the individual prefers will lie ____________ his
22. ____________ budget constraint; he cannot afford to purchase any bundle
23. ____________ that he ____________. Note that when the individual maximizes his utility, the tangent line of the indifference
24. ____________ curve is the ____________ constraint. Thus, the slope of the indifference curve equals the slope of the budget line and
25. ____________ the marginal rate of ____________ equals the price ratio.

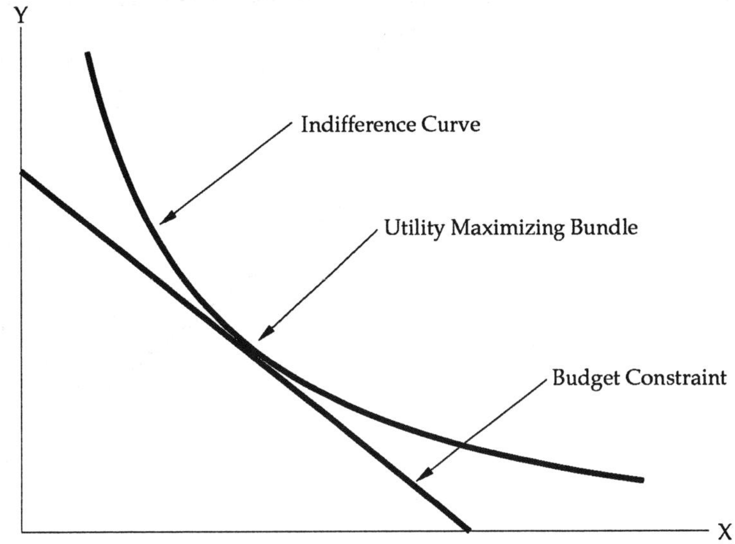

Figure 3.3: *Utility Maximization*

MULTIPLE-CHOICE QUESTIONS

26. ______ An individual's utility
    a. depends on the quantities of goods he consumes.
    b. refers to how valuable he is to society.
    c. is defined to be the satisfaction that he receives from the various activities he pursues.
    d. refers to how adaptable his job skills are.
    e. a and c.

27. ______ To economists a bundle of goods consists of
    a. all goods that can be bundled, that is, all goods that can be transported.
    b. the goods which individuals purchase at a supermarket.
    c. only goods that are perishable.
    d. specific amounts of all goods which individuals consume.
    e. a and b.

28. ______ Economists use utility functions to
    a. measure how much income an individual earns.
    b. describe how an individual ranks various bundles of goods.
    c. describe how firms decide upon the level of production.
    d. describe how firms decide upon the inputs to use.
    e. c and d.

29. ______ When comparing bundles A and B, an individual with consistent preferences will prefer

a. A to B only if he has transitive preferences.
b. A to B only if he can afford to buy A.
c. A to B only if he can afford to buy A, but cannot afford to buy B.
d. A to B, prefer B to A, or find A and B equally attractive.
e. B to A only if both can be afforded.

30. ______ If an individual who has transitive preferences prefers bundle A to B and prefers bundle B to C, then he prefers A to C

a. only if preferences are consistent.
b. only if A contains more of every good.
c. only if he can afford to purchase A.
d. only if he can afford to purchase both.
e. always.

31. ______ An individual's indifference curve

a. is downward sloping.
b. is upward sloping.
c. is a contour line of the utility function.
d. illustrates all the bundles an individual can afford to purchase.
e. a and c.

32. ______ If bundle A lies on an individual's indifference curve and bundle B lies on the same curve the individual

a. prefers A to B, if he can afford A.
b. prefers B to A, if he can afford B.
c. always finds A and B equally attractive.
d. always prefers A to B.
e. always prefers B to A.

33. ______ If bundle A lies on an individual's indifference curve and bundle B lies above the curve, the individual

a. prefers A to B, if he can afford A.
b. prefers B to A, if he can afford B.
c. always finds A and B equally attractive.
d. always prefers A to B.
e. always prefers B to A.

34. ______ If bundle A lies on an individual's indifference curve and bundle B lies below the curve, the individual

a. prefers A to B, if he can afford A.
b. prefers B to A, if he can afford B.
c. always finds A and B equally attractive.
d. always prefers A to B.
e. always prefers B to A.

35. ______ An individual's marginal rate of substitution of X for Y

a. represents the ratio by which the individual is willing to substitute good X for good Y.
b. depends on the bundle presently consumed.
c. represents the ratio by which the individual can trade goods in the marketplace.
d. always equals the price ratio.
e. a and b.

36. ______ Graphically, the marginal rate of substitution is indicated by the slope of the

a. line connecting the origin to the point on the individual's indifference curve that represents the bundle being consumed.
b. indifference curve at the point representing the bundle being consumed.
c. line connecting the origin to the point on the individual's utility function that represents the bundle being consumed.
d. utility function at the point representing the bundle being consumed.
e. b and d.

37. ______ As an individual substitutes more and more X for Y, his marginal rate of substitution of X for Y

a. typically increases.
b. typically decreases.
c. typically remains the same.
d. may increase or remain constant, but cannot decrease.
e. must increase.

38. ______ An individual's budget constraint

a. is upward sloping.
b. is a contour line of the utility function.
c. illustrates all the bundles the individual can afford to purchase.
d. a and b.
e. a and c.

39. ______ The slope of an individual's budget constraint

   a. is the negative of the price ratio.
   b. represents the ratio by which the individual can trade goods in the marketplace.
   c. represents the ratio by which the individual is willing to substitute good X for good Y.
   d. a and b.
   e. a and c.

40. ______ The Y-intercept of an individual's budget constraint equals

   a. his income divided by the price of Y.
   b. his income divided by the price of X.
   c. how much Y the individual can purchase if he buys no X and spends all his income on good Y.
   d. how much X the individual can purchase if he spends half his income on good X.
   e. a and c.

41. ______ When an individual maximizes his utility he consumes a bundle of goods that lies

   a. above the budget constraint.
   b. below the budget constraint.
   c. on the budget constraint.
   d. above his utility curve.
   e. none of the above.

42. ______ When an individual maximizes his utility

   a. the indifference curve passing through his bundle must be tangent to the budget line.
   b. his marginal rate of substitution equals the price ratio.
   c. his marginal rate of substitution must equal the slope of the utility function.
   d. all bundles that he prefers must lie above the budget line.
   e. a, b, and d.

RUNNING GLOSSARY

43. __________ Theory of choice: the interaction of preferences and __________ that causes people to make the choices they do.

44. __________ __________: the pleasure, satisfaction, or need fulfillment that people get from their economic activity.

45. __________ Ceteris paribus assumption: in economic analysis, holding all __________ factors constant so that only the factor being studied is allowed to change.

46. __________ __________ preferences: the assumption that an individual is able to state which of any two possible options is preferred.

47. __________ Transitivity of preferences: the property that if A is preferred to B, and B is preferred to C, then A must be __________ to C.

48. __________ Marginal rate of __________ (MRS): the rate at which an individual is willing to trade one good for another while remaining equally well-off.

49. __________ __________ curve: all the combinations of goods or services that provide the same level of utility.

50. __________ Indifference curve map: a __________ map that shows the utility an individual obtains from all possible consumption options.

51. __________ __________ constraint: the limit that income places on the combinations of goods and services that an individual can buy.

52. __________ Composite good: treating expenditures on several different goods whose relative prices do not change as a __________ good for convenience in analysis.

ANSWERS

1. ceteris
2. bundles
3. exceed
4. equal
5. exceed
6. prefers
7. substitution
8. decreases
9. indifference
10. contour
11. same
12. below
13. on
14. slope
15. income
16. on
17. Y
18. X
19. negative
20. most
21. tangent
22. above
23. prefers
24. budget
25. substitution
26. c
27. d
28. b
29. d
30. e
31. e
32. c
33. e
34. d
35. e
36. b
37. b
38. c
39. d
40. e
41. c
42. e
43. income
44. Utility
45. other
46. Complete
47. preferred
48. substitution
49. Indifference
50. contour
51. Budget
52. single

CHAPTER 4

HOW CHANGES IN INCOME AND PRICES AFFECT CHOICES

WALKING TOUR SUMMARIES

DEMAND FUNCTIONS

We have argued that the bundle of goods an
1. ____________ individual chooses depends upon his ____________ constraint and his preferences. The quantities of good X and Y demanded depends upon the budget constraint and
2. ____________ preferences. An individual's ____________ and the prices of X and Y determine his budget constraint. Therefore, we can represent his *demand function* with the following equation:

$$\text{Quantity of X Demanded} = X = d_X(P_X, P_Y, I; \text{preferences}).$$

HOMOGENEITY: WHAT HAPPENS WHEN ALL PRICES AND INCOME CHANGE BY THE SAME PERCENTAGE?

If all prices and income change by the same percentage, the quantities of X and Y demanded are
3. ____________ ____________. To understand why note that when all prices and income change by the same percentage, the budget
4. ____________ constraint is ____________. Thus, the individual will still choose the same bundle of goods.

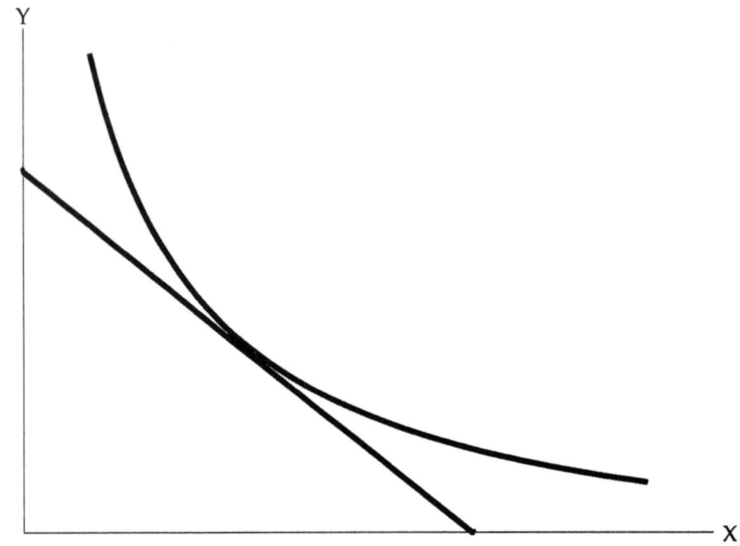

Figure 4.1: *All Prices Change by the Same Percentage*

CHANGE IN INCOME: WHAT HAPPENS WHEN INCOME ALONE CHANGES?

Whenever an individual's income rises and prices do not change, his budget constraint shifts out, away from the
5. ____________ origin. Since the __________ of the budget depends only on the ratio of prices, the slope does not change; thus, the
6. ____________ budget line shifts in a __________ fashion. Such a shift
7. ____________ causes an __________ effect. The income effect represents a change in real purchasing power; the individual can now afford bundles which contain more of both goods. The quantity of X that the individual demands after his income rises may increase, decrease, or remain the same.
8. ____________ Economists refer to a good as __________ whenever the quantity X demanded increases with a rise in income. Alternatively, if an increase in income causes the quantity
9. ____________ demanded to decrease, we call the good __________. An
10. ____________ __________ Curve illustrates the relationship between the quantity of X demanded and income.

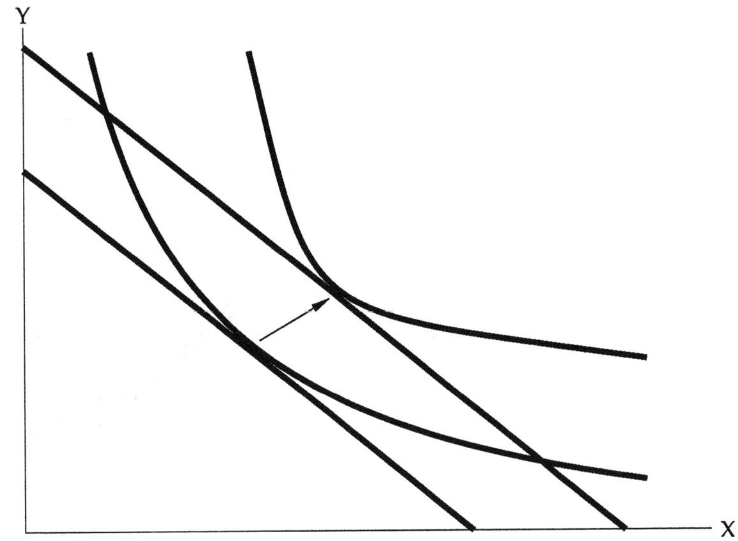

Figure 4.2: *Income Alone Changes*

CHANGE IN A GOOD'S PRICE: WHAT HAPPENS WHEN THE PRICE OF GOOD X ALONE CHANGES?

11. ____________
12. ____________
13. ____________
14. ____________

Whenever the price of good X falls the budget constraint shifts out, but not in a ____________ fashion. It rotates about the ____________-intercept becoming less steep. To understand why recall that the Y-intercept depicts the situation in which the individual spends all his income on good ____________. Since neither income nor the price of good Y has changed, the Y-intercept remains unchanged. The X-intercept (which depicts the situation in which the individual spends all his income on good X) ____________, however, because the price of good X has fallen.

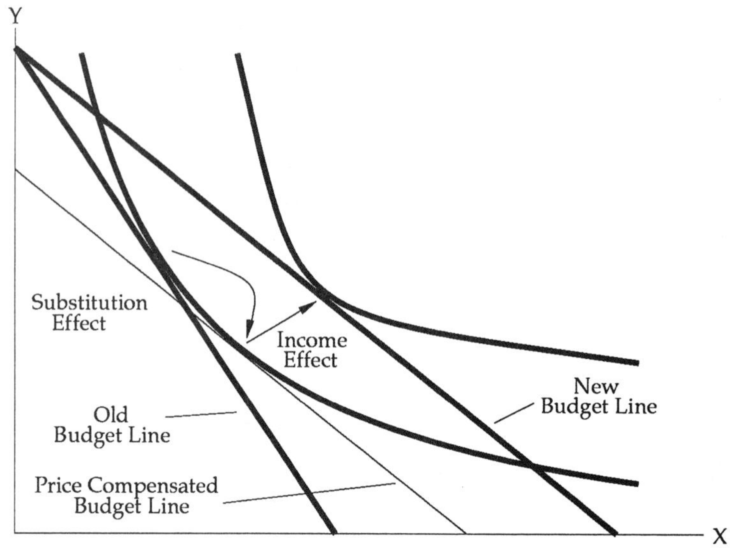

Figure 4.3: *Decrease in the Price of Good X*

Two effects now come into play. The change in the
slope of the budget constraint reflects the fact that good X
15. __________ has become __________ expensive relative to good Y.
Therefore, we would expect the individual to substitute
good X for good Y. If the individual were to stay on the
same indifference curve, he would now substitute X for Y.
16. __________ He would equate his marginal rate of ______________ to
17. __________ the new price ratio. As a result of this __________ effect,
the individual will consume more of good X and less of
good Y. Second, recall that the budget constraint has shifted
out. The fall in the price of X without any change in income
has increased the individual's real purchasing power. There
18. __________ is an __________ effect, also. The individual can now
afford bundles which contain more of both goods. As a
result of the income effect, the individual would consume
19. __________ more good X, if good X is a ______________ good. He
20. __________ would consume less X, if X is __________.

TOTAL EFFECT ON THE QUANTITY OF GOOD X DEMANDED WHEN THE PRICE OF GOOD X CHANGES

21. __________ Whenever good X is __________ the substitution
and income effects work together; a fall in the price of good
22. __________ X will unambiguously lead to a __________ quantity of X
demanded and vice versa. On the other hand, whenever

23. ____________ good X is ____________, the substitution and income effects work against each other. If the price of the good falls, the
24. ____________ substitution effect leads to an ____________ in the quantity
25. ____________ of X while the income effect leads to a ____________. With
26. ____________ an ____________ good the net result depends upon which of the two effects is stronger. A fall in the price decreases the
27. ____________ quantity demanded whenever the ________________ effect
28. ____________ dominates. Economists refer to such cases as ____________ Paradox.

SUBSTITUTES AND COMPLEMENTS

Good X is a (gross) *substitute* for good Y if an increase
29. ____________ in the price of good Y ____________ the quantity of good X
30. ____________ demanded. Good X is a (gross) ____________ of good Y if an increase in the price of good Y decreases the quantity of good demanded.

INDIVIDUAL DEMAND CURVE

An *individual's demand curve* for good X illustrates the relationship between the quantity of good X demanded by the individual and the price of good X. Along a single demand curve, all factors which affect demand besides the price of the good itself do not change. The demand curve for good X will be downward sloping unless the good is a
31. ____________ ____________ good. The demand curve can shift only when a factor relevant to the demand for good X other than the
32. ____________ __________ of good X itself changes. When this happens a
33. ____________ change in ____________ occurs. If the demand curve shifts
34. ____________ to the right, there is an ____________ in demand. If it shifts
35. ____________ to the left, there is a __________ in demand. A change in the price of good X itself never causes the demand curve to
36. ____________ ____________, but rather leads to a movement
37. ____________ ____________ the demand curve. Economists refer to a movement along a demand curve as a change in the
38. ____________ ____________ demanded. An increase in the price of X
39. ____________ ____________ the quantity of good X demanded unless the good is a Giffen good. Alternatively, a decrease in the price increases the quantity demanded.

MULTIPLE-CHOICE QUESTIONS

40. ______ When all prices and income increase by the same percentage an individual's budget constraint will
    a. shift outwards in a parallel fashion.
    b. shift inwards in a parallel fashion.
    c. remain stationary.
    d. shift outwards by rotating about the Y-intercept.
    e. shift outwards by rotating about the X-intercept.

41. ______ When all prices and income increase by the same percentage the quantity of good X demanded will
    a. increase only if X is a normal good.
    b. increase only if X is an inferior good.
    c. always remain the same.
    d. always increase.
    e. always decrease.

42. ______ When income alone increases, an individual's budget constraint will
    a. shift outwards in a parallel fashion.
    b. shift inwards in a parallel fashion.
    c. remain stationary.
    d. shift outwards by rotating about the Y-intercept.
    e. shift outwards by rotating about the X-intercept.

43. ______ When income alone increases, the quantity of X an individual demands will
    a. increase only if X is a normal good.
    b. increase only if X is an inferior good.
    c. always remain the same.
    d. always increase.
    e. always decrease.

44. ______ The Engel curve relates quantity demanded to changes in
    a. price only.
    b. income only.
    c. price and income.
    d. utility.
    e. the marginal rate of substitution.

45. ______ If the quantity demanded increases whenever income rises the good is called
   a. a Giffen good.
   b. a normal good.
   c. an inferior good.
   d. a necessity.
   e. b and d.

46. ______ If the quantity demanded decreases whenever income rises the good is called
   a. a Giffen good.
   b. a normal good.
   c. an inferior good.
   d. a necessity.
   e. a and c.

47. ______ Whenever the price of good X alone decreases, the budget constraint will
   a. shift outwards in a parallel fashion.
   b. shift inwards in a parallel fashion.
   c. remain stationary.
   d. shift outwards by rotating about the Y-intercept.
   e. shift outwards by rotating about the X-intercept.

48. ______ Whenever the price of good X alone decreases, the substitution effect causes the quantity of good X to
   a. increase always.
   b. decrease always.
   c. increase only if good X is normal.
   d. increase only if good X is inferior.
   e. remain unchanged always.

49. ______ Whenever the price of good X alone decreases, the income effect causes the quantity of good X to
   a. increase always.
   b. decrease always.
   c. increase only if good X is normal.
   d. increase only if good X is inferior.
   e. remain unchanged always.

50. ______ If the good is normal and its price falls, the quantity demanded
   a. will increase always.
   b. will decrease always.
   c. will remain the same always.
   d. may increase, decrease, or remain the same.
   e. will never increase.

51. ______ If the good is inferior and its price falls, the quantity demanded
   a. will increase always.
   b. will decrease always.
   c. will remain the same always.
   d. may increase, decrease, or remain the same.
   e. will never increase.

52. ______ If the quantity demanded increases whenever the price increases, the good is called
   a. a Giffen good.
   b. a normal good.
   c. an inferior good.
   d. a necessity.
   e. b and d.

53. ______ If a good is a Giffen good, the good is
   a. normal and the income effect dominates the substitution effect.
   b. normal and the substitution effect dominates the income effect.
   c. inferior and the income effect dominates the substitution effect.
   d. inferior and the substitution effect dominates the income effect.
   e. none of the above.

54. ______ If an increase in the price of good Y leads to an increase in the quantity of good X demanded, good X is
   a. a Giffen good relative to good Y.
   b. an inferior good relative to good Y.
   c. a (gross) substitute of good Y.
   d. a (gross) complement of good Y.
   e. a normal good.

55. ______ If an increase in the price of good Y leads to a decrease in the quantity of good X demanded, good X is

a. a Giffen good relative to good Y.
b. an inferior good relative to good Y.
c. a (gross) substitute of good Y.
d. a (gross) complement of good Y.
e. a normal good.

56. ______ An individual's demand curve for good X illustrates the quantity demanded for

a. every price of good X holding all other factors (relevant to the demand for good X) constant.
b. every income level holding all other factors (relevant to the demand for good X) constant.
c. every price of good Y holding all other factors (relevant to the demand for good X) constant.
d. every price of good X, good Y, and income level.
e. none of the above.

57. ______ An individual's demand curve for good X shifts only when

a. the price of good X changes.
b. any factor relevant to the demand of good X changes.
c. income changes.
d. some factor relevant to the demand for good X other than the price of good X itself changes.
e. a and c.

58. ______ If good X is not a Giffen good, an increase in the price of good X leads to

a. an increase in demand.
b. a decrease in demand.
c. an increase in the quantity demanded.
d. a decrease in the quantity demanded.
e. b and d.

59. ______ If good X is a normal good, an increase in income leads to

a. an increase in demand.
b. a decrease in demand.
c. an increase in the quantity demanded.
d. a decrease in the quantity demanded.
e. b and d.

RUNNING GLOSSARY

60. ____________ ____________ statics: the investigation of new choices people make when conditions change, as compared to the choices they make under the former conditions.

61. ____________ Demand function: a representation of how quantity demanded depends on ____________, income, and preferences.

62. ____________ Homogeneous demand function: demand does not change when prices and income increase in the same ____________.

63. ____________ ____________ good: a good that is bought in greater quantities as income increases.

64. ____________ Substitution effect: the part of the change in quantity demanded of a good whose price has changed that is caused by substitution of the good that is now relatively __________ for the other that is now relatively more costly. A

65. ____________ movement ________ an indifference curve.

66. ____________ ____________ effect: the part of the change in quantity demanded of a good whose price has changed that is caused by the change in real purchasing power that results from the price change.

67. ____________ Giffen's paradox: a situation in which the increase in a good's price leads people to consume ____________ of the good.

68. ____________ Complements: two goods such that when the price of one increases, the quantity demanded of the other ____________.

69. ____________ ____________: two goods such that if the price of one increases, the quantity demanded of the other rises.

70. ____________ Individual demand curve: a graphic representation of the relationship between the ____________ of a good and the quantity of it demanded by a person.

71. ____________ Increase or decrease in ___________ demanded: the increase or decrease in quantity demanded caused by a change in the good's price. Graphically represented by the

72. ____________ movement ___________ a demand curve.

73. ____________ Increase or decrease in ___________: the change in demand for a good caused by changes in the price of another good, income, or preferences. Graphically represented by a

74. ____________ ___________ of the entire demand curve.

ANSWERS

1. budget
2. income
3. unaffected
4. unchanged
5. slope
6. parallel
7. income
8. normal
9. inferior
10. Engle
11. parallel
12. Y
13. Y
14. increases
15. less
16. substitution
17. substitution
18. income
19. normal
20. inferior
21. normal
22. greater
23. inferior
24. increase
25. decrease
26. inferior
27. income
28. Giffin's
29. increases
30. complement
31. Giffen
32. price
33. demand
34. increase
35. decrease
36. shift
37. along
38. quantity
39. decreases
40. c
41. c
42. a
43. a
44. b
45. b
46. c
47. d
48. a
49. c
50. a
51. d
52. a
53. c
54. c
55. d
56. a
57. d
58. d
59. a
60. Comparative
61. prices
62. proportion
63. Normal
64. cheaper
65. along
66. income
67. more
68. falls
69. Substitutes
70. price
71. quantity
72. along
73. demand
74. shift

CHAPTER 5

MARKET DEMAND AND ELASTICITY

WALKING TOUR SUMMARIES

MARKET DEMAND CURVES

A market demand curve illustrates the relationship between the quantity of a good demanded by all potential
1. __________ buyers and the __________ of the good. All other factors which influence demand other than the price of the good itself are held constant. We construct a market demand curve by summing each individual's demand curve
2. __________ __________:

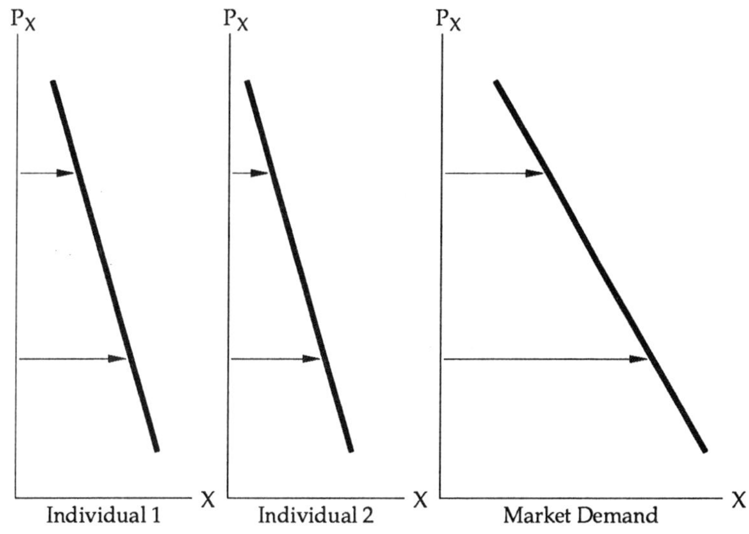

Figure 5.1: *Construction of the Market Demand Curve*

A market demand curve can shift only when
3. __________ something other than the __________ of the good itself changes. Economists refer to a shift of the curve as a
4. __________ __________ in demand. A change in the price of the good itself will never cause the market demand curve to shift. A change in the good's price will cause a movement
5. __________ __________ the market demand curve, however. We refer

to a movement along the curve as a change in the

6. ____________ ____________ demanded.

ELASTICITY

Economists use the notion of elasticity to quantify the relationship between two variables. The price elasticity of demand allows us to estimate by how much the quantity demanded will change when the price of a good changes. It is important to remember that elasticities are always

7. ____________ calculated in ____________ terms.

PRICE ELASTICITY OF DEMAND ($e_{Q,P}$)

The price elasticity of demand measures how

8. ____________ sensitive the quantity demanded is to the ____________. More specifically, the price elasticity of demand equals the percent change in quantity demanded resulting from a one

9. ____________ ____________ change in the price:

$$e_{Q,P} = \frac{\text{Percent Change in Q}}{\text{Percent Change in P}}$$

Except in the case of Giffen's Paradox, the price elasticity of

10. ____________ demand will be ____________.

If the quantity demanded is "very" sensitive to price,

11. ____________ demand is ____________. More specifically, demand is elastic when a 1 percent change in price leads to a more than 1 percent change in quantity demanded. In mathematical

12. ____________ terms, when $e_{Q,P}$ is ____________ than -1, demand is elastic. On the other hand, if the quantity demanded is "not very"

13. ____________ sensitive to price, demand is ____________. More specifically, demand is inelastic when a 1 percent change in price leads to a less than 1 percent change in quantity

14. ____________ demanded. When $e_{Q,P}$ is ____________ than -1, demand is

15. ____________ inelastic. Last, if $e_{Q,P}$ equals -1, demand is ____________ elastic.

PRICE ELASTICITY AND TOTAL EXPENDITURES

Price elasticity of demand explains how total expenditures individuals make to buy a good will respond to price changes. Note that:

Total Expenditures = Price × Quantity.

16. __________ Except for a Giffin good quantity will __________ when
the price decreases and vice versa. Thus, the effect of a price
change on total expenditures depends on whether a price
change leads to a "large" or "small" change in the
17. __________ __________. That is, the effect depends on the price
18. __________ __________ of demand. If demand is elastic, the quantity
demanded is "very" sensitive to the price. A fall in the price
will lead to a "large" increase in quantity causing an
19. __________ __________ in total expenditures. A rise in the price will
20. __________ cause a __________ in total expenditures. On the other
hand, if demand is inelastic, the quantity demanded is "not
very" sensitive to the price. A fall in the price will lead to a
21. __________ "small" increase in quantity causing a __________ in total
22. __________ expenditures. A rise in the price will cause an __________
in total expenditures.

IS THE PRICE ELASTICITY OF DEMAND CONSTANT?

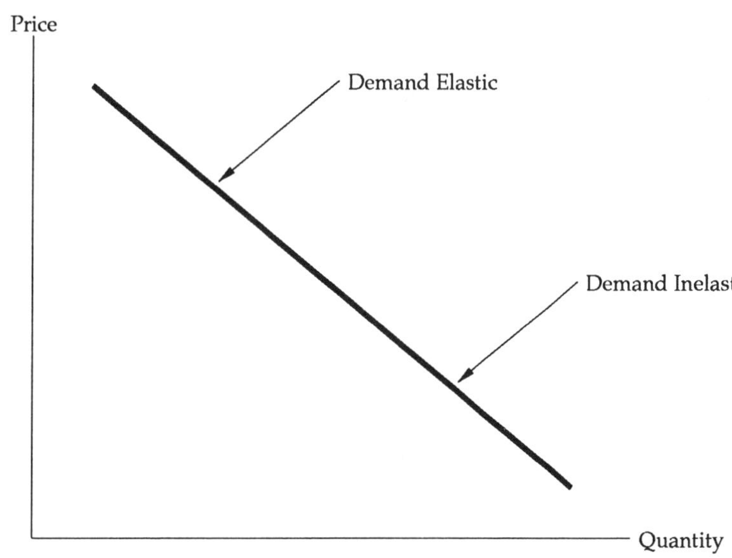

Figure 5.2: *Linear Demand Curve and Elasticity*

The price elasticity of demand need not be the same
at all points on a demand curve. In fact, if the demand
curve is linear (a straight line), the price elasticity of demand
is different at every point. At high prices demand is
23. __________ __________, at low prices demand is inelastic. Note that
the linear case illustrates that slope and elasticity are

different. All points on a linear demand curve have the
24. ___________ same ___________, but they do not have the same elasticity.

INCOME ELASTICITY OF DEMAND

The *income elasticity of demand* measures how sensitive the quantity demanded is to a change in income. More specifically, the income elasticity of demand equals the percent change in the quantity demanded resulting from a
25. ___________ one ___________ change in income:

$$e_{Q,I} = \frac{\text{Percent Change in Q}}{\text{Percent Change in I}}$$

26. ___________ The income elasticity is ___________ for a normal good and
27. ___________ ___________ for an inferior good. Goods for which the
28. ___________ income elasticity exceeds one are called ___________.

CROSS-PRICE ELASTICITY OF DEMAND

The *cross-price elasticity of demand* measures how sensitive the quantity demanded of one good is to a change
29. ___________ in the ___________ of another good. More specifically, the cross-price elasticity of demand equals the ___________
30. ___________ change in the quantity demanded of one good resulting from a one percent change in the price of another good:

$$e_{Q,P'} = \frac{\text{Percent Change in Q}}{\text{Percent Change in P'}}$$

where P' represents the price of the other good.

EMPIRICAL STUDIES OF DEMAND

The most serious difficulty in estimating demand elasticities concerns the *ceteris paribus* assumption. The price elasticity of demand implicitly assumes that only one
31. ___________ determinant of demand, the ___________, changes. Similarly, the income elasticity implicitly assumes that only
32. ___________ ___________ changes. In the real world it is virtually impossible to observe a situation in which only one determinant of demand changes; many factors are changing simultaneously. Fortunately, multiple regression analysis

provides economists with a statistical technique that isolates the effect of a single factor.

MULTIPLE-CHOICE QUESTIONS

33. ______ A good's market demand curve indicates the quantity of the good demanded by
    a. one individual buyer.
    b. all individual buyers who historically purchase the good.
    c. all potential buyers.
    d. the average individual buyer.
    e. b and d.

34. ______ The market demand curve for good X illustrates the quantity demanded by all potential buyers for
    a. every price of good X holding all other factors (relevant to the demand for good X) constant.
    b. every income level holding all other factors (relevant to the demand for good X) constant.
    c. every price of good Y holding all other factors (relevant to the demand for good X) constant.
    d. every price of good X, good Y, and income level.
    e. a and b.

35. ______ The market demand curve for good X shifts only when
    a. the price of good X changes.
    b. any factor relevant to the demand of good X changes.
    c. income changes.
    d. some factor relevant to the demand for good X other than the price of good X changes.
    e. a and d.

36. ______ The market demand curve can be constructed by summing each individual's
    a. Engel curve horizontally.
    b. Engel curve vertically.
    c. demand curve horizontally.
    d. demand curve vertically.
    e. Engel and demand curves horizontally.

37. ______ The price elasticity of demand illustrates how sensitive the quantity demanded is to a change in

a. its own price.
b. income.
c. the price of another good.
d. utility.
e. the marginal rate of substitution.

38. ______ The price elasticity of demand equals

a. the change in the quantity demanded caused by a 1 unit (1 dollar) change in price.
b. the percent change in the quantity demanded caused by a 1 percent change in price.
c. the ratio of the change in the quantity demanded to the change in the price.
d. the ratio of the percent change in the quantity demanded to the percent change in the price.
e. b and d.

39. ______ If a good is a Giffen good, the elasticity of demand must be

a. negative.
b. positive.
c. one.
d. minus one.
e. less than or equal to zero.

40. ______ If the quantity demanded is "very" sensitive to a change in the price, that is, if a 1 percent change in the price leads to a greater than 1 percent change in quantity demanded, then

a. the price elasticity of demand is less than -1.
b. the price elasticity of demand is greater than -1.
c. demand is said to be unit elastic.
d. demand is said to be inelastic.
e. a and c.

41. ______ If the quantity demanded is "not very" sensitive to a change in the price, that is, if a 1 percent change in the price leads to a less than 1 percent change in quantity demanded, then

a. the price elasticity of demand is less than -1.
b. the price elasticity of demand equals -1.
c. demand is said to be elastic.
d. demand is said to be inelastic.
e. demand is said to be unit elastic.

42. ______ If a 1 percent change in the price leads to a 1 percent change in quantity demanded, then

a. the price elasticity of demand is less than -1.
b. the price elasticity of demand is greater than -1.
c. the price elasticity of demand equals -1.
d. demand is said to be elastic.
e. demand is said to be unit inelastic.

43. ______ If the price of a good whose demand is elastic falls, the total expenditures individuals make to purchase the good

a. must increase.
b. must decrease.
c. must remain the same.
d. may increase, decrease, or remain the same.
e. may decrease or remain the same, but cannot increase.

44. ______ If the price of a good whose demand is inelastic falls, the total expenditures individuals make to purchase the good

a. must increase.
b. must decrease.
c. must remain the same.
d. may increase, decrease, or remain the same.
e. will never decrease.

45. ______ If the price of a good whose demand is unit elastic falls, the total expenditures individuals make to purchase the good

a. must increase.
b. must decrease.
c. must remain the same.
d. may increase, decrease, or remain the same.
e. none of the above.

46. ______ A straight line demand curve

a. has price elasticity equal to 1 at all prices.
b. has the same price elasticity at all prices.
c. is elastic at low prices and inelastic at high prices.
d. is inelastic at low prices and elastic at high prices.
e. has a constant marginal rate of substitution.

47. ______ The income elasticity equals

a. the change in the quantity demanded caused by a 1 unit (1 dollar) change in income.
b. the percent change in the quantity demanded caused by a 1 percent change in income.
c. the ratio of the change in the quantity demanded to the change in income.
d. the ratio of the percent change in the quantity demanded to the percent change in the price.
e. b and d.

48. ______ The income elasticity of a normal good is

a. never positive.
b. always positive.
c. always negative.
d. always zero.
e. always one.

49. ______ The income elasticity of an inferior good is

a. always positive.
b. always negative.
c. always zero.
d. always one.
e. never negative.

RUNNING GLOSSARY

50. ____________ ____________ demand: the total quantity of a good or service demanded by potential buyers.

51. ____________ Market demand curve: the relationship between the total quantity demanded of a good or service and its ________ holding all other factors constant.

52. ____________ Elasticity: the measure of the percent change in one variable brought about by a ________ percent change in some other variable.

53. ____________ ________ elasticity of demand: the percent change in the quantity demanded of a good in response to a one percent change in its price.

54. ____________ Income elasticity of demand: the percent change in the quantity demanded of a good in response to a 1 percent change in __________.

55. ____________ __________ price elasticity of demand: the percent change in the quantity demanded of a good in response to a 1 percent change in the price of another good.

ANSWERS

1. price
2. horizontally
3. price
4. change
5. along
6. quantity
7. percentage
8. price
9. percent
10. negative
11. elastic
12. less
13. inelastic
14. greater
15. unit
16. increase
17. quantity
18. elasticity
19. increase
20. decrease
21. decrease
22. increase
23. elastic
24. slope
25. percent
26. positive
27. negative
28. luxuries
29. price
30. percent
31. price
32. income
33. c
34. a
35. d
36. c
37. a
38. e
39. b
40. a
41. d
42. c
43. a
44. b
45. c
46. d
47. b
48. b
49. b
50. Market
51. price
52. one
53. Price
54. income
55. Cross-

CHAPTER 6

FURTHER APPLICATIONS OF THE THEORY OF CHOICE

WALKING TOUR SUMMARIES

COMPENSATED DEMAND CURVES

An ordinary demand curve illustrates how the quantity demanded of a good changes when the good's price changes, while keeping all other prices and
1. ____________ ____________ unchanged. As one moves on a standard demand curve, utility changes. For example, when the price of good X increases, the budget constraint rotates inward,
2. ____________ making the consumer ____________ off:

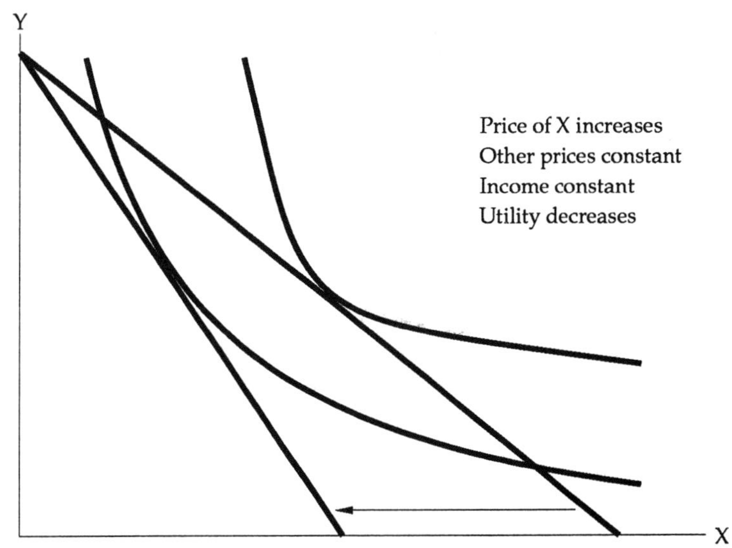

Figure 6.1: *Derivation of an Ordinary Demand Curve*

When moving along an ordinary demand curve the price of
3. ____________ the good itself and utility ____________, all other prices and income remain constant. An ordinary demand curve reflects
4. ____________ both a substitution and ____________ effect.

5. ____________ A ____________ demand curve illustrates how the quantity demanded of a good changes when the good's price changes, while keeping all other prices and utility unchanged. As one moves along a compensated demand
6. ____________ curve, income ____________. As the good's price increases,
7. ____________ the consumer needs ____________ income to keep his utility constant:

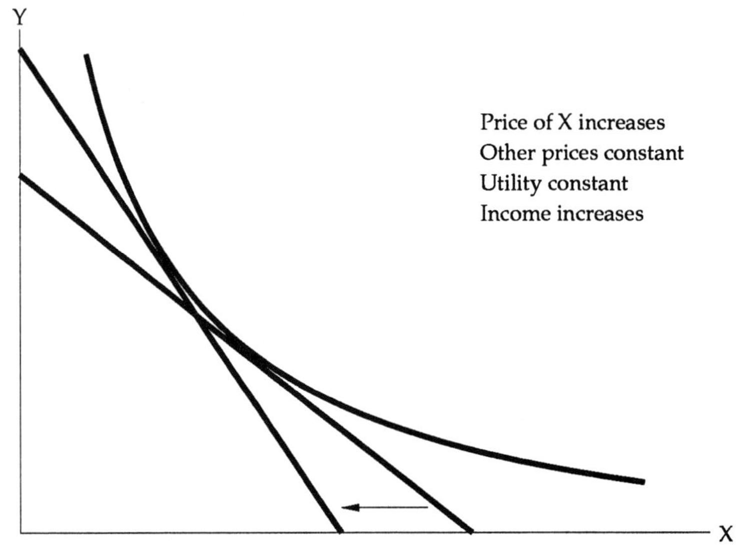

Figure 6.2: *Derivation of a Compensated Demand Curve*

When moving along a compensated demand curve the price of the good itself and income change, all other prices and
8. ____________ ____________ remain constant. The compensated demand
9. ____________ implicitly provides the individual with the ____________ necessary to compensate him for price changes. The compensated demand curve compensates the individual for the income effect that results from a change in the price.
10. ____________ Hence, it reflects only the ____________ effect.

The "triangle" beneath the compensated demand curve and above the price represents the compensation required to keep individuals just as well off, if consumption
11. ____________ of the good were reduced to ____________:

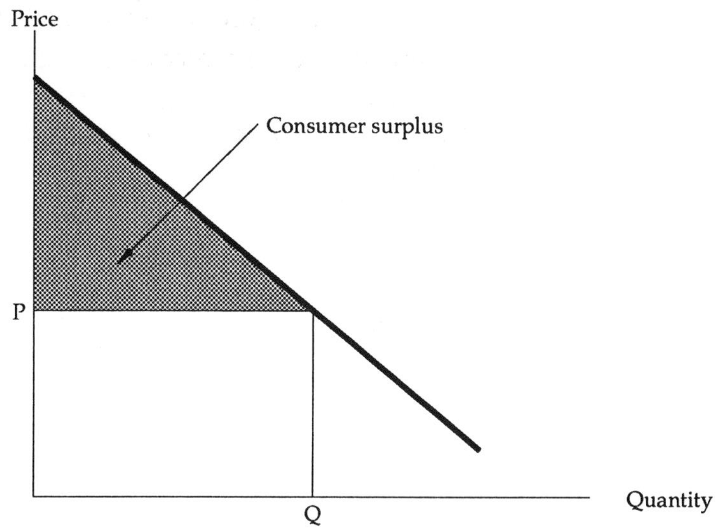

Figure 6.3: *Consumer Surplus*

12. ____________ Economists call this area ____________ surplus. It represents the extra value individuals receive from consuming the good over what they actually pay for it. When prices change, changes in consumer surplus reflect
13. ____________ how the ____________ of individuals is affected.

INDEX NUMBERS

An index number summarizes the information described by two or more economic statistics. The calculation of an index number requires some type of
14. ____________ ____________ scheme. Unfortunately, no perfect weighting scheme exists. Every weighting scheme will mislead one in certain situations. For example, the weighting scheme used
15. ____________ in the Consumer Price Index ____________ the effect of price increases whenever prices increase by different rates. When this occurs, people modify their consumption choices,
16. ____________ responding to the change in relative ____________. The Consumer Price Index does not account for this change in consumption patterns.

GAINS FROM VOLUNTARY TRADE

An individual's marginal rate of substitution (MRS) equals the ratio at which he is willing to substitute two goods. Whenever two individuals have different marginal

rates of substitution both can gain from trade. If they exchange the goods in a ratio between their marginal rates
17. ____________ of ____________, both will become better off. To understand why assume that Smith's MRS of apples for oranges is 5 and Jones' is 1. Now tell Smith to give Jones 3 oranges in exchange for 1 apple:

Smith ⟶ 3 oranges ⟶ Jones
MRS = 5 ⟵ 1 apple ⟵ MRS = 1

Smith is willing to substitute 5 oranges for 1 apple

Jones is willing to substitute 1 orange for 1 apple

18. ____________ Since Smith's MRS equals 5, exchanging ____________ oranges for 1 apple would leave Smith just as well off. Smith only gives up 3 oranges, however; Smith becomes better off. Jones becomes better off, also. Since Jones' MRS
19. ____________ equals 1, exchanging ____________ apple for 1 orange would leave Jones just as well off. Jones actually receives 3
20. ____________ apples for 1 orange, however; Jones becomes ____________ off, too.

While both individuals can benefit from voluntary trade, they need not share the gains equally. They typically negotiate the precise ratio at which the trade occurs. Each argues for those terms that most benefit him. Their skills as
21. ____________ negotiators determine the ____________ of the gains.

EDGEWORTH BOX DIAGRAM

The Edgeworth Box provides a graphical means to
22. ____________ illustrate all the possible ways to ____________ two goods between two individuals. The height of an Edgeworth Box represents the total amount of good Y owned by both individuals. The width represents the total amount of good X owned. The locus of all efficient points in the Edgeworth
23. ____________ Box is called the ____________ curve. If a point is not on the contract curve, the marginal rates of substitution are not equal. It is possible for the individuals to exchange the
24. ____________ goods to make both of them ____________ off. If a point is on the contract curve, however, the marginal rates of
25. ____________ substitution are ____________. The only way to make one person better off is to hurt the other.

MULTIPLE-CHOICE QUESTIONS

26. ______ When moving along an ordinary demand curve
    a. the prices of other goods are constant.
    b. income is constant.
    c. utility is constant.
    d. a and b.
    e. a and c.

27. ______ When moving along a compensated demand curve
    a. the prices of other goods are constant.
    b. income is constant.
    c. utility is constant.
    d. a and b.
    e. a and c.

28. ______ Consumer surplus equals
    a. what consumers spend on the good.
    b. what consumers spend on the good plus the profits firms earn.
    c. the value consumers place on being able to consume a good in excess of what they pay for it.
    d. the area beneath the compensated demand curve.
    e. what people actually pay for the good plus the compensation they would demand to voluntarily stop consuming the good.

29. ______ Consumer surplus equals
    a. the area beneath the ordinary demand curve.
    b. the area beneath the ordinary demand curve lying above the price.
    c. the area beneath the compensated demand curve.
    d. the area beneath the compensated demand curve lying above the price.
    e. none of the above.

30. ______ The Consumer Price Index typically
    a. overstates the effects of income changes.
    b. overstates the effects of price increases.
    c. understates the effects of price increases.
    d. may overstate or understate the effects of price increases.
    e. precisely reflects the effects of price increases.

31. ______ The marginal rate of substitution indicates

a. how a firm can substitute labor for capital while keeping production constant.
b. how production of one good can be substituted for the production of another.
c. how an individual is willing to substitute the consumption of one good for another.
d. how a firm can substitute the production of a good today with the production of that good in the future.
e. a and c.

32. ______ The marginal rate of substitution is indicated by the slope of

a. a consumer's compensated demand curve.
b. a firm's indifference curve.
c. the production possibility curve.
d. a consumer's ordinary demand curve.
e. a consumer's indifference curve.

33. ______ Whenever two individuals have different marginal rates of substitution, trade between them

a. can help both.
b. must help both.
c. must hurt both.
d. must hurt at least one.
e. only helps one.

34. ______ Assume that Mr. Smith's marginal rate of substitution of good X for good Y is 2 and that Mr. Jones' is 5. If Mr. Smith trades 1 unit of good X to Mr. Jones in exchange for 3 units of good Y,

a. both Mr. Smith and Mr. Jones will be helped.
b. both Mr. Smith and Mr. Jones will be hurt.
c. Mr. Smith will be helped, Mr. Jones hurt.
d. Mr. Smith will be hurt, Mr. Jones helped.
e. it is impossible to tell if either is helped or hurt.

35. ______ Assume that Mr. Smith's marginal rate of substitution of good X for good Y is 2 and that Mr. Jones' is 5. If Mr. Smith trades 1 unit of good X to Mr. Jones in exchange for 1 unit of good Y,

a. both Mr. Smith and Mr. Jones will be helped.
b. both Mr. Smith and Mr. Jones will be hurt.
c. Mr. Smith will be helped, Mr. Jones hurt.
d. Mr. Smith will be hurt, Mr. Jones helped.
e. it is impossible to tell if either is helped or hurt.

36. ______ An Edgeworth box illustrates

a. all the possible ways to divide income between two individuals.
b. all the possible ways to divide utility between two individuals.
c. all the possible ways to divide two goods between two individuals.
d. all the inefficient ways to divide two goods between two individuals.
e. none of the above.

37. ______ The contract curve illustrates

a. the efficient ways to divide two goods between two individuals.
b. the efficient ways to divide income between two individuals.
c. each individual's demand curve.
d. all points where the individual's marginal rates of substitution are equal.
e. a and d.

RUNNING GLOSSARY

Compensated demand curve: a demand curve drawn on the
38. ____________ assumption that other prices and ____________ are held
constant. Income effects of price changes are compensated
39. ____________ for along the curve and it reflects only ____________ effects.

40. ____________ ____________ surplus: the extra value individuals receive from consuming a good over what they pay for it. The maximum amount people would be willing to pay for the right to consume a good at its current price.

41. ____________ ____________ number: an average of many different trends in one number.

Consumer price index (CPI): the current value of the market
basket of goods and services purchased by a typical
42. ____________ household compared to a ____________ year value of the
same market basket.

43. ____________ Pareto ___________ allocation: an allocation of available resources in which no mutually beneficial trading opportunities are unexploited. That is, an allocation in which no one person can be made better off without

44. ____________ someone else being made ___________ off.

45. ____________ Contract curve: the set of all ___________ allocations of the existing goods in an exchange situation. Points off that curve are necessarily inefficient, since individuals can be made unambiguously better off by moving to the curve.

ANSWERS

1. income
2. worse
3. change
4. income
5. compensated
6. changes
7. more
8. utility
9. income
10. substitution
11. zero
12. consumer
13. welfare
14. averaging
15. overstates
16. prices
17. substitution
18. 5
19. 1
20. better
21. distribution
22. allocate
23. contract
24. better
25. equal
26. d
27. c
28. c
29. d
30. b
31. c
32. e
33. a
34. a
35. d
36. c
37. e
38. utility
39. substitution
40. Consumer
41. Index
42. base
43. efficient
44. worse
45. efficient

CHAPTER 7

UNCERTAINTY AND INFORMATION

WALKING TOUR SUMMARIES

PROBABILITY AND EXPECTED VALUE

1. ___________ The ___________ of a particular outcome in a game is the relative frequency that the outcome would occur if the game were played many, many times. For example, when a coin is tossed, the probability of a head equals 1/2 (assuming of course that someone has not doctored the
2. ___________ coin). The ___________ value of a game with several uncertain prizes equals the size of the prize that the player will win on average. If the expected value of a game equals
3. ___________ the cost of playing it, we call the game ___________.

RISK AVERSION

4. ___________ Individuals are typically risk ___________; that is,
5. ___________ individuals do not choose to participate in ___________
6. ___________ games. ___________ marginal utility of income explains

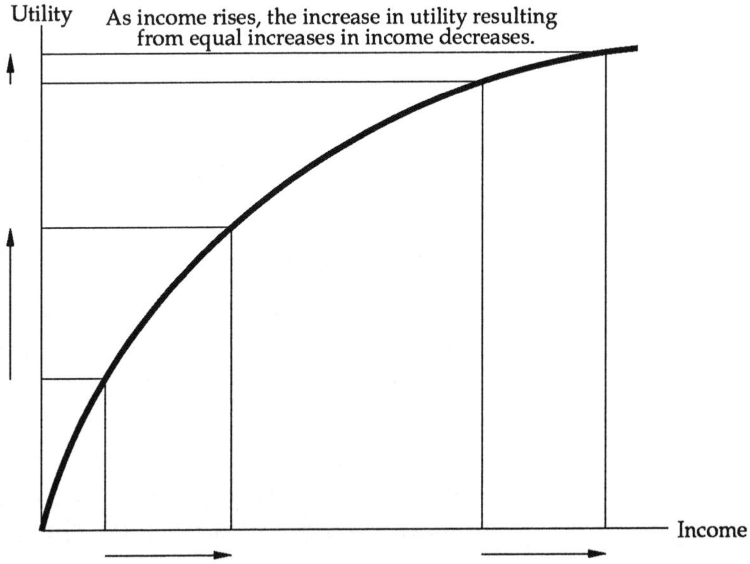

Figure 7.1: *Diminishing Marginal Utility of Income*

why individuals are risk averse. Although additional
income always raises an individual's utility, the increase in
utility resulting from equal increments of income becomes
7. ____________ less and less as income ___________. This means that while
a fair game is fair in terms of dollars, it is not fair in terms of
8. ____________ ___________. Consider a game in which one wins $1,000 if
a head appears on a coin toss, but loses $1,000 for a tail. The
game is fair in terms of dollars, but not in terms of utility. In
9. ____________ terms of utility, the $1,000 loss brings ___________ pain
than the $1,000 win brings pleasure. Thus, risk
10. ____________ ___________ individuals refuse to play this game.

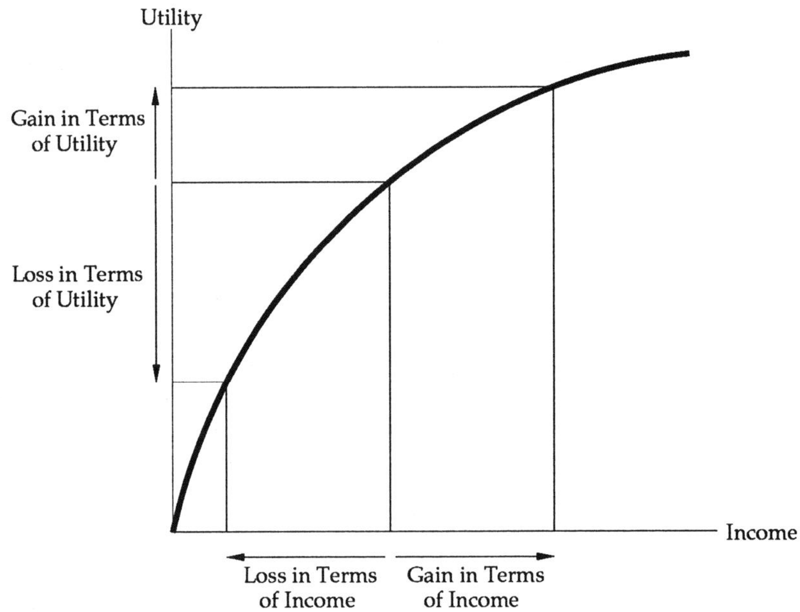

Figure 7.2: *Risk Aversion*

METHODS FOR REDUCING RISK

Individuals purchase insurance to reduce risk.
11. ____________ Because individuals are risk ___________, they are willing
to give up some income to avoid risk. An actuarially
12. ____________ ___________ insurance premium makes a risk-averse
individual better off. In terms of income, the expected
13. ____________ losses from the risky outcome would ___________ the
premium. In terms of utility, the expected pain of the risky
losses would exceed the pain of paying the premium.
14. ____________ Insurance companies must charge a premium ___________
than the actuarially fair value to avoid losses, however. A
risk-averse individual may or may not purchase such a

policy. His actions depend on how risk averse he is and also by how much the actual premium exceeds the actuarially fair premium. Insurance companies do not offer policies to
15. ___________ cover all types of risks; some are ___________. Some types of risk are so rare and unpredictable that no one can
16. ___________ estimate actuarially fair premiums. ___________ selection can lead to uninsured risks when insurance companies and potential customers do not both have accurate assessments
17. ___________ of the risks involved. ___________ hazard can limit coverage when purchasing the policy affects the behavior of the policyholders.

18. ___________ Risk ___________ individuals reduce risk by diversifying
19. ___________ their assets. By not "___________ all your eggs in one basket," individuals increase their utility.

ECONOMICS OF INFORMATION

All uncertain situations share one similar
20. ___________ characteristic, the lack of complete ___________.
21. ___________ Individuals implicitly or explicitly ___________ how much information to acquire. Information is similar to most economic goods in some respects, but is different in other ways. The decision concerning how much information to acquire is similar. Individuals weigh the benefits against the costs, as we do for goods. This explains why some individuals acquire more information than others. Some assess the benefits to be higher or the costs to be lower. Unlike most goods, however, it is often very difficult for an individual who has gathered information to prevent
22. ___________ ___________ from using it. Patent laws try to protect inventors by giving the exclusive rights to their inventions. These laws do not enable the inventor to garner
23. ___________ ___________ the benefits of his ideas, however. Information acquisition activities benefit not only the
24. ___________ individual bearing the costs, but ___________ also. Economists believe that financial markets react quickly to
25. ___________ new information. The ___________ markets hypothesis asserts that market prices accurately reflect all available information.

Economists often use a utility-maximizing model to understand how individuals behave when facing uncertainty. An individual is assumed to face two possible
26. ___________ outcomes, two ___________ of the world. In the graph

below, C_1 represents consumption if state 1 results; C_2 consumption if state 2 results. Each point on the certainty line represents a situation in which consumption is the

27. ____________ ____________ regardless of the state of the world. That is, along the certainty line, there is no uncertainlty, our individual's consumption is unaffected by the state of the world. Points not on the certainty line represent situations in which the amount of consumption depends on the state of the world. By purchasing insurance, an individual would

28. ____________ move ____________ the certainty line.

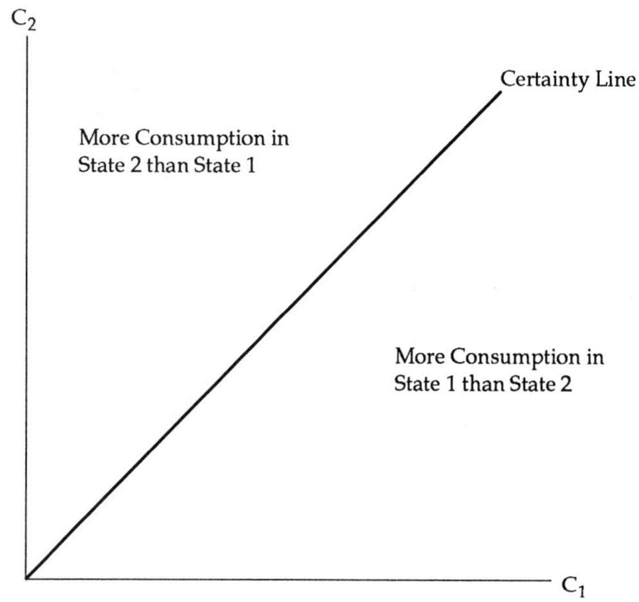

Figure 7.3: *Certainty Line and States of the World*

MULTIPLE-CHOICE QUESTIONS

29. ______ The probability of an event is
   a. the relative frequency with which the outcome would occur.
   b. what a player would win on average if a game were played many, many times.
   c. what a player can be assured of winning if he plays a game once.
   d. what a player can be assured of losing if he plays a game once.
   e. the difference between c and d.

30. ______ The expected value of a game is

a. the relative frequency that each outcome would occur if the game were played many, many times.
b. what a player would win on average if the game were played many, many times.
c. what a player can be assured of winning if he plays the game once.
d. what a player can be assured of losing if he plays the game once.
e. the difference between c and d.

31. ______ If a game is fair, the cost of playing the game

a. is greater than its expected value.
b. is less than its expected value.
c. equals its expected value.
d. is unrelated to its expected value.
e. equals its expected value times the probability of winning.

32. ______ Individuals are

a. usually risk averse.
b. usually risk takers.
c. usually risk neutral.
d. always risk neutral.
e. never risk averse.

33. ______ A risk-averse individual will

a. want to play a fair game.
b. not want to play a fair game.
c. be indifferent about playing a fair game.
d. be undecided about playing a fair game.
e. always gamble at the race track.

34. ______ Risk aversion can be explained by

a. increasing marginal utility of income.
b. decreasing marginal utility of income.
c. constant marginal utility of income.
d. constant marginal rate of substitution.
e. b and d.

35. ______ If an individual is a risk averter

a. a $1,000 loss brings more pain than a $1,000 gain brings pleasure.
b. a $1,000 gain brings more pleasure than a $1,000 loss brings pain.
c. a $1,000 loss brings just as much pain as a $1,000 gain brings pleasure.
d. his marginal rate of substitution is constant.
e. his marginal utility of income is increasing.

36. ______ A risk may be uninsurable if insurance would lead to

a. adverse selection.
b. moral hazard.
c. a premium which is more than fair.
d. a and b.
e. a and c.

37. ______ Information is similar to most goods in that

a. all the benefits enjoyed by acquiring information are enjoyed by the individual who incurs the cost of acquiring it.
b. some of the benefits enjoyed by acquiring information are not enjoyed by the individual who incurs the cost of acquiring it.
c. individuals decide to acquire information whenever the benefits exceed the costs.
d. individuals decide to acquire information whenever the benefits are positive.
e. a and c.

38. ______ Information is dissimilar from most goods in that

a. all the benefits enjoyed by acquiring information are enjoyed by the individual who incurs the cost of acquiring it.
b. some of the benefits enjoyed by acquiring information are not enjoyed by the individual who incurs the cost of acquiring it.
c. individuals decide to acquire information whenever the benefits exceed the costs.
d. individuals decide to acquire information whenever the benefits are positive.
e. a and c.

RUNNING GLOSSARY

39. ___________ ___________: the relative frequency with which an event occurs.

40. ___________ Expected value: the _________ outcome from an uncertain gamble.

41. ___________ Fair games: games that cost their ___________ value.

42. ___________ Risk aversion: the tendency of people to refuse to accept ___________ games.

43. ___________ ___________ insurance: insurance for which the premium is equal to the expected value of the loss.

44. ___________ Averse selection: the possibility that individuals know more about their expected ___________ than do insurers (or other market participants).

45. ___________ ___________ hazard: the effect that having insurance has on the behavior of the insured.

46. ___________ ___________: the spreading of risk among several options rather than choosing only one.

47. ___________ Efficient markets hypothesis: the hypothesis that all information is reflected in prevailing market ___________.

ANSWERS

1. probability
2. expected
3. fair
4. averse
5. fair
6. Diminishing
7. rises
8. utility
9. more
10. averse
11. averse
12. fair
13. equal
14. greater
15. uninsurable
16. Averse
17. Moral
18. averse
19. putting
20. information
21. decide
22. others
23. all
24. others
25. efficient
26. states
27. same
28. toward
29. a
30. b
31. c
32. a
33. b
34. b
35. a
36. d
37. c
38. b
39. Probability
40. average
41. expected
42. fair
43. Fair
44. losses
45. Moral
46. Diversification
47. prices

PART 2

CHOICE AND DEMAND

WALKING TOUR PROBLEMS

UTILITY MAXIMIZATION

1. Suppose that the price of good X is \$6.00 and the price of good Y is \$2.00. An individual whose income is \$600.00 purchases a bundle of goods containing 60 units of good X and 120 units of good Y. The individual's marginal rate of substitution is 2.

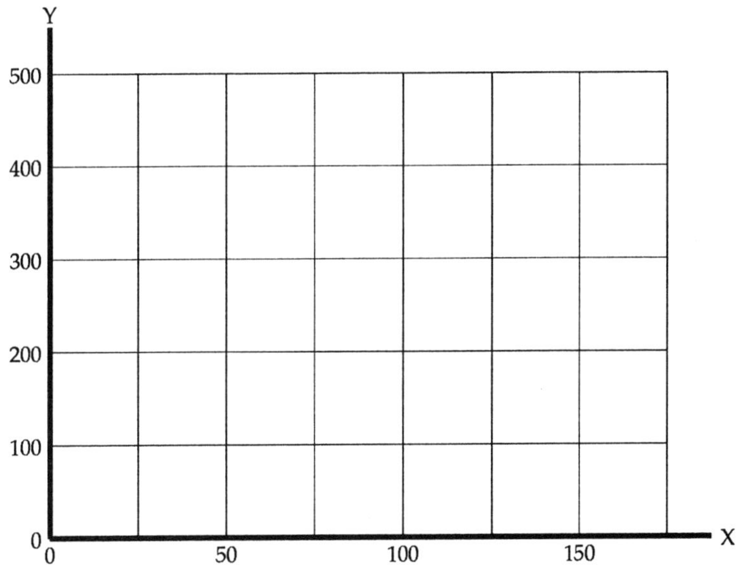

a. Plot the budget line on the above diagram.

b. What is the X-intercept of the individual's budget line?

The X-intercept of the individual's budget line depicts the situation in which all income is spent on good
1. ____________ ____________. Since income is \$600.00 and the price of good X is \$6.00, the individual would purchase
2. ____________ ____________ units of X if all income were spent on good X.

The answer is 100.

c. What is the Y-intercept of the individual's budget line?

3. ____________ The ____________ of the individual's budget line depicts the situation in which all income is spent on good Y. Since income is $600.00 and the price of good Y is $2.00, the individual would purchase

4. ____________ ____________ units of Y if all income were spent on good Y.

The answer is 300.

d. Does the bundle of goods purchased more than exhaust, less than exhaust, or exactly exhaust the individual's income?

The bundle contains 60 units of good X and 120 units of good Y. Since the price of good X is $6.00,

5. ____________ $____________ is spent on good X; since the price of

6. ____________ good Y is $2.00, $____________ is spent on good Y. A

7. ____________ total of $____________ is spent to purchase the bundle exactly exhausting the individual's income.

The answer is exactly exhaust.

e. Is the individual maximizing utility? Should more, less, or the same amount be spent on X to maximize utility?

The price ratio is ($6.00/$2.00) = 3 whereas the individual's marginal rate of substitution is 2.

8. ____________ ____________ is not being maximized because the marginal rate of substitution does not equal the price ratio.

The answer is no.

Since the price ratio is 3, if the individual purchases 1 less unit of good X he can afford to buy 3 more units of good Y. Since the individual's marginal rate of

9. ____________ substitution is 2, only ____________ additional units of good Y are required to keep him just as well off

when he consumes 1 less unit of good X. Consequently, by purchasing 1 less unit of good X and 3 more units of good Y the individual
10. ____________ becomes ____________ off.

The answer is spend less on good X.

2. Suppose that the price of good X is $5.00 and the price of good Y is $2.00. An individual whose income is $400.00 purchases a bundle of goods containing 60 units of good X and 40 units of good Y. The individual's marginal rate of substitution is 1.25.

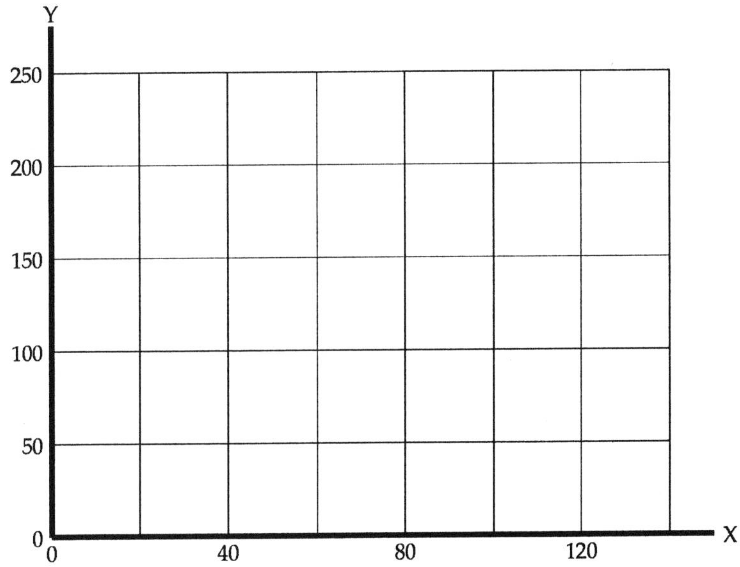

a. Plot the budget line on the above diagram.

b. What is the X-intercept of the individual's budget line?

11. ____________ The ____________ of the individual's budget line depicts the situation in which all income is spent on good X. Since income is $400.00 and the price of good X is $5.00, the individual would purchase
12. ____________ ____________ units of X if all income were spent on good X.

The answer is 80.

c. What is the Y-intercept of the individual's budget line?

The Y-intercept of the individual's budget line depicts the situation in which all income is spent on good

13. ____________

14. ____________

____________. Since income is $400.00 and the price of good Y is $2.00, the individual would purchase ____________ units of Y if all income were spent on good Y.

The answer is 200.

d. Does the bundle of goods purchased more than exhaust, less than exhaust, or exactly exhaust the individual's income?

15. ____________

16. ____________

17. ____________

The bundle contains 60 units of good X and 40 units of good Y. Since the price of good X is $5.00, $____________ is spent on good X; since the price of good Y is $2.00, $____________ is spent on good Y. A total of $380.00 is spent to purchase the bundle ____________ the individual's income.

The answer is less than exhaust.

e. Is the individual maximizing utility? Should more, less, or the same amount be spent on X to maximize utility?

Since the individual is not spending all his income, he is not maximizing utility.

The answer is no.

Since the individual is not spending all his income, he can purchase more of good X and good Y thereby increasing his utility.

The answer is spend more on both goods.

3. Suppose that the price of good X is \$10.00 and the price of good Y is \$2.00. An individual whose income is \$1000.00 purchases a bundle of goods containing 40 units of good X and 300 units of good Y. The individual's marginal rate of substitution is 8.

a. What is the X-intercept of the individual's budget
18. ____________ line?

b. What is the Y-intercept of the individual's budget
19. ____________ line?

20. ____________ c. Does the bundle exhaust the individual's income?

21. ____________ d. Is the individual maximizing utility? Should more,
less, or the same amount be spent on X to maximize
22. ____________ utility?

4. Suppose that the price of good X is \$2.00 and the price of good Y is \$4.00. An individual whose income is \$1000.00 purchases a bundle of goods containing 300 units of good X and 100 units of good Y. The individual's marginal rate of substitution is 0.5.

a. What is the X-intercept of the individual's budget
23. ____________ line?

b. What is the Y-intercept of the individual's budget
24. ____________ line?

25. ____________ c. Does the bundle exhaust the individual's income?

26. ____________ d. Is the individual maximizing utility? Should more,
less, or the same amount be spent on X to maximze
27. ____________ utility?

5. Suppose that the price of good X is \$4.00 and the price of good Y is \$2.00. An individual whose income is \$1200.00 purchases a bundle of goods containing 100 units of good X and 400 units of good Y. The individual's marginal rate of substitution is 6.

a. What is the X-intercept of the individual's budget
28. ____________ line?

b. What is the Y-intercept of the individual's budget
29. ____________ line?

30. ____________ c. Does the bundle exhaust the individual's income?

31. ____________ d. Is the individual maximizing utility? Should more, less, or the same amount be spent on X to maximize
32. ____________ utility?

INCOME AND SUBSTITUTION EFFECTS

1. Initially the price of good X is \$1.00, the price of good Y is \$2.00, and income is \$100.00. Income increases from \$100.00 to \$150.00. Good X is a normal good.

a. Plot the old and new budget lines on the above diagram.

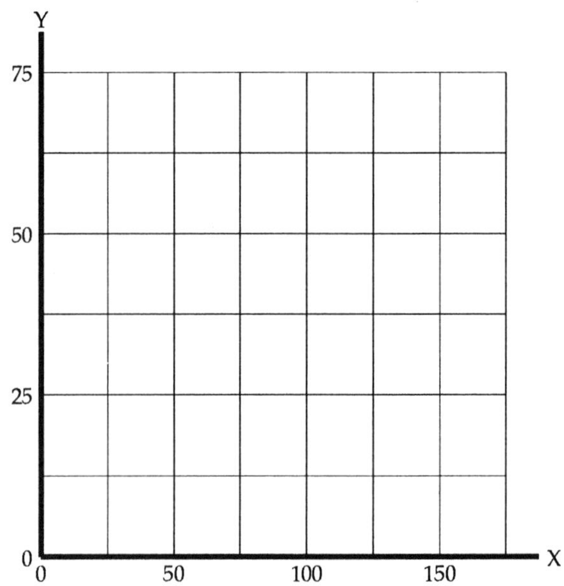

b. What happens to the slope of the budget line?

The slope of the budget line depends on the
33. ___________ ___________ ratio. Since neither the price of good X nor the price of good Y has changed, the slope is
34. ___________ ___________.

The answer is nothing.

c. Is there a substitution effect? As a result, does the utility maximizing quantity of X increase, decrease, or remain the same?

Since the slope of the budget line is unchanged, there
35. ___________ is ___________ substitution effect.

The answer is no. The utility maximizing quantity of X is unaffected.

d. What happens to the X-intercept of the budget line?

The X-intercept of the budget line illustrates the situation when the consumer spends all his income
36. ___________ on good ___________. Initially, since the price of good X was $1.00 and income was $100.00, the X-
37. ___________ intercept was ___________. After income rises from $100.00 to $150.00, the X-intercept increases to
38. ___________ ___________.

The answer is it increases from 100 to 150.

e. What happens to the Y-intercept of the budget line?

39. ___________ The ___________ of the budget line illustrates the situation when the consumer spends all his income on good Y. Initially, since the price of good Y was $2.00 and income was $100.00, the Y-intercept was
40. ___________ ___________. After income rises from $100.00 to
41. ___________ $150.00, the Y-intercept increases to ___________.

The answer is it increases from 50 to 75.

f. Is there an income effect? As a result, does the utility maximizing quantity of X increase, decrease, or remain the same?

42. ____________ The budget line has shifted ____________; consequently there is an income effect.

The answer is yes.

For a normal good when the budget line shifts outward, the utility maximizing quantity of the good

43. ____________ ____________; when the budget line shifts

44. ____________ ____________, the utility maximizing quantity of the good decreases. Since good X is normal and the budget line has shifted outward, the quantity of good

45. ____________ X ____________ as a consequence of the income effect.

The answer is it increases.

g. Accounting for both the income and substitution effects how is the utility maximizing quantity of good X affected?

46. ____________ Since there is ____________ substitution effect and the income effect leads to the consumption of more X, the

47. ____________ quantity of good X ____________.

The answer is it increases.

2. Initially the price of good X is $1.00, the price of good Y is $2.00, and income is $100.00. Income decreases from $100.00 to $50.00. Good X is an inferior good.

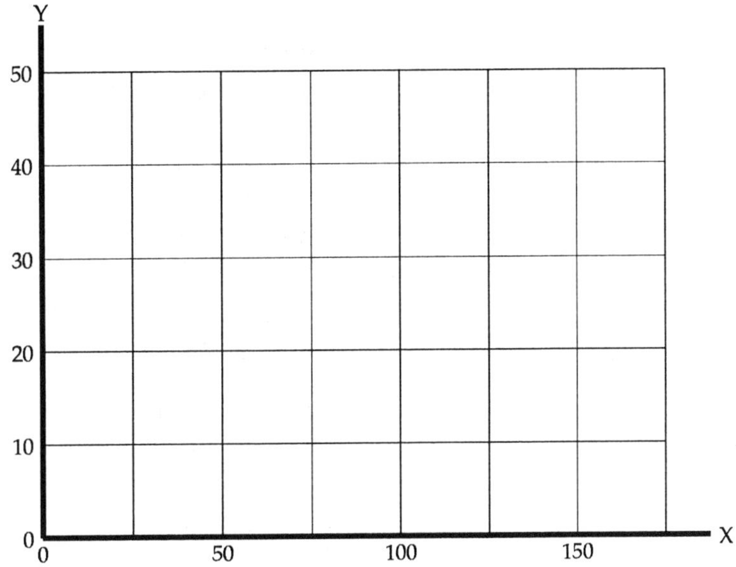

a. Plot the old and new budget lines on the above diagram.

b. What happens to the slope of the budget line?

48. ____________ The slope of the budget line depends on the price ratio. Since neither the price of good X nor the price of good Y has changed, the slope is ____________.

The answer is nothing.

c. Is there a substitution effect? As a result, does the utility maximizing quantity of X increase, decrease, or remain the same?

49. ____________ Since the slope of the budget line is ____________, there is no substitution effect.

The answer is no.

d. What happens to the X-intercept of the budget line?

50. ____________ The ____________ of the budget line illustrates the situation when the consumer spends all his income on good X. Initially, since the price of good X was

	\$1.00 and income was \$100.00, the X-intercept was
51. ____________	____________. After income falls from \$100.00 to
52. ____________	\$50.00, the X-intercept decreases to ____________.

The answer is it decreases from 100 to 50.

e. What happens to the Y-intercept of the budget line?

	The Y-intercept of the budget line illustrates the situation when the consumer spends all his income
53. ____________	on good ____________. Initially, since the price of good Y was \$2.00 and income was \$100.00, the Y-
54. ____________	intercept was ____________. After income falls from \$100.00 to \$50.00, the Y-intercept decreases to
55. ____________	____________.

The answer is it decreases from 50 to 25.

f. Is there an income effect? As a result, does the utility maximizing quantity of X increase, decrease, or remain the same?

56. ____________	The budget line has shifted ____________; consequently there is an income effect.

The answer is yes.

	For an inferior good when the budget line shifts outward, the utility maximizing quantity of the good
57. ____________	____________; when the budget line shifts
58. ____________	____________, the utility maximizing quantity of the good increases. Since good X is inferior and the budget line has shifted inward, the quantity of good
59. ____________	X ____________.

The answer is it increases.

g. Accounting for both the income and substitution effects how is the utility maximizing quantity of good X affected?

	Since there is no substitution effect and the income effect leads to the consumption of more X, the
60. ____________	quantity of good X ____________.

The answer is it increases.

3. Initially the price of good X is $1.00, the price of good Y is $2.00, and income is $100.00. The price of good X decreases from $1.00 to $.50. Good X is a normal good.

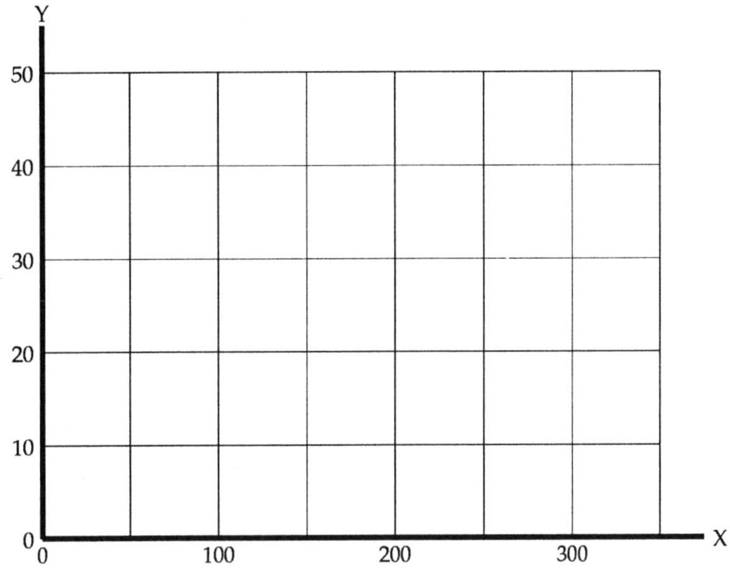

a. Plot the old and new budget lines on the above diagram.

b. What happens to the slope of the budget line?

The slope of the budget line depends on the
61. ____________ ____________ ratio; the slope equals the negative of
the price of good X divided by the price of good Y.
62. ____________ Since the price of good X has ____________, the price
ratio has declined and the budget line is
63. ____________ ____________ steeply sloped.

The answer is it becomes less steeply sloped.

c. Is there a substitution effect? As a result, does the utility maximizing quantity of X increase, decrease, or remain the same?

64. ____________ Since the slope of the budget line has ____________,
there is a substitution effect.

The answer is yes.

65. ____________ Good X has become ____________ expensive relative to good Y; as a consequence of the substitution effect, the utility maximizing quantity of good X

66. ____________ ____________.

The answer is it increases.

d. What happens to the X-intercept of the budget line?

The X-intercept of the budget line illustrates the situation when the consumer spends all his income

67. ____________ on good ____________. Initially, since the price of good X was $1.00 and income was $100.00, the X-

68. ____________ intercept was ____________. After the price of good X falls from $1.00 to $.50, the X-intercept increases to 200.

The answer is it increases from 100 to 200.

e. What happens to the Y-intercept of the budget line?

The Y-intercept of the budget line illustrates the situation when the consumer spends all his income

69. ____________ on good ____________. Initially, since the price of good Y was $2.00 and income was $100.00, the Y-

70. ____________ intercept was ____________. Since neither the price of good Y nor income has changed, the Y-intercept is unchanged.

The answer is nothing.

f. Is there an income effect? As a result, does the utility maximizing quantity of X increase, decrease, or remain the same?

The budget line has shifted outward; consequently there is an income effect.

The answer is yes.

71. ____________ For a ____________ good when the budget line shifts outward, the utility maximizing quantity of the good increases; when the budget line shifts inward, the utility maximizing quantity of the good

72. ____________ ____________. Since good X is normal and the budget

73. ____________ line has shifted outward, the quantity of good X ____________ as a consequence of the income effect.

The answer is it increases.

g. Accounting for both the income and substitution effects how is the utility maximizing quantity of good X affected?

74. ____________ Both the income and substitution effects lead to the consumption of ____________ X. The utility maximizing quantity of good X increases.

The answer is it increases.

4. Initially the price of good X is $1.00, the price of good Y is $2.00, and income is $100.00. The price of good X increases from $1.00 to $2.00. Good X is a normal good.

75. ____________ a. What happens to the slope of the budget line?

76. ____________
77. ____________ b. Is there a substitution effect? Does the quantity of X increase, decrease, or remain the same?

78. ____________ c. What happens to the X-intercept of the budget line?

79. ____________ d. What happens to the Y-intercept of the budget line?

80. ____________
81. ____________ e. Is there an income effect? Does the quantity of X increase, decrease, or remain the same?

82. ____________ f. Accounting for both the income and substitution effects, how is the utility maximizing quantity of good X affected?

5. Initially the price of good X is $1.00, the price of good Y is $2.00, and income is $100.00. The price of good X increases from $1.00 to $2.00. Good X is an inferior good.

83. ____________ a. What happens to the slope of the budget line?

84. ____________ b. Is there a substitution effect? Does the quantity of X
85. ____________ increase, decrease, or remain the same?

86. ____________ c. What happens to the X-intercept of the budget line?

87. ____________ d. What happens to the Y-intercept of the budget line?

88. ____________ e. Is there an income effect? Does the quantity of X
89. ____________ increase, decrease, or remain the same?

f. Accounting for both the income and substitution effects, how is the utility maximizing quantity of
90. ____________ good X affected?

6. Initially the price of good X is $1.00, the price of good Y is $2.00, and income is $100.00. The price of good X decreases from $1.00 to $.50. Good X is an inferior good.

91. ____________ a. What happens to the slope of the budget line?

92. ____________ b. Is there a substitution effect? Does the quantity of X
93. ____________ increase, decrease, or remain the same?

94. ____________ c. What happens to the X-intercept of the budget line?

95. ____________ d. What happens to the Y-intercept of the budget line?

96. ____________ e. Is there an income effect? Does the quantity of X
97. ____________ increase, decrease, or remain the same?

f. Accounting for both the income and substitution effects, how is the utility maximizing quantity of
98. ____________ good X affected?

SHIFTS AND MOVEMENTS ALONG DEMAND CURVES

1. The income elasticity of demand is .50 and the price elasticity of demand is -.50. Initially income is $20,000, the price is $.60, and the quantity is 1000. Income increases from $20,000 to $22,000.

   a. Will the demand curve shift? Does it shift to the right, left, or remain stationary?

   The demand curve can shift only if something other
   99. ____________ than the ____________ of the good itself changes.
   Since income has risen, the demand curve will
   100. ____________ ____________.

   The answer is yes.

   101. ____________ Income rises from $20,000 to $22,000, a ____________
   percent increase. Since the income elasticity of
   demand is .50, a 10 percent change in income causes a
   102. ____________ ____________ percent change in the quantity. The
   demand curve will shift to the right by 5 percent of
   103. ____________ 1000, which is ____________.

   The answer is it shifts to the right by 50.

   b. Is there a change in demand?

   104. ____________ A change in demand refers to a ____________ of the
   demand curve. Since the demand curve has shifted
   105. ____________ to the right by 50, demand has ____________ by 50.

   The answer is yes, an increase in demand.

   c. Will there be a movement along the demand curve? By how much do we move along the demand curve?

   A movement along the demand curve occurs only if
   106. ____________ the ____________ of the good itself changes. Since the
   107. ____________ price is unchanged, there is ____________ movement
   along the demand curve.

   The answer is no.

d. Is there a change in the quantity demanded?

108. ____________
109. ____________

A change in the quantity demanded refers to a movement __________ the demand curve. Since there has not been a movement along the demand curve, there has been no change in the __________ demanded.

The answer is no.

2. The income elasticity of demand is .50 and the price elasticity of demand is -.50. Initially income is $20,000, the price is $.60, and the quantity is 1000. The price increases from $.60 to $.72.

a. Will the demand curve shift? Does it shift to the right, left, or remain stationary?

110. ____________
111. ____________

The demand curve can __________ only if something other than the price of the good itself changes. Since income has not changed, the demand curve will __________ shift.

The answer is no.

b. Is there a change in demand?

112. ____________
113. ____________

A change in demand refers to a __________ of the demand curve. Since the demand curve has not shifted, there is __________ change in demand.

The answer is no.

c. Will there be a movement along the demand curve? By how much do we move along the demand curve?

114. ____________
115. ____________

A movement along the demand curve occurs only if the __________ of the good itself changes. Since the price has changed, there will be a movement __________ the demand curve.

The answer is yes.

116. ____________ The price has increased from $.60 to $.72, which is a ____________ percent increase. Since the price elasticity of demand is -.50, a 20 percent increase in

117. ____________ the price will lead to a ____________ percent decrease in the quantity. The quantity decreases by 10 percent

118. ____________ of 1000, which is ____________.

The answer is by a decrease of 100.

d. Is there a change in the quantity demanded?

119. ____________ A change in the quantity demanded refers to a movement ____________ the demand curve. There has been a movement along the demand curve

120. ____________ because the price has ____________; the quantity

121. ____________ demanded has decreased by ____________.

The answer is yes, a decrease of 100.

3. The income elasticity of demand is .50 and the price elasticity of demand is -1.00. Initially income is $20,000, the price is $.60, and the quantity is 1000. The price decreases from $.60 to $.54.

122. ____________ a. Will the demand curve shift? Does it shift to the

123. ____________ right, left, or remain stationary?

124. ____________ b. Is there a change in demand?

125. ____________ c. Will there be a movement along the demand curve?

126. ____________ By how much do we move along the demand curve?

127. ____________ d. Is there a change in the quantity demanded?

4. The income elasticity of demand is 1.00 and the price elasticity of demand is -1.00. Initially income is $20,000, the price is $.60, and the quantity is 1000. Income decreases from $20,000 to $15,000.

128. ____________ a. Will the demand curve shift? Does it shift to the
129. ____________ right, left, or remain stationary?

130. ____________ b. Is there a change in demand?

131. ____________ c. Will there be a movement along the demand curve?
132. ____________ By how much do we move along the demand curve?

133. ____________ d. Is there a change in the quantity demanded?

5. The income elasticity of demand is .50 and the price elasticity of demand is -1.00. Initially income is $20,000, the price is $.60, and the quantity is 1000. Income increases from $20,000 to $24,000 and the price decreases from $.60 to $.48.

134. ____________ a. Will the demand curve shift? Does it shift to the
135. ____________ right, left, or remain stationary?

136. ____________ b. Is there a change in demand?

137. ____________ c. Will there be a movement along the demand curve?
138. ____________ By how much do we move along the demand curve?

139. ____________ d. Is there a change in the quantity demanded?

ANSWERS

1. X
2. 100
3. Y-intercept
4. 300
5. 360
6. 240
7. 600
8. Utility
9. 2
10. better
11. X-intercept
12. 80
13. Y
14. 200
15. 300
16. 80
17. less than
18. 100
19. 500
20. Yes
21. No
22. Consume more X
23. 500
24. 250
25. Yes
26. Yes
27. Consume the same
28. 300
29. 600
30. Yes
31. No
32. Consume more X
33. price
34. unchange
35. no
36. X
37. 100
38. 150
39. Y-intercept
40. 50
41. 75
42. outward
43. increases
44. inward
45. increases
46. no
47. increases
48. unchanged
49. unchanged
50. X-intercept
51. 100
52. 50
53. Y
54. 50
55. 25
56. inward
57. decreases
58. inward
59. increases
60. increases
61. price
62. fallen
63. less
64. changed
65. less
66. increases
67. X
68. 100
69. Y
70. 50
71. normal
72. decreases
73. increases
74. more
75. More steep
76. Yes
77. Decreases
78. Decreases
79. No change
80. Yes
81. Decreases
82. Decreases
83. Less steep
84. Yes
85. Decreases
86. Decreases
87. No change
88. Yes
89. Increases
90. One cannot tell
91. Less steep
92. Yes
93. Increases
94. Increases
95. No change
96. Yes
97. Decreases
98. One cannot tell
99. price
100. shift
101. 10
102. 5
103. 50
104. shift
105. increased
106. price
107. no
108. along
109. quantity
110. shift
111. not
112. shift
113. no
114. price
115. along
116. 20
117. 10
118. 100
119. along
120. changed
121. 100
122. No
123. Stationary
124. No
125. Yes
126. Increase of 100

127. Yes
128. Yes
129. Leftward by 250
130. Yes
131. No
132. No change
133. No
134. Yes
135. Rightward by 100
136. Yes
137. Yes
138. Increase of 200
139. Yes

PART 3

FIRMS, PRODUCTION, AND SUPPLY

CHAPTER 8

PRODUCTION

WALKING TOUR SUMMARIES

PRODUCTION FUNCTION

A firm's production function summarizes what the
1. ____________ firm knows about using inputs to produce ____________:

Quantity of Output = Q = f(K,L,M,...)

K equals the units of capital used, L units of labor, and M units of raw materials. It is convenient to simplify the presentation by focusing attention on the capital and labor:

Q = f(K,L)

MARGINAL PHYSICAL PRODUCTIVITY: WHAT HAPPENS TO OUTPUT WHEN THE FIRM CHANGES ONE INPUT WITHOUT CHANGING ANY OTHER INPUTS

A firm's marginal physical productivity of labor equals the change in output resulting from the use of one additional unit of labor while keeping all other
2. ____________ ____________ constant. This can be expressed more mathematically:

$$\text{Marginal Physical Productivity of Labor} = MP_L = \frac{\text{Change in Output}}{\text{Change in Labor Input}}$$

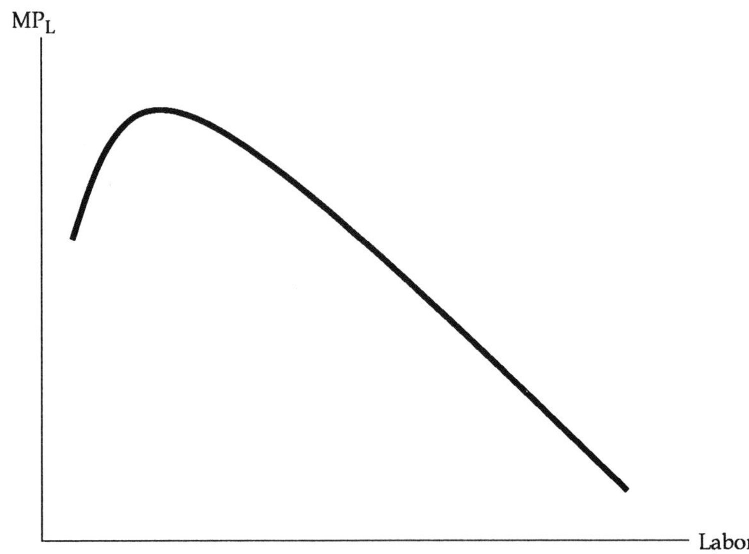

Figure 8.1: *Marginal Productivity of Labor*

DIMINISHING MARGINAL PHYSICAL PRODUCTIVITY

3. ____________ As a firm uses more and more labor without changing the amount of other inputs used, the marginal physical productivity of labor will ___________.

AVERAGE PHYSICAL PRODUCTIVITY

4. ____________ A firm's average physical productivity of labor refers to how much output is produced per unit of labor; that is, average physical productivity equals the ___________ of output to labor:

$$\text{Average Physical Productivity of Labor} = AP_L = \frac{\text{Output}}{\text{Labor Input}}$$

THE TOTAL PRODUCTIVITY, MARGINAL PRODUCTIVITY, AND AVERAGE PRODUCTIVITY CURVES

The total productivity of labor curve illustrates how a
firm's total production of output is affected when it uses
5. ____________ more and more labor without changing any ___________
inputs. At low levels of labor usage, output increases
rapidly as additional labor is used, but eventually due to
6. ____________ ___________ marginal productivity the increase in output
will slow. The firm may even reach a point where it cannot
produce more output. Using additional labor beyond this
point would cause output to decrease. The marginal
physical productivity of labor equals the ___________ of
7. ____________ the total labor productivity curve. The slope illustrates how
output will change when the firm uses one additional unit
8. ____________ of labor. The ___________ productivity of labor equals the
slope of the ray connecting the origin and the relevant point
on the total productivity curve.

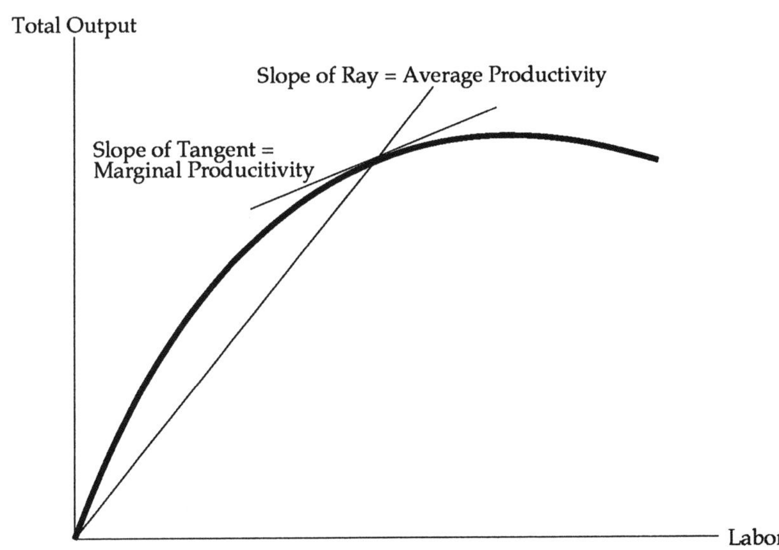

Figure 8.2: *Total, Marginal, and Average Productivity*

ISOQUANT MAPS: HOW INPUTS CAN BE SUBSTITUTED FOR EACH OTHER TO KEEP OUTPUT CONSTANT

To construct an isoquant first choose a level of
9. ____________ ___________ and then find all the different combinations of
capital and labor that will allow the firm to produce that

level of output. An isoquant is just a contour line of the
10. ____________ ____________ function. Any two combinations of labor and
11. ____________ capital lying on the ____________ isoquant will produce the
same level of output. A combination on an isoquant will
produce more output than a combination lying
12. ____________ ____________ the curve. Any combination lying above an
13. ____________ isoquant will produce ____________ than a combination on
the curve.

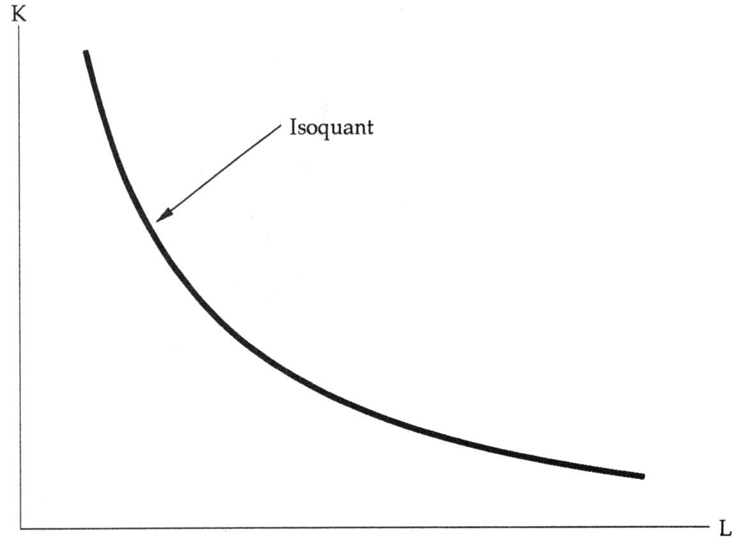

Figure 8.3: *Isoquant*

RATE OF TECHNICAL SUBSTITUTION

A firm's rate of technical substitution of labor for capital equals the amount by which capital can be reduced when one more unit of labor is used in order to keep the
14. ____________ quantity produced ____________:

$$\text{Rate of Technical Substitution} = \text{RTS}$$
$$= \frac{\text{Change in Capital}}{\text{Change in Labor}}$$

while holding output constant. A firm's rate of technical substitution depends upon the amount of capital and labor it is now using. As the firm substitutes more and more labor
15. ____________ for capital, its rate of technical substitution ____________.
Economists call this diminishing rate of technical substitution.

ISOQUANTS AND THE RATE OF TECHNICAL SUBSTITUTION

16. ____________ The ____________ of a firm's isoquant equals the ratio by which the firm can substitute labor for capital while keeping production constant. The slope of a firm's isoquant
17. ____________ and its rate of ____________ substitution represent the same thing.

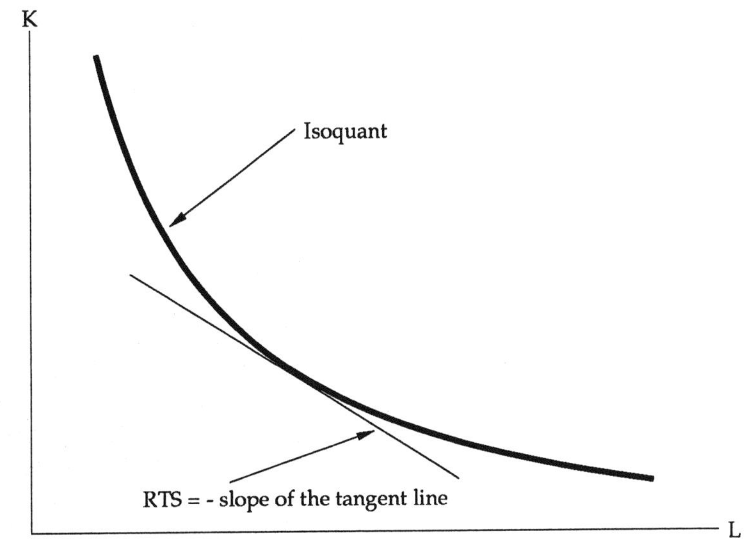

Figure 8.4: *Rate of Technical Substitution*

RETURNS TO SCALE: HOW OUTPUT IS AFFECTED WHEN ALL INPUTS ARE INCREASED SIMULTANEOUSLY

A production function exhibits constant returns to
18. ____________ scale, if a doubling of all inputs exactly ____________
19. ____________ output; ____________ returns to scale, if a doubling of all inputs less than doubles output; and increasing returns to
20. ____________ scale, if a doubling of all inputs ____________ than doubles output.

CHANGES IN TECHNOLOGY

Technological innovation allows a firm to produce the same amount of output with fewer inputs. Therefore, technological change causes a firm's isoquants to shift
21. ____________ ____________, toward the origin.

MULTIPLE-CHOICE QUESTIONS

22. ______ A production function describes how
    a. an individual can turn goods into utility.
    b. an individual can turn inputs into utility.
    c. a firm can turn goods into output.
    d. a firm can turn inputs into output.
    e. a and d.

23. ______ A firm's marginal physical productivity of labor equals
    a. the change in the firm's output resulting from the use of one additional unit of labor without changing any other inputs.
    b. the firm's total output divided by the units of labor used.
    c. the ratio of the change in output to the change in labor input without changing any other inputs.
    d. the ratio of total output to labor input.
    e. a and c.

24. ______ As a firm uses more and more labor without changing any other inputs its marginal physical productivity of labor eventually will
    a. increase.
    b. decrease.
    c. remain constant.
    d. equal marginal cost.
    e. b and d.

25. ______ A firm's average physical productivity of labor equals
    a. the change in the firm's output resulting from the use of one additional unit of labor without changing any other inputs.
    b. the firm's total output divided by the units of labor used.
    c. the ratio of the change in output to the change in labor input without changing any other inputs.
    d. the ratio of marginal physical productivity to labor input.
    e. b and d.

26. ______ A firm's total product of labor curve
    a. relates total output to all inputs used.
    b. is a contour line of the production function.
    c. illustrates all the combinations of capital and labor which will produce a constant level of output.
    d. relates output to the amount of labor used keeping all other inputs constant.
    e. a and b.

27. ______ Graphically, a firm's marginal physical productivity of labor equals the slope of the

a. total product of labor curve at the relevant point.
b. straight line connecting the origin with the relevant point on the total product of labor curve.
c. average productivity of labor curve at the relevant point.
d. straight line connecting the origin with the relevant point on the average productivity of labor curve.
e. a and c.

28. ______ Graphically, a firm's average physical productivity of labor equals the slope of the

a. total product of labor curve at the relevant point.
b. straight line connecting the origin with the relevant point on the total product of labor curve.
c. average productivity of labor curve at the relevant point.
d. straight line connecting the origin with the relevant point on the average productivity of labor curve.
e. a and c.

29. ______ A firm's isoquant

a. relates output to the amount of labor used keeping all other inputs constant.
b. relates total output to all inputs used.
c. is a contour line of the production function.
d. illustrates all the combinations of capital and labor which will produce a constant level of output.
e. c and d.

30. ______ A firm's rate of technical substitution of labor for capital

a. equals the amount by which capital can be reduced when one more unit of labor is used while keeping the level of production constant.
b. equals the ratio of capital used to labor used.
c. reflects the ratio by which capital and labor can be substituted in order to keep output constant.
d. equals the ratio of total output to inputs.
e. a and c.

31. ______ A firm's rate of technical substitution

a. always increases whenever labor and capital are increased by the same percentage.
b. always decreases whenever labor and capital are increased by the same percentage.
c. depends on the amount of labor and capital being used presently.
d. is constant.
e. a and c.

32. ______ Graphically, a firm's rate of technical substitution is reflected by the slope of the

a. isoquant at the relevant point.
b. line connecting the origin with the relevant point on the isoquant.
c. production function at the relevant point.
d. line connecting the origin with the relevant point on the production function.
e. a and d.

33. ______ As a firm moves along an isoquant substituting more and more labor for capital, the rate of technical substitution

a. typically increases.
b. typically decreases.
c. always remains the same.
d. may increase or remain constant, but cannot decrease.
e. always increases.

34. ______ Returns to scale indicate how a firm's total output changes whenever

a. only one input changes.
b. all but one input changes.
c. all inputs change.
d. no inputs change.
e. none of the above.

35. ______ If a firm's production function exhibits increasing returns to scale, a doubling of all inputs will

a. less than double output.
b. more than double output.
c. exactly double output.
d. not affect output.
e. increase the rate of technical substitution.

36. _____ If a firm's production function exhibits constant returns to scale, a doubling of all inputs will
   a. less than double output.
   b. more than double output.
   c. exactly double output.
   d. not affect output.
   e. increase the rate of technical substitution.

RUNNING GLOSSARY

37. __________ Firm: any organization that turns __________ into outputs.

38. __________ __________ function: the mathematical relationship between inputs and outputs.

39. __________ Marginal physical productivity: the __________ output that can be produced by one more unit of a particular input while holding all other inputs constant.

40. __________ Average productivity: the __________ of total output produced to the quantity of a particular input employed.

41. __________ __________ map: a contour map of a firm's production function.

Isoquant: a curve that shows the various combinations of
42. __________ __________ that will produce the same amount of output.

43. __________ Marginal rate of __________ substitution: the negative of the slope of an isoquant. This shows the amount by which
44. __________ capital input can be reduced while holding the __________ constant when one more unit of labor input is added.

45. __________ __________ to scale: the rate at which output increases in response to proportional increases in all inputs.

Fixed proportions production function: a production
46. __________ function in which the input must be used in a __________ ratio to one another.

Technical progress: a shift in the production function that allows a given output level to be produced using
47. __________ __________ inputs.

ANSWERS

1. output
2. inputs
3. diminish
4. ratio
5. other
6. diminishing
7. slope
8. average
9. output
10. production
11. same
12. below
13. more
14. constant
15. decreases
16. slope
17. technical
18. doubles
19. decreasing
20. more
21. in
22. d
23. e
24. b
25. b
26. d
27. a
28. b
29. e
30. e
31. c
32. a
33. b
34. c
35. b
36. c
37. inputs
38. Production
39. additional
40. ratio
41. isoquant
42. inputs
43. technical
44. output
45. Returns
46. fixed
47. less

CHAPTER 9

COSTS

WALKING TOUR SUMMARIES

BASIC CONCEPTS OF COSTS

The production of any good requires the use of
1. ___________ resources. ___________ cost refers to the other goods
foregone when we use resources to produce the good in
2. ___________ question. The ___________'s concept of cost refers to the
firm's out-of-pocket expenses. That is, what the firm must
pay to others for using the resources it employs.
3. ___________ ___________ cost refers what the firm must pay for the
resources it uses to keep those resources employed at the
firm. Putting it differently, economic cost is the
4. ___________ ___________ someone else would pay to use the resources
the firm employs. That is, the remuneration the resources
would receive in their best alternative use.

Economic profit equals total revenue less
5. ___________ ___________ cost. Economic profit of an owner-operated
firm equals the income the owner receives from the firm
6. ___________ ___________ what is necessary to keep the owner operating
7. ___________ his firm; that is, less the ___________ someone would pay
the owner to work elsewhere.

COST-MINIMIZING INPUT CHOICE

Once the firm decides upon its level of production,
the firm will produce its output using the input combination
8. ___________ that ___________ total costs. The firm produces its chosen
level of output in the least costly way whenever its rate of
9. ___________ ___________ substitution equals the ratio of the wage and
10. ___________ rental rates. To understand why recall that an ___________
represents all the combinations of labor and capital that can
produce a given level of output. We wish to find that
combination of labor and capital, that point on the isoquant,
which minimizes the firm's total costs. In light of our
previous assumption that a firm's only inputs are labor and
capital, a firm's total costs are:

$$\text{Total Costs} = TC = wL + vK$$

where w= wage rate of labor

v = rental rate of capital

The combinations of labor and capital which keep total costs
11. ____________ constant lie on a straight line with ____________ equal to -w/v. The least costly way to produce the firm's chosen level of production is the point on the isoquant which is
12. ____________ ____________ to the equal total cost curve. In this situation all less costly combinations of labor and capital lie
13. ____________ ____________ the isoquant. This means that the firm cannot reduce its total costs without decreasing its level of production.
14. ____________ A firm's ____________ path illustrates how the cost-minimizing combination of labor and capital changes with the firm's level of output changes. To construct the expansion path find the cost-minimizing combination of
15. ____________ labor and capital for each level of ____________. The expansion path is the locus of these points. A negatively sloped expansion path indicates that higher levels of
16. ____________ production result in using ____________ of one input.
17. ____________ Economists call such an input ____________.

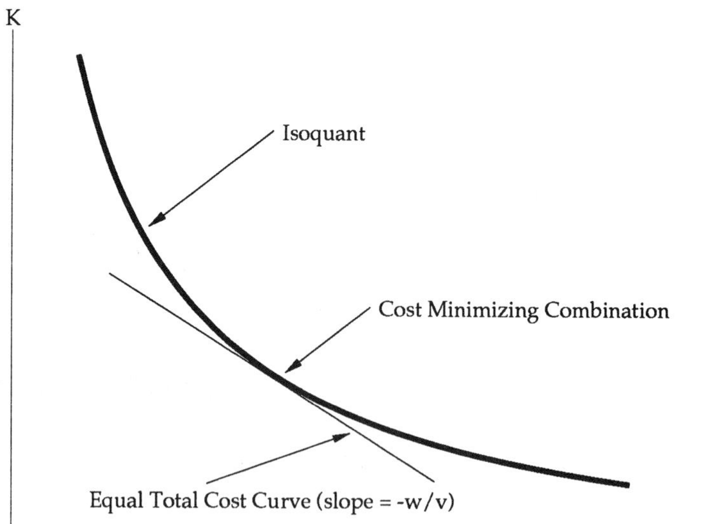

Figure 9.1: *Cost Minimzing Combination*

TOTAL COST CURVE

A firm's total cost curve illustrates the costs the firm
18. __________ incurs when it produces different levels of __________.
The total cost curve passes through the origin. If the firm
produces no output, it uses no inputs, and its total costs are
19. __________ __________. Also, the total cost curve is always upward
sloping. To produce more output, the firm must employ
20. __________ more inputs which __________ its total costs. The total
cost curve is a straight line whenever the production
21. __________ function exhibits __________ returns to scale; inputs and
hence costs expand proportionally as output rises. The total
cost curve is concave whenever the production function
22. __________ exhibits __________ returns to scale; inputs and hence
costs expand more than proportionally as output rises. Last,
23. __________ the total cost curve is convex with __________ returns to
scale.

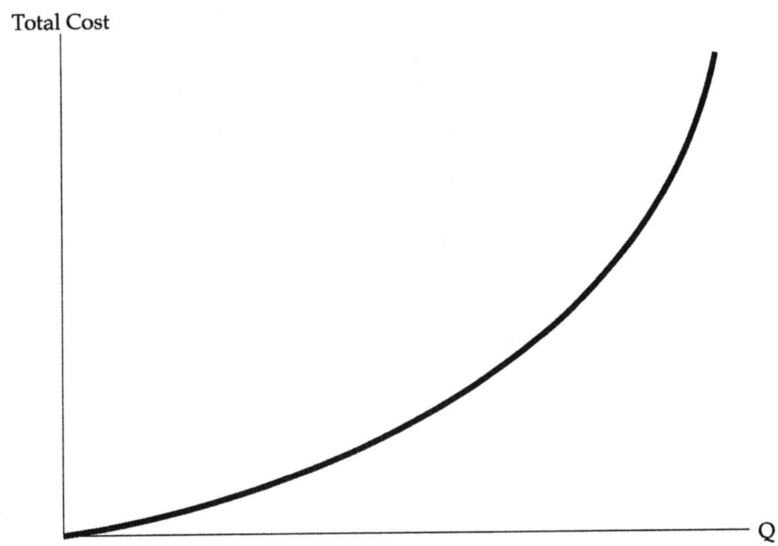

Figure 9.2: *Total Cost Curve*

MARGINAL COST CURVE

A firm's marginal cost equals the change in total cost
24. __________ resulting from the production of __________ additional
unit of output:

$$\text{Marginal Cost} = MC = \frac{\text{Change in Total Cost}}{\text{Change in Quantity}}$$

Graphically, marginal cost is the slope of the total cost curve. It is constant when the production function exhibits
25. ____________ ____________ returns to scale. Marginal cost is increasing
26. ____________ with ____________ returns to scale and decreasing with
27. ____________ ____________ returns to scale. If the production function exhibits increasing returns to scale for low levels of production and decreasing returns to scale for high levels,
28. ____________ the marginal cost curve will be ____________-shaped.

AVERAGE COST CURVE

A firm's average cost equals its total costs divided by
29. ____________ the ____________; that is, average cost is the ratio of total costs to quantity:

$$\text{Average Cost} = AC = \frac{\text{Total Cost}}{\text{Quantity}}$$

Graphically, average cost equals the slope of the ray from the origin to the total cost curve.

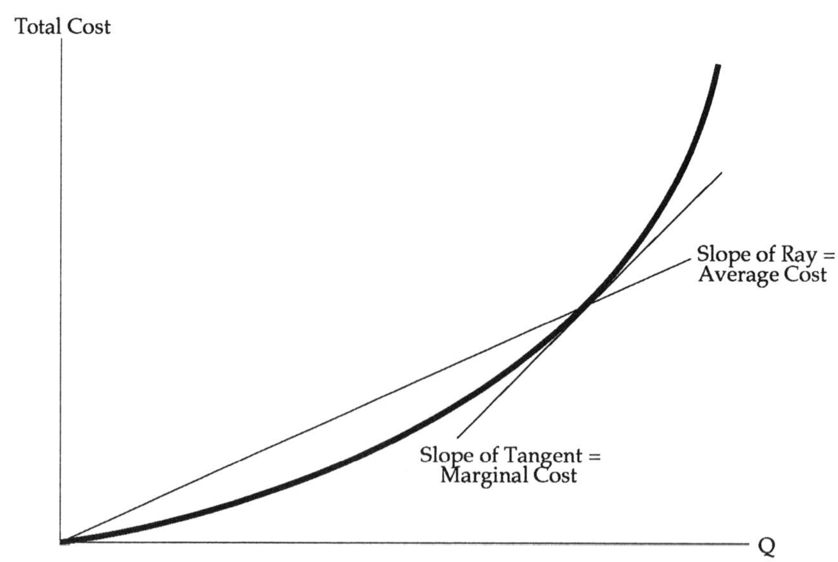

Figure 9.3: *Total, Marginal, and Average Cost*

AVERAGE AND MARGINAL COST CURVES

If the marginal cost curve is U-shaped, the average total cost curve will be U-shaped also. When the average
30. ____________ cost curve is falling, marginal cost must be ____________ than average cost; if the average cost of production decreases when an additional unit is produced, the cost of producing the additional unit itself (marginal cost) must be
31. ____________ ____________ than the average. Similarly, when average
32. ____________ cost is rising marginal cost must ____________ average cost; if the average cost of production increases when an additional unit is produced, the cost of producing the additional unit itself (the marginal cost) must be
33. ____________ ____________ than the average. Since marginal cost must be less than average cost when the average is falling and marginal cost must be greater than average cost when the
34. ____________ average is rising, marginal cost must ____________ average cost when the average is at its minimum. The marginal and
35. ____________ average cost curves ____________ at the point of minimum average cost.

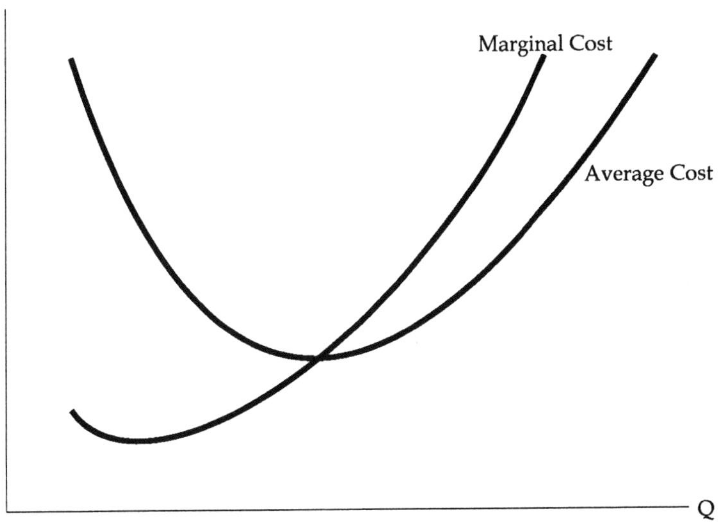

Figure 9.4: *Marginal and Average Cost Curves*

DISTINCTION BETWEEN THE SHORT RUN AND THE LONG RUN

36. ____________ In the ____________ run the firm can vary all input while in the short run some inputs are fixed. Typically,

37. ____________ ____________ is assumed to be fixed. In the short run total costs can be divided into two components:

$$STC = SFC + SVC$$

38. ____________ Costs that are fixed in the short run are called ____________ costs, denoted by SFC. Similarly, economists call costs

39. ____________ associated with the variable inputs ____________ costs, denoted by SVC. Fixed costs are constant, unaffected by the level produced. Variable costs, on the other hand, change as the level of production changes. Short-run average total cost

40. ____________ equals short-run total cost divided by ____________:

$$SAC = \frac{STC}{Q} = \frac{SFC}{Q} + \frac{SVC}{Q}$$

Typically, the short-run average total cost curve is

41. ____________ ____________ -shaped. The short-run marginal cost curve

42. ____________ eventually becomes ____________ sloping as a result of diminishing marginal productivity. These two curves

43. ____________ intersect at the point of ____________ average total cost.

THE RELATIONSHIP BETWEEN SHORT-RUN AND LONG-RUN CURVES

44. ____________ In the long run the firm can change ____________ its inputs. In the short run the firm can change only

45. ____________ ____________ inputs. Because the firm has more flexibility in the long run than in the short run, long-run costs are

46. ____________ typically ____________ than short-run costs.

MULTIPLE-CHOICE QUESTIONS

47. ______ Opportunity cost of producing a good refers to
    a. the goods that must be forgone in order to produce the good in question.
    b. the out-of-pocket expenses a firm incurs when producing the good.
    c. the remuneration that must be made in order to keep all the resources used to produce the good in place.
    d. the most someone else would pay to use the resources now producing the good.
    e. the out-of-pocket payments the firm makes for the resources used to produce the good.

48. ______ The accountant's cost of producing a good refers to
    a. the goods that must be forgone in order to produce the good in question.
    b. the remuneration that must be made in order to keep all the resources used to produce the good in place.
    c. the most someone else would pay to use the resources now producing the good.
    d. the out-of-pocket payments the firm makes for the resources used to produce the good.
    e. b and d.

49. ______ The economist's cost of producing a good refers to
    a. the goods that must be forgone in order to produce the good in question.
    b. the out-of-pocket expenses a firm incurs when producing the good.
    c. the remuneration that must be made in order to keep all the resources used to produce the good in place.
    d. the most someone else would pay to use the resources now producing the good.
    e. c and d.

50. ______ The economic profit of an owner-operated firm equals
    a. total revenues less economic costs.
    b. total revenue less the firm's out-of-pocket costs.
    c. the income the owner receives from the firm less what is necessary to keep the owner operating his firm.
    d. the income the owner receives from the firm less the most someone else would pay the owner to work elsewhere.
    e. a, c, and d.

51. ______ A firm's equal total cost curve

a. reflects all the combinations of labor and capital that will produce a given level of output.
b. reflects all the combinations of labor and capital that cost the firm the same amount.
c. is upward sloping.
d. is horizontal.
e. b and d.

52. ______ The slope of a firm's equal total cost curve

a. reflects the ratio of the wage rate to the rental rate for capital.
b. reflects the firm's marginal rate of substitution.
c. equals zero.
d. reflects the price of the good produced.
e. a and d.

53. ______ In order to produce a given amount of output at the lowest possible cost, a firm will choose the input combination at which

a. its rate of technical substitution equals the wage-rental ratio.
b. its ratio of labor to capital used equals the wage-rental ratio.
c. its ratio of the average labor productivity to the average capital productivity equals the wage-rental ratio.
d. the amount of labor used is minimized.
e. b and d.

54. ______ A firm's expansion path illustrates

a. all the combinations of labor and capital that will produce a given level of output.
b. the total costs a firm incurs producing each level of output.
c. the cost-minimizing combinations of labor and capital for each level of output.
d. the firm's marginal cost curve.
e. c and d.

55. ______ If an input is inferior, a firm's expansion path will be

a. horizontal.
b. upward sloping.
c. downward sloping.
d. U-shaped.
e. impossible to describe without additional information.

56. ______ A firm's total cost curve

a. cannot be downward sloping.
b. is always downward sloping.
c. is always horizontal.
d. may be upward sloping, downward sloping, or horizontal.
e. is impossible to describe without additional information.

57. ______ If a firm's production function exhibits increasing returns to scale the total cost curve is

a. a straight upward sloping line.
b. an upward sloping curve that bends downward.
c. an upward sloping curve that bends upward.
d. a downward sloping curve.
e. impossible to describe without additional information.

58. ______ If a firm's production function exhibits constant returns to scale the total cost curve is

a. a straight upward sloping line.
b. an upward sloping curve that bends downward.
c. an upward sloping curve that bends upward.
d. a downward sloping curve.
e. impossible to describe without additional information.

59. ______ A firm's marginal cost equals

a. the change in total cost resulting from the production of one additional unit of output.
b. the ratio of total cost to output.
c. the ratio of the change in a firm's total cost to a change in output.
d. average cost at all levels of production.
e. a and c.

60. ______ Graphically, a firm's marginal cost equals the slope of

a. its average cost curve at the relevant point.
b. the straight line connecting the origin with the relevant point on its average cost curve.
c. its total cost curve at the relevant point.
d. the straight line connecting the origin with the relevant point on its total cost curve.
e. a and c.

61. ______ In the short run a firm

a. can vary all inputs.
b. can vary only some inputs.
c. can vary no inputs.
d. cannot change its level of production.
e. c and d.

62. ______ In the long run a firm

a. can vary all inputs.
b. can vary only some inputs.
c. can vary no inputs.
d. cannot change its level of production.
e. c and d.

63. ______ Costs associated with those inputs that a firm cannot vary in the short run are called

a. total costs.
b. accountant's costs.
c. variable costs.
d. fixed costs.
e. b and d.

64. ______ Costs associated with those inputs that a firm can vary in the short run are called

a. total costs.
b. accountant's costs.
c. variable costs.
d. fixed costs.
e. b and d.

65. ______ In the short run a firm's average total cost curve is typically

a. upward sloping.
b. downward sloping.
c. flat.
d. U-shaped.
e. upward sloping or flat.

66. ______ If a firm's marginal cost is greater than its average cost, its

a. average cost curve must be falling.
b. average cost curve must be rising.
c. average cost curve may be rising, falling, or flat.
d. marginal cost curve must be falling.
e. marginal cost curve must be rising.

67. ______ If a firm's marginal cost is less than average cost, its
   a. average cost curve must be falling.
   b. average cost curve must be rising.
   c. average cost curve may be rising, falling, or flat.
   d. marginal cost curve must be falling.
   e. marginal cost curve must be rising.

68. ______ A firm's average cost curve and marginal cost curve intersect at the point of minimum
   a. marginal cost.
   b. average cost.
   c. total cost.
   d. average variable cost.
   e. a and b.

69. ______ A firm's short-run costs are
   a. always less than its long-run costs.
   b. never less than its long-run costs.
   c. sometimes less than its long-run costs and sometimes greater than its long-run costs.
   d. unrelated to its long-run costs.
   e. always greater than its long-run costs.

RUNNING GLOSSARY

70. ____________ Opportunity cost: the cost of a good or service as measured by the alternative uses that are ____________ by producing the good or service.

71. ____________ ____________ cost: the concept that goods or services cost what was paid for them.

72. ____________ ____________ cost: the cost concept that goods or services cost the amount required to keep them in their present use; the amount that they would be worth in their next best alternative use.

73. ____________ Wage rate: the cost of hiring one ____________ for one hour.

74. ____________ ____________ rate: the cost of hiring one machine for one hour.

75. ____________ Economic____________: the difference between a firm's total revenues and its total economic costs.

76. ____________ Expansion path: the locus of cost-minimizing ____________ combinations a firm will choose to produce various levels of output (when the prices of inputs are held constant).

77. ____________ Average cost: total costs divided by ____________.

78. ____________ Marginal cost: the additional cost of producing one ____________ unit of output.

79. ____________ ____________ run: the period of time in which a firm must consider some inputs absolutely fixed in making its decisions.

80. ____________ Long run: the period of time in which a firm may consider ____________ of its inputs to be variable in making its decisions.

81. ____________ Fixed costs: cost associated with inputs that are fixed in the ____________ run.

82. ____________ ____________ costs: costs associated with inputs that can be varied in the short run.

ANSWERS

1. Opportunity
2. accountant
3. Economic
4. most
5. economic
6. less
7. most
8. minimizes
9. technical
10. isoquant
11. slope
12. tangent
13. below
14. expansion
15. production
16. less
17. inferior
18. output
19. zero
20. increase
21. constant
22. increasing
23. decreasing
24. one
25. constant
26. decreasing
27. increasing
28. U
29. quantity
30. less
31. less
32. exceed
33. greater
34. equal
35. intersect
36. long
37. capital
38. fixed
39. variable
40. quantity
41. U
42. upward
43. minimum
44. all
45. variable
46. less
47. a
48. d
49. e
50. e
51. b
52. a
53. a
54. c
55. c
56. a
57. b
58. a
59. e
60. c
61. b
62. a
63. d
64. c
65. d
66. b
67. a
68. b
69. b
70. foregone
71. Accounting
72. Economic
73. worker
74. Rental
75. profits
76. input
77. output
78. more
79. Short
80. all
81. short
82. Variable

CHAPTER 10

PROFIT MAXIMIZATION AND SUPPLY

WALKING TOUR SUMMARIES

PROFIT MAXIMIZATION

Economists typically assume that the goal of a firm is to maximize profits:

Profits = Total Revenue + Total Costs
= TR + TC

1. ___________ Total revenue equals price times ___________:

$$TR = P \times Q$$

PROFIT MAXIMIZATION AND MARGINALISM

2. ___________ Marginal ___________ equals the additional revenue the firm obtains from the sale of one additional unit of
3. ___________ output. Marginal ___________ equals the additional cost the firm incurs from the production of one additional unit of output. To maximize profits the firm will produce the level
4. ___________ of output at which marginal revenue ___________
5. ___________ marginal cost. Whenever marginal revenue ___________ marginal cost the production and sale of one additional unit of output will increase total revenues more than total costs. Therefore profits will rise with additional production. Alternatively, whenever marginal revenue is less than
6. ___________ marginal cost, profits will ___________ with reduced production. To maximize profits, marginal revenue must
7. ___________ ___________ marginal cost.

MARGINAL REVENUE

8. ___________ If a firm is a price ___________, the firm's output decision does not affect the price. In this case the firm's
9. ___________ marginal revenue ___________ the price. Whenever the

firm produces one additional unit of output, its total
10. ____________ revenues rise by an amount ____________ to the price.

On the other hand, if the price falls whenever the firm
11. ____________ increases production marginal revenue will be ____________ than the price. To understand why assume that the quantity is initially 50 units and that the sale of one additional unit causes the price to fall from \$1.00 to \$.99. Recall that
12. ____________ marginal revenue equals the change in total ____________ resulting from the sale of one additional unit of production. The sale of one additional unit of production affects total revenue in two ways:

1. The sale of the additional unit itself causes total revenues to rise by an amount equal to the price. The sale of the 51st unit by itself produces \$.99 of additional revenues.

2. The sale of the additional unit causes the price to fall from \$1.00 to \$.99. The lower price means that the firm will collect fewer revenues from the other units sold. Revenues collected from the other 50 units decrease from \$50.00 (50 × \$1.00) to \$49.50 (50 × \$.99).

As a consequence of the second effect, marginal revenue is
13. ____________ less than the ____________.

MARGINAL REVENUE AND PRICE ELASTICITY

To understand the relationship between marginal revenue and elasticity of demand recall that the elasticity of demand indicates how sensitive the quantity demanded is to a change in the price:

$$e_{Q,P} = \frac{\text{Percent Change in Quantity}}{\text{Percent Change in Price}}$$

Total revenue equals price times quantity:

$$TR = P \times Q.$$

If demand is inelastic, marginal revenue will be negative.
14. ____________ While a fall in the price will ____________ the quantity, it will not increase it by "very much" when demand is
15. ____________ inelastic. Hence, total revenues will ____________. Marginal revenue equals the change in total revenues

resulting from the sale of one additional unit of output. Since total revenues fall as the quantity increases, marginal

16. ____________ revenue must be ____________. On the other hand, if
17. ____________ demand is elastic, marginal revenue will be ____________.

MARGINAL REVENUE CURVE

Every demand curve has a marginal revenue curve associated with it. The demand curve can be thought of as
18. ____________ the ____________ revenue curve. The demand curve illustrates the revenue per unit (that is, the price) yielded by alternative output choices. Whenever the demand curve is downward sloping, additional production causes average
19. ____________ revenue to ____________. The sale of an additional unit of output causes average revenue to fall. The extra revenue
20. ____________ produced by the additional unit sold must be ____________ than the average. Hence when the demand curve is downward sloping the marginal revenue curve lies
21. ____________ ____________ the demand curve.

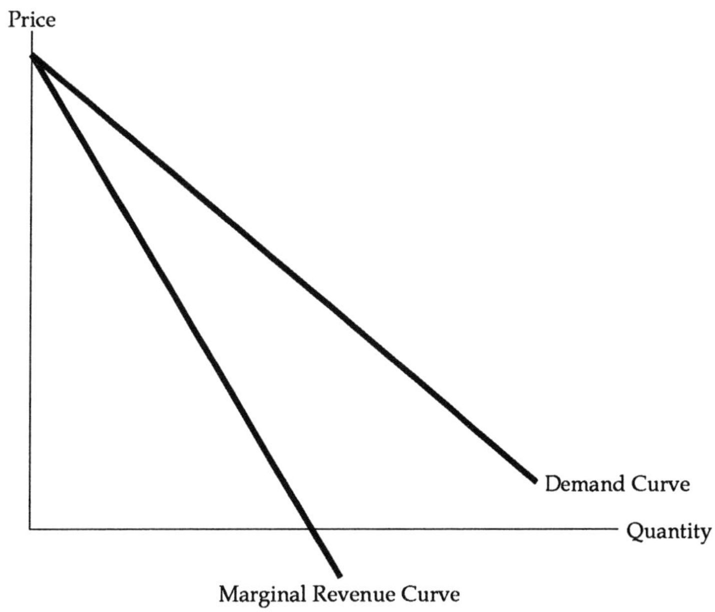

Figure10.1: *Downward Sloping Demand and Marginal Revenue*

CONTROVERSY OVER THE PROFIT MAXIMIZATION HYPOTHESIS

When the owners of firms respond to questionnaires, they seldom rank profits as their only goal. Furthermore, they even deny having the information needed to compare marginal revenue and marginal cost. In view of the economist's reliance on the profit maximization assumption this is troublesome. Milton Friedman argues that we

22. ____________ ______________ judge the validity of the profit maximization hypothesis in this way, however. We should judge models by how accurately they predict real-world events. In fact, the profit maximization hypothesis is extremely accurate in predicting many aspects of firms' behavior. A second reason why most economists favor the

23. ____________ profit maximization hypothesis is the ___________ principle. In many industries firms must maximize profits to survive. Otherwise, they would go out of business or their management would be taken over by others.

Other hypotheses to explain firm behavior have been

24. ____________ advanced. Baumol suggested that ___________ maximization may better explain firm behavior. Revenue maximizing firms would expand output beyond profit maximizing levels. Another alternative, the markup pricing

25. ____________ hypothesis, appears to be quite similar to ___________ maximization. Some empirical evidence suggests that markups vary in a way that is entirely consistent with profit maximization.

SHORT-RUN SUPPLY BY A PRICE-TAKING FIRM

To maximize profits a firm produces the level of

26. ____________ output at which marginal revenue ___________ marginal cost. A price-taking firm's marginal revenue equals the

27. ____________ ___________. Putting both parts together, a profit-maximizing, price-taking firm produces the level of output

28. ____________ at which ___________ equals marginal cost. Therefore, the firm's individual supply curve is its marginal cost curve.

Before moving on we must amend this last statement to cover those situations in which the price is "very low." If the price falls below the firm's average variable cost, the

29. ____________ firm will find it advantageous to ___________ in the short run. To understand this keep in mind a simple rule: a firm

30. ____________ will shut down when it ___________ more by operating than it loses by shutting down.

31. ___________ When the ___________ is less than average variable costs, the firm's total revenues do not cover its variable costs:

$$P < AVC$$

$$P < \frac{VC}{Q}$$

$$P \times Q < VC \qquad \text{Profit} = TR - TC$$

$$TR < VC \qquad \text{Profit} = TR - (FC - VC)$$

$$\text{Profit} = (TR - VC) - FC$$

32. ___________ By operating the firm loses ___________ than its fixed costs, whenever price is less than average variable costs. On the other hand, if a firm shuts down, total revenues and variable
33. ___________ costs are zero; the firm loses only its ___________ costs. A firm will shut down whenever the price falls short of
34. ___________ ___________ variable cost.

MULTIPLE-CHOICE QUESTIONS

35. _____ Economists typically assume that firms
   a. maximize sales.
   b. maximize revenues.
   c. maximize profits.
   d. maximize costs.
   e. are completely unpredictable.

36. _____ A firm's total revenue equals
   a. price times the quantity it sells.
   b. price times its average cost.
   c. average cost times the quantity it sells.
   d. marginal cost times the quantity it sells.
   e. a and c.

37. _____ To maximize profits a firm produces the level of output at which its
   a. marginal revenue equals price.
   b. average cost is minimized.
   c. marginal revenue equals its marginal cost.
   d. average cost equals the price.
   e. c and d.

38. ______ A firm's marginal cost equals

a. the additional revenue the firm obtains from the sale of one additional unit of output.
b. total costs divided by output.
c. the ratio of total costs to output.
d. the additional costs the firm incurs from the production of one additional unit of output.
e. the additional profits the firm obtains from the production and sale of one additional unit of output.

39. ______ A firm's marginal revenue equals

a. the additional revenue the firm obtains from the sale of one additional unit of output.
b. total revenue divided by output.
c. the ratio of total revenue to output.
d. the additional costs the firm incurs from the production of one additional unit of output.
e. the additional profits the firm obtains from the production and sale of one additional unit of output.

40. ______ If a firm's marginal revenue exceeds its marginal cost, additional production will

a. decrease its costs.
b. increase its revenues by more than its costs.
c. increase its costs by more than its revenues.
d. decrease its profits.
e. a and b.

41. ______ If a firm's marginal cost exceeds it marginal revenue, additional production will

a. decrease its costs.
b. increase its revenues by more than its costs.
c. increase its costs by more than its revenues.
d. increase its profits.
e. b and d.

42. ______ If a firm is a price taker

a. its output decisions will not affect the price.
b. additional production by the firm will lower the price.
c. its marginal revenue will equal the price.
d. its marginal revenue will be less than the price.
e. a and c.

43. ______ If price falls whenever the firm increases production, marginal revenue will

a. equal the initial price.
b. equal the new price.
c. be less than the price.
d. be greater than the new price.
e. a and d.

44. ______ A good's price elasticity of demand reflects how sensitive the quantity demanded is to a change in

a. the price of the good in question.
b. income.
c. the price of another good.
d. consumer preferences.
e. b and c.

45. ______ The price elasticity of demand equals

a. the change in the quantity demanded caused by a 1 unit (1 dollar) change in price.
b. the percent change in the quantity demanded caused by a 1 percent change in income.
c. the ratio of the change in the quantity demanded to the change in the price.
d. the ratio of the percent change in the quantity demanded to the percent change in the price.
e. a and c.

46. ______ If a firm faces an inelastic demand curve for the good it produces, then the firm's marginal revenue

a. must be negative.
b. must be positive.
c. must be zero.
d. may be positive, negative, or zero.
e. is never negative.

47. ______ If a firm faces an elastic demand curve for the good it produces, then the firm's marginal revenue

a. must be negative.
b. must be positive.
c. must be zero.
d. may be positive, negative, or zero.
e. equals minus one.

48. ______ Most economists support the use of the profit maximization hypothesis because

a. most firm managers rank profits as their only goal when they are polled.
b. the hypothesis has proven to be an accurate predictor of firm behavior in the real world.
c. of the survivorship principle.
d. no other hypothesis has been advanced.
e. b and c.

49. ______ The survivorship principle argues that in order to survive a firm must

a. maximize profits.
b. maximize sales.
c. become a monopolist.
d. merge with its competitors.
e. a and d.

50. ______ A profit-maximizing firm in a perfectly competitive industry will at all times produce the level of output at which price equals its

a. average cost regardless of the relationship between price and average variable cost.
b. average cost as long as price exceeds average variable cost.
c. marginal cost regardless of the relationship between price and average variable cost.
d. marginal cost as long as price exceeds average variable cost.
e. a and d.

51. ______ An individual firm's supply curve is its

a. marginal cost curve.
b. marginal cost curve as long as price exceeds average variable cost.
c. average cost curve.
d. average cost curve as long as price exceeds average variable cost.
e. a and c.

52. ______ If a firm were to operate when the price is less than its average variable cost

a. variable costs exceed total revenues.
b. total costs exceed total revenues.
c. losses are less than fixed costs.
d. losses are greater than fixed costs.
e. a, b, and d.

53. _____ In the short run whenever the price is less than average variable cost the firm will

a. shut down.
b. exit the industry.
c. expand production.
d. continue to operate.
e. c and d.

RUNNING GLOSSARY

54. ___________ ___________ revenue: the extra revenue a firm receives when it sells one more unit of output.

Price taker: a firm or individual whose decisions regarding buying or selling have no effect on the prevailing market
55. ___________ ___________ of a good or service.

56. ___________ ___________ principle: the idea that in competitive markets, only profit-maximizing firms are likely to survive.

Revenue maximization: a goal for firms in which they work
57. ___________ to maximize their total ___________ rather than profits.

58. ___________ ___________ pricing: determining the selling price of a good by adding a percentage to the average cost of producing it.

Shutdown price: the price below which the firm will choose
59. ___________ to produce no output in the ___________ run. Equal to
60. ___________ minimum average ___________ cost.

ANSWERS

1. quantity
2. revenue
3. cost
4. equals
5. exceeds
6. rise
7. equal
8. taker
9. equals
10. equal
11. less
12. revenue
13. price
14. increase
15. fall
16. negative
17. positive
18. average
19. fall
20. less
21. beneath
22. cannot
23. survivorship
24. revenue
25. profit
26. equals
27. price
28. price
29. shut down
30. loses
31. price
32. more
33. fixed
34. average
35. c
36. a
37. c
38. d
39. a
40. b
41. c
42. e
43. c
44. a
45. d
46. a
47. b
48. e
49. a
50. d
51. b
52. e
53. a
54. Marginal
55. price
56. Survivorship
57. revenue
58. Markup
59. short
60. variable

CHAPTER 11

FURTHER APPLICATIONS OF THE THEORY OF THE FIRM

WALKING TOUR SUMMARIES

CONTRACTS WITH WORKERS

1. ____________ While most workers do not have ____________ contracts with their employer, virtually all have clear understandings about their duties and their pay. Typically, when a firm hires a new worker, he will not be a very productive employee at first. The new worker does not have all the skills that are important for his particular job.
2. ____________ The new worker must be ____________; he must learn these
3. ____________ job-specific skills, a process that is ____________ to the firm. Firms try to keep these costs low by encouraging workers to
4. ____________ ____________ with the firm thereby reducing the need to train new workers. Firms have an incentive to develop
5. ____________ ____________-term relationships (explicit or implicit contracts) with their employees.

The attractiveness of long-term relationships explains why firms are often reluctant to hire new or lay off present employees when demand changes temporarily. If demand
6. ____________ for a firm's product were to ____________ temporarily, the firm might be reluctant to lay off a present employee. A laid-off worker may seek employment elsewhere. The firm would lose the job-specific skills the worker had acquired, if the worker finds another job. Thus, to continue the long-
7. ____________ term relationship, the firm hesitates to ____________ workers. Similarly, pay based on seniority, pension plans based on years of service, and bonuses based on the success
8. ____________ of the firm are ways to promote a ____________-term relationship between firms and employees.

CONTRACTS WITH MANAGERS

9. __________ In many firms those who __________ the firm's capital are not the same individuals as those who manage the operation of the firm. The manager acts as an
10. __________ __________ for the owner. This separation of ownership and management creates a conflict: The owner is concerned
11. __________ with the firm's __________ while the manager is concerned with benefits. The manager (who is not the sole
12. __________ owner) will operate the firm to produce __________ profit and more benefits than the owner would like. Management contracts lessen this conflict. These contracts provide
13. __________ __________ with incentives to encourage profit-maximizing behavior. The contracts represent a compromise. Profits will be greater than in the pure agent case, but less than the owner-operated case.

THE MARKET FOR FIRMS

If a firm is inefficiently managed, its costs will be
14. __________ __________ than they need be. A new management team could take over and presumably reduce costs and
15. __________ __________ the firm's profits, thereby aiding the firm's owners. The takeover of a corporation is no simple matter, however; there are significant costs involved. Typically, the new management must negotiate complex borrowing arrangements. Furthermore, existing management may pursue defensive ploys making a takeover more
16. __________ __________. Consequently, we would expect a takeover to succeed only when substantial management inefficiencies exist, when a new management team could produce major cost savings.

MULTIPLE-CHOICE QUESTIONS

17. _____ Typically when a worker is first hired his productivity is
    a. relatively high.
    b. relatively low.
    c. always negative.
    d. always positive.
    e. a and d.

18. ______ As a new employee works at his job longer and longer his productivity will

a. increase.
b. decrease.
c. remain the same.
d. approach zero.
e. b and d.

19. ______ A worker's productivity typically increases the longer he is employed on a new job because he

a. receives on-the-job training.
b. learns job-specific skills.
c. attends formal education classes.
d. becomes more familiar with the his new job.
e. a, b, and d.

20. ______ As a consequence of training costs firms have an incentive to

a. encourage short-term relationships with their employees.
b. encourage long-term relationships with their employees.
c. hire and fire workers frequently.
d. never rehire laid-off workers.
e. a and c.

21. ______ In order to encourage long-term relationships with their employees firms

a. always insist on formal contracts.
b. often are reluctant to lay off workers.
c. often advocate seniority systems.
d. are reluctant to institute pension plans.
e. b and c.

22. ______ When the ownership and management of a firm is separated

a. the owner acts as the manager's agent.
b. the owner and manager typically have identical interests.
c. the owner and manager typically have different interests.
d. a and b.
e. a and c.

23. ______ Contracts between owners and managers
   a. completely resolve their conflicting interests.
   b. partially resolve their conflicting interests.
   c. encourage managers to become more concerned with benefits.
   d. encourage managers to become more concerned with profits.
   e. b and d.

24. ______ If a firm is inefficiently managed
   a. costs are higher than they need to be.
   b. new management could increase the firm's profits.
   c. it will undoubtably be taken over by a new management team in a very short period of time.
   d. a and b.
   e. a, b, and c.

25. ______ The takeover of a corporation
   a. is a very simple matter.
   b. is typically welcomed by the present managers.
   c. typically requires simple borrowing arrangements.
   d. is often fought by the present managers.
   e. c and d.

26. ______ One would expect takeovers to succeed
   a. when the present management team is inefficient in even the smallest way.
   b. when new management could achieve any reduction in costs no matter how small.
   c. when new management could achieve any increase in profits no matter how small.
   d. only when the firm is very poorly managed by the present management team.
   e. a, b, and c.

RUNNING GLOSSARY

27. ____________ ___________: the role of making economic decisions for another party, for example the manager of a firm being hired to act for the owner.

28. ____________ Job-specific skills: skills learned on a ____________ that enable a worker to do a specific job better.

29. ____________ Efficient wage: a wage above the market wage paid to encourage a worker to ____________ with a firm.

ANSWERS

1. formal
2. trained
3. costly
4. stay
5. long
6. fall
7. lay off
8. long
9. own
19. agent
11. profits
12. less
13. managers
14. greater
15. increase
16. difficult
17. b
18. a
19. e
20. b
21. e
22. c
23. e
24. d
25. d
26. d
27. Agent
28. job
29. remain

PART 3

FIRMS, PRODUCTION, AND SUPPLY

WALKING TOUR PROBLEMS

COST MINIMIZATION

1. The wage rate of labor is \$20.00 and the rental rate of capital is \$10.00. The firm's rate of technical substitution is 1.0.

   a. What is the wage-rental ratio; that is, what is the wage rate divided by the rental rate?

   The wage rate is \$20.00 and the rental rate is \$10. The
1.__________ wage-rental ratio is __________.

   The answer is 2.0.

   b. Can the firm reduce costs without decreasing its level of output? Should the firm use more, less, or the same amount of labor?

   Since the wage-rental ratio does not equal the rate of
2.__________ technical substitution, the firm __________ reduce
its costs without producing less output.

   The answer is yes.

   The firm's rate of technical substitution is 1.0; if the
3.__________ firm uses 1 less unit of labor, __________ additional
unit of capital is required to keep the level of production constant. The wage-rental ratio is 2.0; if
4.__________ the firm hires 1 less unit of labor, __________
additional units of capital can be hired while keeping its total costs constant. Consequently, if the firm hires 1 less unit of labor and 1 additional unit of capital, production will remain the same and total costs will
5.__________ __________.

The answer is hire less labor and more capital.

2. The wage rate of labor is $30.00 and the rental rate of capital is $10.00. The firm's rate of technical substitution is 4.0.

   a. What is the wage-rental ratio; that is, what is the wage rate divided by the rental rate?

6.____________ The wage rate is $30.00 and the rental rate is $10. The wage-rental ratio is ____________.

   The answer is 3.0.

   b. Can the firm reduce costs without decreasing its level of output? Shoud the firm use more, less, or the same amount of labor?

   Since the wage-rental ratio does not equal the rate of technical substitution, the firm can reduce its costs

7.____________ ____________ producing less output.

   The answer is yes.

   The firm's rate of technical substitution is 4.0; if the firm uses 1 more unit of labor, 4 fewer units of capital can be used while keeping the level of production

8.____________ ____________. The wage-rental ratio is 3.0; if the firm

9.____________ hires 1 more unit of labor, ____________ fewer units of capital must be hired to keep its total costs constant. Consequently, if the firm hires 1 more unit of labor and 4 fewer units of capital, production will

10.____________ remain the same and total costs will ____________.

   The answer is hire more labor and less capital.

3. The wage rate of labor is $20.00 and the rental rate of capital is $10.00. The firm's rate of technical substitution is 2.0.

   a. What is the wage-rental ratio; that is, what is the

11.____________ wage rate divided by the rental rate?

b. Can the firm reduce costs without decreasing its level
12. ____________ of output? Should the firm use more, less, or the
13. ____________ same amount of labor?

4. The wage rate of labor is $5.00 and the rental rate of capital is $10.00. The firm's rate of technical substitution is 0.8.

a. What is the wage-rental ratio; that is, what is the
14. ____________ wage rate divided by the rental rate?

b. Can the firm reduce costs without decreasing its level
15. ____________ of output? Should the firm use more, less, or the
16. ____________ same amount of labor?

5. The wage rate of labor is $20.00 and the rental rate of capital is $10.00. The firm's rate of technical substitution is 0.5.

a. What is the wage-rental ratio; that is, what is the
17. ____________ wage rate divided by the rental rate?

b. Can the firm reduce costs without decreasing its level
18. ____________ of output? Should the firm use more, less, or the
19. ____________ same amount of labor?

PROFIT MAXIMIZATION AND SHUTDOWN

1. The price is $.60. A firm is producing 100 units of output; its marginal revenue is $.60, its marginal cost is $.50, its average cost is $.65, and its average variable cost is $.30.

a. Is the firm operating in a perfectly competitive industry?

In a perfectly competitive industry firms are price
20. ____________ ____________; a firm's marginal revenue equals the
21. ____________ ____________. Since both the price and marginal
revenue are $.60, the industry is perfectly competitive.

The answer is yes.

b. Is the firm maximizing its profits? Should the firm produce more, less, or the same amount of output?

To determine whether a firm is maximizing its profits, compare its marginal revenue with its

22.____________ ____________. Since marginal revenue exceeds

23.____________ marginal cost profits are ____________ being maximized.

The answer is no.

The production and sale of one additional unit of

24.____________ output will increase total revenues by $____________ (marginal revenue) and increase total costs by $.50

25.____________ (____________); profits increase when the additional unit is produced.

The answer is produce more.

c. What is the firm's total revenue?

26.____________ Total revenue equals ____________ times quantity. The price is $.60 and the quantity is 100; total revenue

27.____________ equals $____________.

The answer is $60.00.

d. What is the firm's total cost?

28.____________ Total cost equals ____________ cost times quantity. Average cost is $.65 and the quantity is 100; total cost

29.____________ equals $____________.

The answer is $65.00.

e. Are the firm's profits currently positive, negative, or zero?

The most straightforward way of answering this question is to calculate profits. Profits equal the

30.____________ ____________ between the firm's total revenue and total cost: $60.00 less $65.00, that is negative

31.____________ $____________. Another way to determine the sign of the firm's profits is to compare price and

32.__________ __________ cost. Total revenue equals price times
33.__________ __________. Total cost equals average cost times
34.__________ __________. Consequently if price exceeds average
35.__________ cost, profit is __________; if average cost exceeds
price, profit is negative; if price equals average cost,
36.__________ profit is __________. Since average cost is $.65 and
37.__________ price is $.60, profits are currently __________.

The answer is negative.

f. Would it be advantageous for the firm to shut down rather than to continue its current mode of operation?

To determine whether or not a firm should shut
38.__________ down compare __________ and average variable
cost. Total cost equals the sum of fixed and variable
cost. Whenever average variable cost exceeds
39.__________ __________, variable cost (which equals average
variable cost times quantity) exceeds total revenue
(which equals price times quantity) and the firm
40.__________ incurs a loss that __________ its fixed cost;
consequently, whenever average variable cost
exceeds price, it is advantageous for the firm to
41.__________ __________ thereby incurring a loss just equal to its
fixed cost. On the other hand, whenever price
42.__________ __________ average variable costs it is
advantageous for the firm to continue to operate.
Since price is $.60 and average variable cost is $.30,
43.__________ the firm will __________ to operate.

The answer is no.

2. The price is $.80. A firm is producing 200 units of output; its marginal revenue is $.80, its marginal cost is $.80, its average cost is $1.25, and its average variable cost is $.90.

a. Is the firm operating in a perfectly competitive industry?

In a perfectly competitive industry firms are price
44.__________ __________; a firm's marginal revenue equals
45.__________ the __________. Since both the price and marginal
revenue are $.80, the industry is perfectly
competitive.

The answer is yes.

b. Is the firm maximizing its profits? Should the firm produce more, less, or the same amount of output?

To determine whether a firm is maximizing its
46.____________ profits, compare its marginal ____________ with its
marginal cost. Since marginal revenue equals
47.____________ marginal cost, profits ____________ being maximized.

The answer is yes.

c. What is the firm's total revenue?

48.____________ Total revenue equals ____________ times quantity.
The price is $.80 and the quantity is 200; total revenue
49.____________ equals $____________.

The answer is $160.00.

d. What is the firm's total cost?

50.____________ Total cost equals ____________ cost times quantity.
Average cost is $1.25 and the quantity is 200; total
51.____________ cost equals $____________.

The answer is $250.00.

e. Are the firm's profits currently positive, negative, or zero?

The most straightforward way of answering this
question is to calculate profits. Profits equal the
52.____________ difference between the firm's total ____________ and
total cost: $160.00 less $250.00, that is negative
53.____________ $____________. Another way to determine the sign of
54.____________ the firm's profits is to compare ____________ and
average cost. Total revenue equals
55.____________ ____________________ times quantity. Total cost
56.____________ equals ____________________ cost times quantity.
57.____________ Consequently if price ____________ average cost,
58.____________ profit is positive; if average cost ____________ price,
profit is negative; if price equals average cost, profit is

zero. Since average cost is $1.25 and price is $.80, profits are currently negative.

The answer is negative.

f. Would it be advantageous for the firm to shut down rather than to continue its current mode of operation?

To determine whether or not a firm should shut
59.______ down compare ______ and average variable cost. Total costs equal the sum of fixed and variable
60.______ cost. Whenever average variable cost ______ price, variable cost (which equals average variable cost times quantity) exceeds total revenue (which equals price times quantity) and the firm incurs a loss
61.______ that ______ its fixed cost; consequently, whenever average variable cost exceeds price, it is advantageous for the firm to shut down thereby incurring a loss just equal to its fixed cost. On the other hand, whenever price exceeds average variable costs it is advantageous for the firm to continue to operate. Since price is $.80 and average variable cost is $.90, it is advantageous for the firm to
62.______ ______.

The answer is yes.

3. The price is $1.10. A firm is producing 1000 units of output; its marginal revenue is $.90, its marginal cost is $1.00, its average cost is $1.05, and its average variable cost is $.60.

63.______ a. Is the firm maximizing its profits? Should the firm
64.______ produce more, less, or the same amount of output?

65.______ b. What is the firm's total revenue?

66.______ c. What is the firm's total cost?

d. Are the firm's profits currently positive, negative, or
67.______ zero?

e. Would it be advantageous for the firm to shut down
68.______ rather than to continue its current mode of operation?

4. The price is $2.00. A firm is producing 500 units of output; its marginal revenue is $2.00, its marginal cost is $2.00, its average cost is $1.50, and its average variable cost is $.90.

69.______________
70.______________ a. Is the firm maximizing its profits? Should the firm produce more, less, or the same amount of output?

71.______________ b. What is the firm's total revenue?

72.______________ c. What is the firm's total cost?

73.______________ d. Are the firm's profits currently positive, negative, or zero?

74.______________ e. Would it be advantageous for the firm to shut down rather than to continue its current mode of operation?

5. The price is $1.50. A firm is producing 1000 units of output; its marginal revenue is $.90, its marginal cost is $.80, its average cost is $1.80, and its average variable cost is $1.40.

75.______________
76.______________ a. Is the firm maximizing its profits? Should the firm produce more, less, or the same amount of output?

77.______________ b. What is the firm's total revenue?

78.______________ c. What is the firm's total cost?

79.______________ d. Are the firm's profits currently positive, negative, or zero?

80.______________ e. Would it be advantageous for the firm to shut down rather than to continue its current mode of operation?

ANSWERS

1. 2.0
2. can
3. 1
4. 2
5. decrease
6. 3.0
7. without
8. constant
9. 3
10. decrease
11. 2.0
12. No
13. The same amount
14. 0.5
15. Yes
16. More labor
17. 2.0
18. Yes
19. More labor
20. takers
21. price
22. marginal cost
23. not
24. .60
25. marginal cost
26. price
27. 60.00
28. average
29. 65.00
30. difference
31. 5.00
32. average
33. quantity
34. quantity
35. positive
36. zero
37. negative
38. price
39. price
40. exceeds
41. shut down
42. exceeds
43. continue
44. takers
45. price
46. revenue
47. are
48. price
49. 160.00
50. average
51. 250.00
52. revenue
53. 90.00
54. price
55. price
56. average
57. exceeds
58. exceeds
59. price
60. exceeds
61. exceeds
62. shut down
63. No
64. Produce less
65. $1100.00
66. $1050.00
67. Positive
68. Continue to operate
69. Yes
70. The same amount
71. $1000.00
72. $750.00
73. Positive
74. Continue to operate
75. No
76. Produce more
77. $1500.00
78. $1800.00
79. Negative
80. Shut down

PART 4

THE PERFECTLY COMPETITIVE MODEL

CHAPTER 12

PRICING IN A PERFECTLY COMPETITIVE MARKET

WALKING TOUR SUMMARIES

PRICING IN THE VERY SHORT RUN

1. ____________ In the very short run there is ____________ supply response; the quantity supplied is fixed. Firms do not have time to adjust their production levels; they will supply the same quantity of goods regardless of the price. In the very
2. ____________ short run the supply curve is ____________.

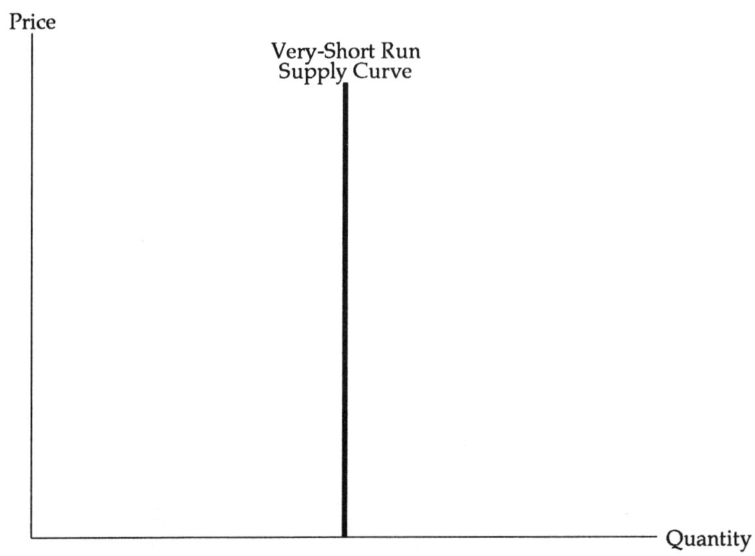

Figure 12.1: *Very Short-Run Supply*

SHORT-RUN SUPPLY

In the short run the number of firms in an industry is
3. ____________ ___________; that is, firms can neither exit nor enter the industry. Each firm can adjust its production level by
4. ____________ varying some (but not all) of its ___________, however.
5. ____________ The firm's short-run supply curve is its ___________ cost curve (as long as price exceeds average variable cost):

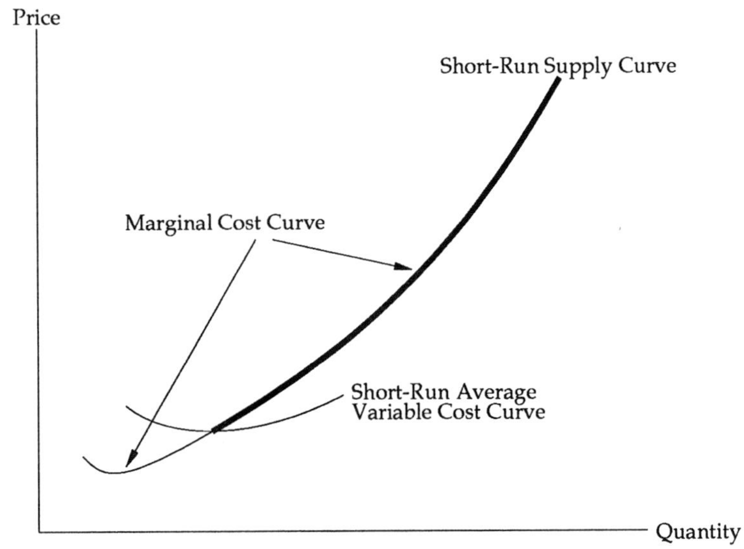

Figure 12.2: *A Firm's Short-Run Supply Curve*

6. ____________ The ___________ summation of each firm's individual short-run supply curve yields the upward sloping short-run market supply curve:

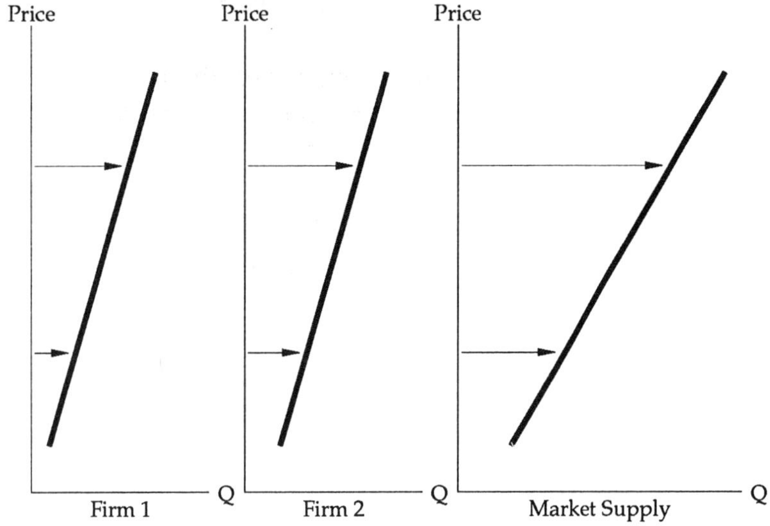

Figure 12.3: *The Market Short-Run Supply Curve*

SHORT-RUN PRICE DETERMINATION

The equilibrium is the price-quantity combination
7. ____________ represented by the ____________ of the market demand and supply curves. At the equilibrium the quantity demanded
8. ____________ ____________ the quantity supplied. If the price were below the equilibrium level, a shortage would exist and market
9. ____________ forces would push the price to ____________. Alternatively, if the price were above the equilibrium, there would be
10. ____________ ____________ and the price would fall.

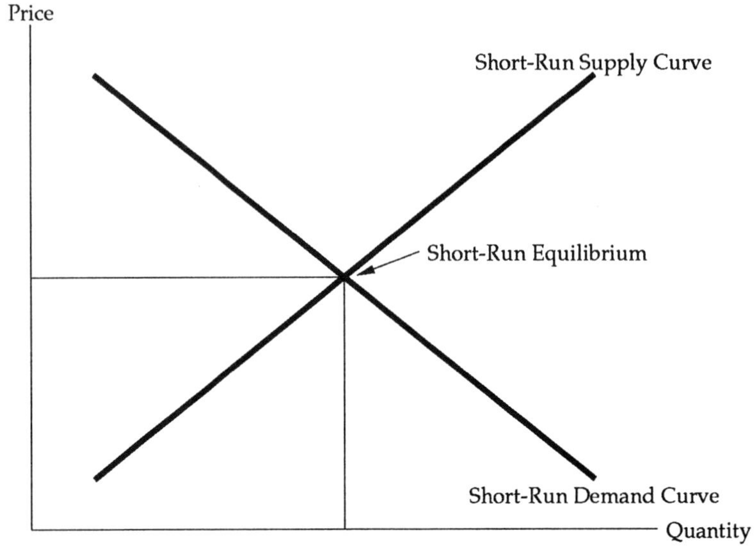

Figure 12.4: *Short-Run Market Equilibrium*

If a market which is initially in equilibrium
experiences an increase in demand, the equilibrium will be
11. ____________ destroyed. The quantity demanded will ____________ the
quantity supplied and the price will rise. In the very short
run, the quantity supplied is fixed. The price rises until the
12. ____________ quantity demanded ____________ the fixed quantity
supplied. That is, in the very short run the price adjusts so
as to ration the fixed quantity supplied among those who
demand the good. While firms cannot respond in the very
short run, they are able to adjust their production levels in
13. ____________ the ____________ run. The short-run market supply curve is
now relevant. A new equilibrium will be established where
14. ____________ quantity demanded ____________ the quantity supplied.
15. ____________ The new equilibrium price will be ____________ than the
16. ____________ initial equilibrium price, but ____________ than the price
established in the very short run. The new equilibrium
17. ____________ quantity ____________ the initial equilibrium quantity.

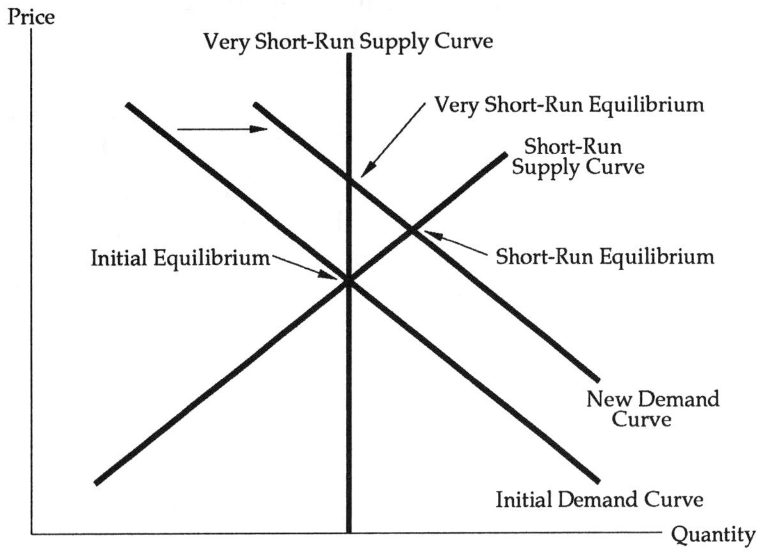

Figure 12.5: *Response to an Increase in Demand*

SHIFTS IN SUPPLY AND DEMAND CURVES

The demand curve for a good can shift only when
something affecting demand changes other than the
18. ____________ ____________ of the good itself. When this happens
19. ____________ economists say that a ____________ in demand occurs. A
change in the price of a good itself will never cause the
20. ____________ demand curve for that good to ____________. A change in
21. ____________ the price leads to a movement ____________ the demand
curve. Economists refer to a movement along a demand
22. ____________ curve as a change in the ____________ demanded.
23. ____________ The ____________ curve for a good can shift only
when something affecting supply changes other than the
price of the good itself. When this happens economists say
that a change in supply occurs. A change in the
24. ____________ ____________ of a good itself will never cause the supply
curve for that good to shift. A change in the price leads to a
movement along the supply curve. Economists refer to a
25. ____________ movement ____________ a supply curve as a change in the
quantity supplied.

SHORT-RUN SUPPLY ELASTICITY

The elasticity of supply indicates how sensitive the
26. ____________ quantity supplied is to a change in the ____________. More
precisely, the elasticity of supply equals the percent change

27. ____________ in the quantity supplied resulting from a one ____________ change in the price:

$$\text{Supply Elasticity} = \frac{\text{Percent Change in Quantity Supplied}}{\text{Percent Change in Price}}$$

Whenever the quantity supplied is "very sensitive" to the
28. ____________ price economists say that supply is ____________. More precisely, supply is elastic whenever a one percent change in price leads to a more than one percent change in quantity supplied. Alternatively, if the quantity supplied is "not very
29. ____________ sensitive," supply is ____________. Last, if a one percent
30. ____________ change in the price leads to a ____________ percent change in quantity supplied, supply is unit elastic. In the very short
31. ____________ run supply is completely ____________ because the quantity supplied cannot change, the quantity supplied is completely insensitive to the price. In the short run supply can be elastic, inelastic, or unit elastic because the quantity
32. ____________ supplied ____________ whenever the price increases.

SHIFTS IN DEMAND AND SUPPLY CURVES AND THE IMPORTANCE OF ELASTICITIES

For a given shift of the supply curve the equilibrium price will change less and less (and the equilibrium quantity
33. ____________ changes more and more) as demand elasticity ____________. For a given shift of the demand curve the equilibrium price will change less and less (and the equilibrium quantity
34. ____________ changes more and more) as supply elasticity ____________.

THE LONG RUN

35. ____________ In the long run, supply responses are ____________ flexible than in the short run for two reasons. First, firms
36. ____________ can ____________ all inputs in the long run while in the short run firms can adjust only variable inputs. Second,
37. ____________ firms can ____________ or exit an industry in the long run in response to profit opportunities.

A long-run equilibrium differs from a short-run equilibrium in two ways. First, firms must be maximizing their profits with respect to all inputs. This means that marginal revenue (which equals price in a perfectly
38. ____________ competitive market) must equal long-run ____________ cost. Second, firms must have no incentive to enter or leave the

industry. This condition is met whenever economic profits
39. ____________ equal ___________. If economic profits are negative, firms
40. ____________ have an incentive to ___________ the industry; positive
profits cause firms to enter.

Economic profits are zero whenever price equals
41. ____________ ___________ cost. To understand why recall that total
revenues equal price times quantity and observe that total
costs equal average cost times quantity:

$$\begin{aligned} \text{Profits} &= \text{TR} - \text{TC} \\ &= P \times Q - AC \times Q \\ &= (P - AC) \times Q \end{aligned}$$

42. ____________ Profits will be ___________ whenever price equals average
cost. In summary, a long-run equilibrium in a perfectly
competitive market requires both marginal cost and average
cost to equal the price:

$$P = MC = AC$$

Furthermore, recall that the marginal cost and average cost
43. ____________ curves intersect at ___________ average cost; consequently,
44. ____________ price will equal minimum average cost in a ___________-
run equilibrium.

LONG-RUN SUPPLY CURVE

The long-run supply curve represents all the price-
45. ____________ quantity combinations that are ___________-run equilibria.
To find one point on the long-run supply curve first choose
a level of demand; in a graph, choose a demand curve. With
the short-run supply curve you can now determine the
current equilibrium. At this equilibrium does the price
equal average cost? If so, you have found one point on the
long-run supply curve. If not, changes will occur in the long
46. ____________ run. Suppose that price exceeds ___________ cost; profits
47. ____________ are positive which leads to ___________ in the long run.
48. ____________ Entry shifts the short-run supply curve to the ___________
49. ____________ causing the price to ___________. Entry continues until
price equals average cost at which time you have now found
one point of the long-run supply curve. By considering all
possible positions of the demand curve we can construct the
long-run supply curve by following this procedure.

50. ____________ If the industry is a ___________ cost industry, the entry of new firms does not affect the cost of existing firms
51. ____________ and the long-run supply curve is ___________. Alternatively, in an increasing cost industry, entry
52. ____________ ___________ the cost of existing firms and the long-run
53. ____________ supply curve is ___________ sloping. Last, the long-run
54. ____________ supply curve is downward sloping in a ___________ cost industry.
55. ____________ Supply is ___________ elastic in the long run than in the short run. In the long run firms can adjust production
56. ____________ levels more easily because they can vary ___________, not just some, inputs; therefore, each firm's production level will
57. ____________ be more sensitive to the ___________. The possibility of
58. ____________ entry and exit makes the quantity supplied ___________ sensitive to the price also.

MULTIPLE-CHOICE QUESTIONS

59. ______ In the very short run

a. the quantity of output a firm produces is fixed.
b. the quantity of output a firm produces can be changed.
c. some (but not all) inputs the firm uses can be changed.
d. all inputs the firm uses can be changed.
e. b and c.

60. ______ In the short run

a. the quantity of output a firm produces is fixed.
b. the quantity of output a firm produces can be changed.
c. some (but not all) inputs the firm uses can be changed.
d. all inputs the firm uses can be changed.
e. b and c.

61. ______ In the long run

a. the quantity of output a firm produces can be changed.
b. all inputs the firm uses can be changed.
c. firms can enter or exit the industry.
d. a and b.
e. a, b, and c.

62. ______ In the short run the market supply curve is

a. the horizontal sum of each firm's individual supply curve.
b. the horizontal sum of each firm's average cost curve.
c. the horizontal sum of each firm's average cost curve as long as price exceeds average variable cost.
d. the horizontal sum of each firm's marginal cost curve as long as price is less than average variable cost.
e. a and d.

63. ______ If the (actual) price exceeds the equilibrium price, market forces tend to make the

a. price increase until it equals the equilibrium price.
b. price decrease until it equals the equilibrium price.
c. equilibrium price increase until it equals the price.
d. equilibrium price decrease until it equals the price.
e. b and c.

64. ______ In the very short run an increase in demand will lead to

a. an increase in price and an increase in quantity.
b. an increase in price and a decrease in quantity.
c. an increase in price and no change in quantity.
d. a decrease in price and an increase in quantity.
e. a decrease in price and a decrease in quantity.

65. ______ In the short run an increase in demand will lead to

a. an increase in price and an increase in quantity.
b. an increase in price and a decrease in quantity.
c. an increase in price and no change in quantity.
d. a decrease in price and an increase in quantity.
e. a decrease in price and a decrease in quantity.

66. ______ A good's elasticity of supply indicates how sensitive the quantity supplied is to a change in

a. the price of the good in question.
b. income.
c. price of another good.
d. consumer preferences.
e. a and b.

67. ______ The elasticity of supply equals

a. the change in the quantity supplied caused by a 1 unit (1 dollar) change in price.
b. the percent change in the quantity supplied caused by a 1 percent change in price.
c. the ratio of the change in the quantity supplied to the change in the price.
d. the ratio of the percent change in the price to the percent change in the quantity demanded supplied.
e. b and d.

68. ______ Whenever the elasticity of supply exceeds 1, supply is said to be

a. elastic.
b. unit elastic.
c. inelastic, but not completely inelastic.
d. completely inelastic.
e. normal.

69. ______ Whenever the elasticity of supply equals 1, supply is said to be

a. elastic.
b. unit elastic.
c. inelastic, but not completely inelastic.
d. completely inelastic.
e. normal.

70. ______ Whenever the elasticity of supply is between 0 and 1, supply is said to be

a. elastic.
b. unit elastic.
c. inelastic, but not completely inelastic.
d. completely inelastic.
e. normal.

71. ______ Whenever the elasticity of supply equals 0, supply is said to be

a. elastic.
b. unit elastic.
c. inelastic, but not completely inelastic.
d. completely inelastic.
e. normal.

72. ______ In the very short run the elasticity of supply
   a. is elastic.
   b. is unit elastic.
   c. is inelastic, but not completely inelastic.
   d. is completely inelastic.
   e. may be elastic, inelastic, or unit elastic.

73. ______ In the short run, a firm's economic profits
   a. must be positive.
   b. must be negative.
   c. must be zero.
   d. may be positive, negative, or zero.
   e. cannot be zero.

74. ______ In long-run equilibrium, a firm's economic profits
   a. must be positive.
   b. must be negative.
   c. must be zero.
   d. may be positive, negative, or zero.
   e. cannot be zero.

75. ______ A firm's profits must be positive whenever the price is
   a. greater than marginal cost.
   b. greater than average cost.
   c. greater than average variable cost.
   d. less than marginal cost.
   e. less than average cost.

76. ______ A firm's profits must be negative whenever the price is
   a. greater than marginal cost.
   b. greater than average cost.
   c. greater than average variable cost.
   d. less than marginal cost.
   e. less than average cost.

77. ______ The long-run supply curve
   a. represents all the price-quantity combinations that are long-run equilibria.
   b. is the vertical sum of each firm's average cost curve.
   c. is the vertical sum of each firm's marginal cost curve.
   d. is the horizontal sum of each firm's average cost curve.
   e. is the horizontal sum of each firm's marginal cost curve.

78. ______ In a constant cost industry the entry of new firms
   a. increases the costs of firms already in the industry.
   b. decreases the costs of firms already in the industry.
   c. has no effect on the costs of firms already in the industry.
   d. may increase, decrease, or have no effect on the costs of firms already in the industry.
   e. none of the above.

79. ______ In an increasing cost industry the entry of new firms
   a. increases the costs of firms already in the industry.
   b. decreases the costs of firms already in the industry.
   c. has no effect on the costs of firms already in the industry.
   d. may increase, decrease, or have no effect on the costs of firms already in the industry.
   e. none of the above.

80. ______ In a constant cost industry the long-run supply curve
   a. is upward sloping.
   b. is downward sloping.
   c. is horizontal.
   d. is U-shaped.
   e. may have any shape.

81. ______ In an increasing cost industry the long-run supply curve
   a. is upward sloping.
   b. is downward sloping.
   c. is horizontal.
   d. is U-shaped.
   e. may have any shape.

RUNNING GLOSSARY

82. ____________ Supply response: the change in quantity of output in response to a change in ____________ conditions.

83. ____________ Market period: a short period of time during which quantity supplied is ____________.

Equilibrium price: the price at which the quantity demanded by buyers of a good is equal to the quantity

84. ____________ ____________ of the good by sellers.

85. ____________ ____________ supply curve: the relationship between market price and quantity supplied of a good in the short run.

86. ____________ External price effects: effects that changes in the level of production of an industry have on the prices of ____________ to that industry.

87. ____________ Short-run elasticity of supply: the percent change in quantity supplied in the short run in response to a ____________ percent change in price.

88. ____________ ____________ cost industry: an industry in which entry or exit of firms has no effect on the cost curves of the firms in the industry.

89. ____________ Tax incidence theory: the study of the final burden of a tax after considering all market ____________ to it.

90. ____________ Increasing cost industry: an industry in which the entry of firms ____________ the costs of the firms in the industry.

91. ____________ Long-run elasticity of supply: the percent change in quantity ____________ in the long run in response to a 1 percent change in price.

92. ____________ Decreasing ____________ industry: an industry in which the entry of firms decreases the costs of the firms in the industry.

ANSWERS

1. no
2. vertical
3. fixed
4. inputs
5. marginal
6. horizontal
7. intersection
8. equals
9. rise
10. surplus
11. exceed
12. equals
13. short
14. equals
15. higher
16. lower
17. exceeds
18. price
19. change
20. shift
21. along
22. quantity
23. supply
24. price
25. along
26. price
27. percent
28. elastic
29. inelastic
30. one
31. inelastic
32. increases
33. increases
34. increases
35. more
36. change
37. enter
38. marginal
39. zero
40. exit
41. average
42. zero
43. minimum
44. long
45. long
46. average
47. entry
48. right
49. fall
50. constant
51. horizontal
52. increases
53. upward
54. decreasing
55. more
56. all
57. price
58. more
59. a
60. e
61. e
62. a
63. b
64. c
65. a
66. a
67. b
68. a
69. b
70. c
71. d
72. d
73. d
74. c
75. b
76. e
77. a
78. c
79. a
80. c
81. a
82. demand
83. fixed
84. supplied
85. Short-run
86. inputs
87. one
88. Constant
80. reactions
90. increases
91. supplied
92. cost

CHAPTER 13

APPLYING THE COMPETITIVE MODEL

WALKING TOUR SUMMARIES

CONSUMER AND PRODUCER SURPLUS

Consumer surplus equals the total value that individuals receive from consuming a good, less what they
1. ____________ ____________ for the good at the current price, their total expenditures. Producers surplus equals the total value
2. ____________ producers receive for a good, their total ____________, less the opportunity costs they incur by producing the good. Geometrically, consumer surplus is the area beneath the
3. ____________ ____________ curve that lies above the price; producer surplus is the area above the supply curve that lies beneath
4. ____________ the ____________.

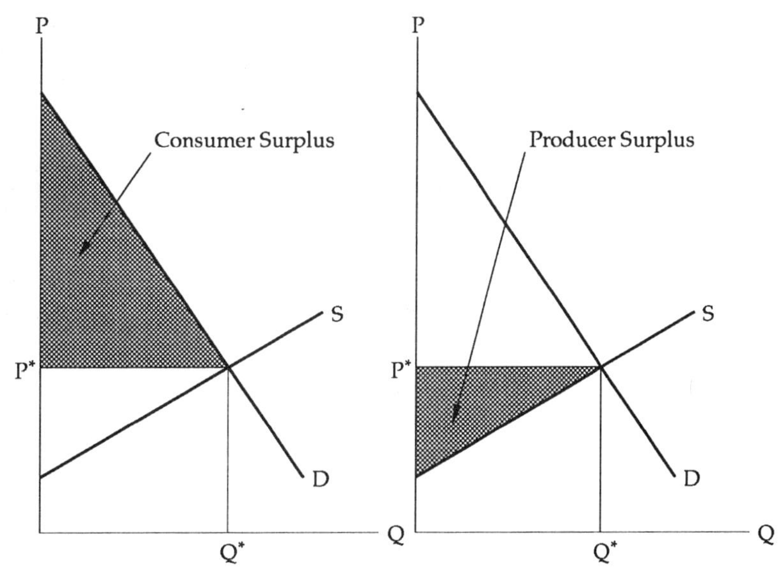

Figure 13.1: *Consumer Surplus and Producer Surplus*

The short-run supply curve is the horizontal sum of
5. ____________ each firm's ____________ cost curve (as long as price exceeds average variable cost). Consequently, in the short run, producer surplus equals total revenues less variable costs;

that is, producer surplus equals short-run profits plus
6. ___________ short-run ___________ costs.

In the long-run equilibrium profits equal
7. ___________ ___________ and there are no fixed costs. The slope of the long-run supply curve depends on whether the firms in the industry experience increasing, constant, or decreasing costs. If the firms experience increasing costs the long-run
8. ___________ supply curve will be ___________ sloping reflecting the fact that the payments received by the firms' inputs
9. ___________ ___________ as output expands. In the long run, producers surplus equals the difference between the payments these inputs receive at the current price less the payments they
10. ___________ would receive if the industry produced ___________ output.

PRICE CONTROLS AND SHORTAGES

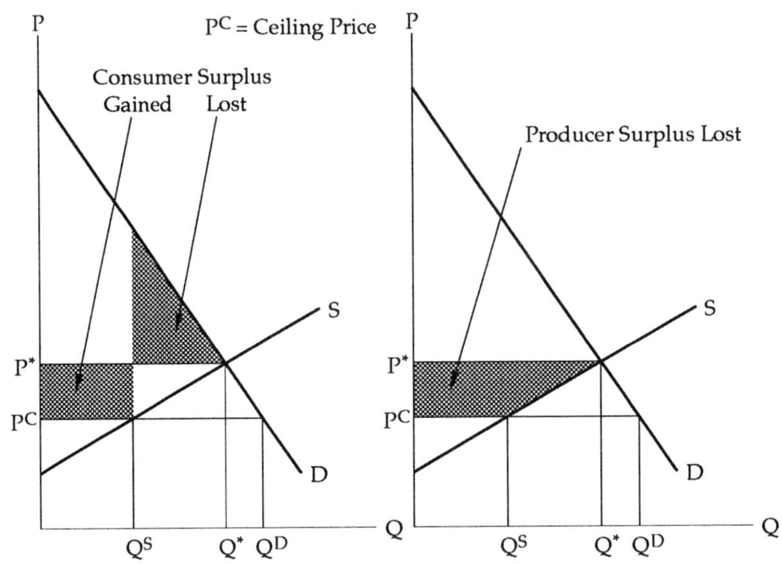

Figure 13.2: *Price Controls*

When the government imposes a price ceiling below the equilibrium price, both the consumers and the producers of the good are affected. Such a price ceiling creates a
11. ___________ ___________: The quantity demanded exceeds the quantity supplied. Some consumers are unable to buy as much of the good as they would like at the below-equilibrium price. Accordingly, some consumers are helped and some hurt. Those able to purchase the good at the below equilibrium
12. ___________ price experience a ___________ in consumer surplus; those
13. ___________ unable to purchase it experience a ___________ in

14. ____________ 15. ____________ consumer surplus. On the other hand, the producers experience an unambiguous ____________ in producer surplus. In net, the losses ____________ the gains; the price ceiling produces a welfare loss.

TAX INCIDENCE

16. ____________ 17. ____________ 18. ____________ 19. ____________ 20. ____________ 21. ____________

The study of tax incidence recognizes that economic interactions can shift the burden of a tax from those legally obilged to pay it to others. A specific tax creates a wedge between what consumers pay and what firms get to keep. In particular, the price viewed from the standpoint of the consumers ____________ the price as seen through the eyes of the firm by an amount just equal to the tax. Typically, the tax ____________ the price as seen by the consumers, thereby ____________ consumer surplus. The tax lowers the price as seen by the firms, thereby ____________ producer surplus. The elasticities of demand and supply determine how the losses are distributed between individuals and firms. The relatively inelastic group will bear ____________ of the burden. The combined loss in consumer and producer surplus exceeds the tax revenue raised; this difference is referred to as the ____________ loss or excess burden of the tax.

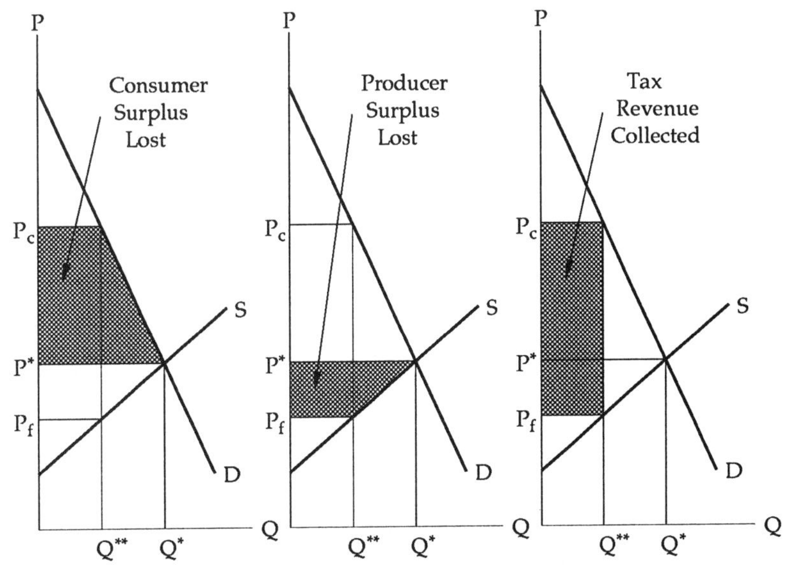

Figure 13.3: *Tax Incidence*

TRADE RESTRICTIONS

When a country opens its borders to the free trade of a good both consumers and producers are typically affected. In particular, if the world price is less than the domestic price, free trade would cause domestic production to

22. ____________ ____________ and domestic consumption to increase.
23. ____________ Consumer surplus would ____________ and producer surplus would decrease. In net, there is a welfare gain
24. ____________ because the gain in consumer surplus ____________ the loss in producer surplus.

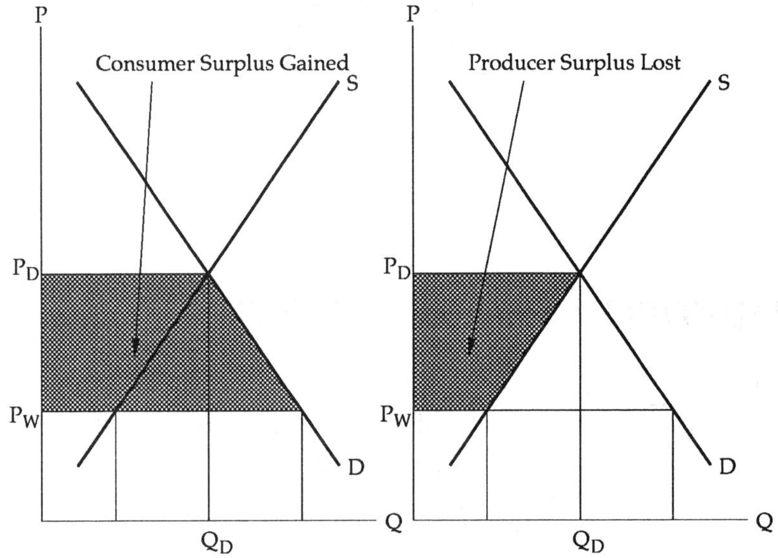

Figure 13.4: *Free Trade*

A tariff would have the effect of increasing the price

25. ____________ within the country to a level ____________ the world price. Starting at the free trade position, a tariff would reduce consumer surplus and increase producer surplus. There is a welfare loss, however, because the gain in producer surplus plus the revenue generated by the tariff falls short of the loss
26. ____________ in ____________surplus.

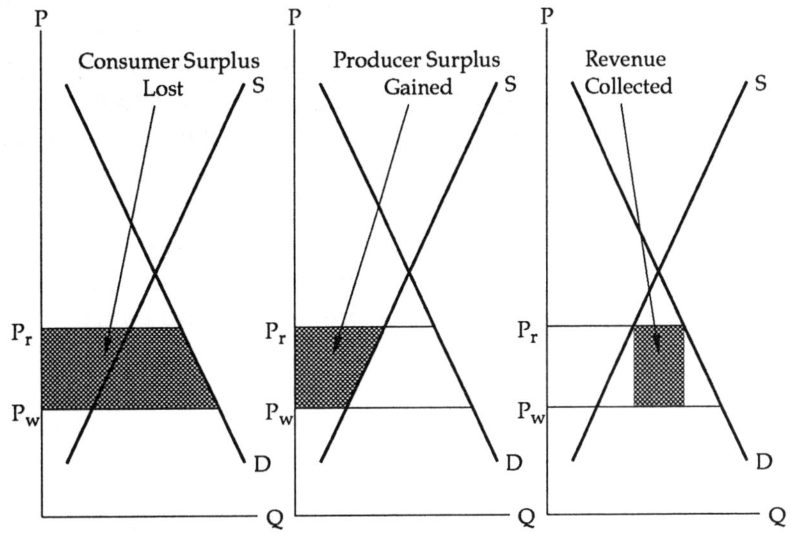

Figure 13.5: *Effect of a Tariff*

MULTIPLE-CHOICE QUESTIONS

27. ______ Consumer surplus equals
   a. the total value placed on the consumption of the good at its current price less what is actually paid for the good.
   b. what is actually paid for the good less the total value placed on the consumption of the good at its current price.
   c. the total revenue received for the good less the opportunity cost of producing the good.
   d. the opportunity cost of producing the good less the total revenue received for the good.

28. ______ Producer surplus equals
   a. the total value placed on the consumption of the good at its current price less what is actually paid for the good.
   b. what is actually paid for the good less the total value placed on the consumption of the good at its current price.
   c. the total revenue received for the good less the opportunity cost of producing the good.
   d. the opportunity cost of producing the good less the total revenue received for the good.
   e. none of the above.

29. ______ Geometrically, consumer surplus equals the area beneath the
  a. demand curve and above the price.
  b. price and above the demand curve.
  c. supply curve and above the price.
  d. price and above the supply curve.
  e. demand curve.

30. ______ Geometrically, producer surplus equals the area beneath the
  a. demand curve and above the price.
  b. price and above the demand curve.
  c. supply curve and above the price.
  d. price and above the supply curve.
  e. supply curve.

31. ______ In the short run, producer surplus equals
  a. the difference between what the firms' inputs currently earn and what the inputs would earn if the industry produced nothing.
  b. zero.
  c. profits less fixed costs.
  d. profits plus fixed costs.
  e. a and d.

32. ______ In the long run, producer surplus equals
  a. the difference between what the firms' inputs currently earn and what the inputs would earn if the industry produced nothing.
  b. zero.
  c. profits less fixed costs.
  d. profits plus fixed costs.
  e. a and d.

33. ______ The imposition of a price ceiling below the equilibrium price
  a. increases producer surplus.
  b. decreases producer surplus.
  c. produces a welfare loss.
  d. b and c.
  e. has no effect.

34. ______ The imposition of a price ceiling above the equilibrium price
  a. increases producer surplus.
  b. decreases producer surplus.
  c. produces a welfare loss.
  d. b and c.
  e. has no effect.

35. ______ The imposition of a tax typically

a. increases consumer surplus and increases producer surplus.
b. increases consumer surplus and decreases producer surplus.
c. decreases consumer surplus and increases producer surplus.
d. decreases consumer surplus and decreases producer surplus.
e. has no effect.

36. ______ The imposition of a tax on a good typically

a. results a dead weight loss.
b. burdens those related to the production of the good.
c. burdens those related to the consumption of the good.
d. a, b, and, c.
e. has no effect.

37. ______ Whenever the domestic price exceeds the world price, the opening of a country to free trade

a. increases consumer surplus and increases producer surplus.
b. increases consumer surplus and decreases producer surplus.
c. decreases consumer surplus and increases producer surplus.
d. decreases consumer surplus and decreases producer surplus.
e. has no effect.

RUNNING GLOSSARY

38. ____________ ____________ surplus: the difference between the value individuals place upon the consumption of a good at its current price and what individuals actually pay for the good.

39. ____________ Producer surplus: the difference between what firms actually ____________ for the good and the opportunity cost of producing the good.

40. ____________ Tax incidence: the study of how economic interactions ____________ the burden of the tax from those legally obilged to pay it to others.

41. ____________ ____________ loss: losses in consumer and producer surplus that are not transferred to others.

42. ____________ Tariff: a tax on an ____________ good.

ANSWERS

1. pay
2. revenue
3. demand
4. price
5. marginal
6. fixed
7. zero
8. upward
9. increase
10. no
11. shortage
12. gain
13. loss
14. loss
15. exceed
16. exceeds
17. raises
18. reducing
19. reducing
20. more
21. deadweight
22. decrease
23. increase
24. exceeds
25. above
26. consumer
27. a
28. c
29. a
30. d
31. d
32. a
33. d
34. e
35. d
36. d
37. b
38. Consumer
39. receive
40. shift
41. Deadweight
42. imported

CHAPTER 14

GENERAL EQUILIBRIUM AND ECONOMIC EFFICIENCY

WALKING TOUR SUMMARIES

PERFECTLY COMPETITIVE PRICE SYSTEM

The perfectly competitive model assumes that:

1. ____________ 1. There is a ____________ number of people
buying each good and supplying each
productive input. Each individual takes all
2. ____________ ____________ as given and maximizes his
utility.

3. ____________ 2. There is a ____________ number of firms
4. ____________ producing each ____________ and purchasing
each productive input. Each firm takes all
5. ____________ prices as given and maximizes its ____________.

Instead of considering a single market in isolation,
general equilibrium studies the interconnection of the
markets for goods and inputs. Typically, a change in
demand and/or supply in one market will ultimately affect
6. ____________ ____________ other markets. For example, if the demand for
one particular good increases, the price of that good
7. ____________ ____________. The incomes of workers producing the good
8. ____________ will ____________ and consequently their demand for all
other goods will be affected. This of course will affect the
prices of other goods and the incomes of workers producing
the goods.

EFFICIENCY IN PRODUCTION

When resources are allocated efficiently the only way
9. ____________ to increase the production of one good is to ____________
the production of some other good. Resources are allocated

inefficiently if more of one good can be produced,
10. ____________ ____________ producing less of any other good.

A firm's rate of technical substitution (RTS) indicates how the firm can substitute labor for capital while keeping
11. ____________ production ____________. Technical efficiency requires the
12. ____________ rate of technical substitution to be ____________ for each good produced.

To understand why suppose that the rates are not equal; for example, suppose that the RTS for cars is 2 while the RTS for trucks is 1. Now shift one unit of labor from the production of trucks to cars and simultaneously shift one unit of capital from cars to trucks.

Cars ←	1 labor	← Trucks
RTS = 2 →	1 capital	→ RTS = 1
Car production remains constant whenever 1 labor is substituted for 2 capital		Truck production remains constant whenever 1 labor is substituted for 1 capital

For trucks there is one less unit of labor and one more
13. ____________ unit of capital; truck production will not be ____________.
Since the RTS is 1 for trucks, production remains constant
14. ____________ whenever ____________ unit of labor is substituted for one
unit of capital. For cars there is one more unit of labor and
15. ____________ one less unit of capital; car production will ____________.
Since the RTS is 2 for cars, production remains constant
16. ____________ whenever ____________ units of capital are substituted for
one unit of labor; hence, production will increase whenever only one unit of capital is exchanged for one unit of labor.

EFFICIENT INPUT USE AND THE EDGEWORTH PRODUCTION BOX

The Edgeworth Box provides a graphical means to
17. ____________ illustrate all the possible ways to ____________ two inputs
between two firms. A particular point in the box represents
18. ____________ ____________ input use only when the isoquants passing
through the point are tangent. When the isoquants are
19. ____________ tangent, the rates of ____________ substitution are equal. If
the isoquants intersect, the rates of technical substitution are
20. ____________ not equal. The firms can produce more of ____________
goods by reallocating the inputs between them.

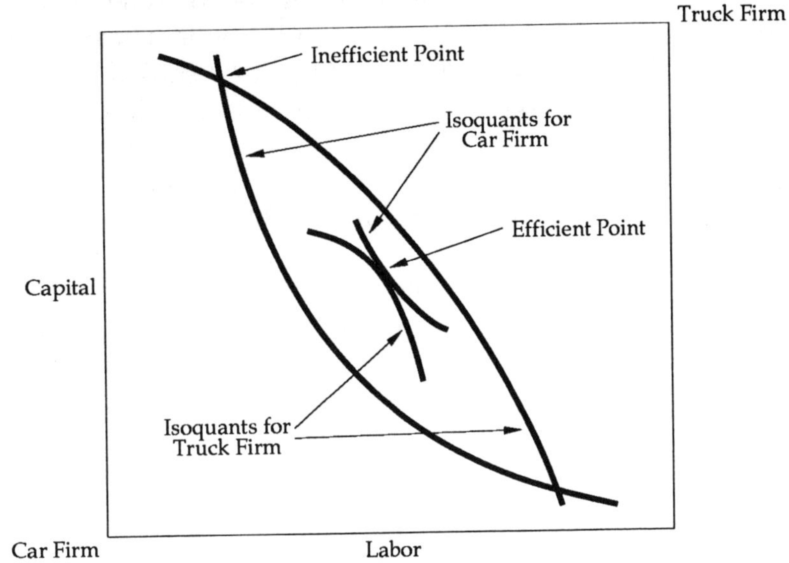

Figure 14.1: *Edgeworth Production Box*

PRODUCTION POSSIBILITY CURVE

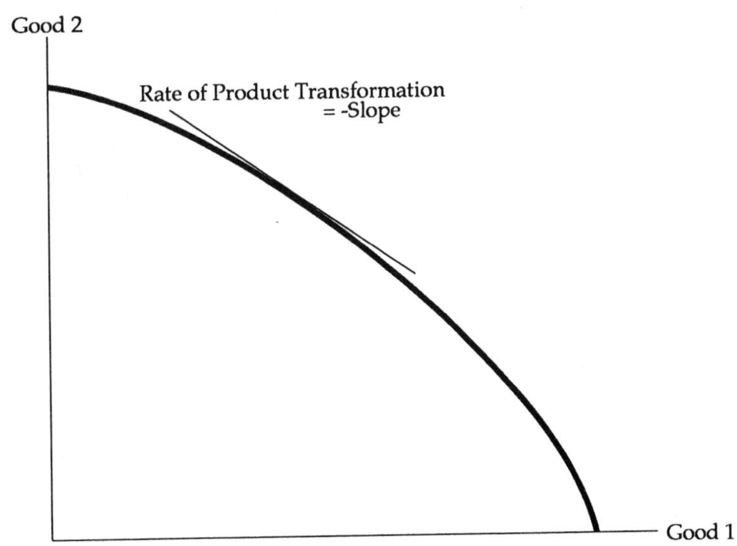

Figure 14.2: *Production Possibilities Curve*

The production possibility frontier illustrates the alternative outputs of X and Y that can be produced with the fixed amounts of inputs available to an economy. An economy operating at a point inside its production

21. ____________ possibility frontier is operating ____________ because the production of one good can be increased without reducing

the production of the other good. An economy operating
22. ____________ ____________ the frontier is efficient; the only way to
23. ____________ produce more of one good is to ____________ the production
of the other good.

RATE OF PRODUCT TRANSFORMATION IS THE RATIO OF MARGINAL COSTS

The rate of product transformation (RPT) indicates
how the production of good X can be substituted for the
production of good Y given the fixed amount of resources
24. ____________ available to an economy. Geometrically, the ____________ of
the production possibility frontier reflects the rate of
product transformation. The rate of product transformation
25. ____________ equals the ____________ of marginal costs:

$$RPT = \frac{\text{Marginal Cost of Good X}}{\text{Marginal Cost of Good Y}}$$

To understand why suppose that the MC_X equals 6 and the
MC_Y equals 2. To produce one additional unit of good X,
26. ____________ ____________ dollars worth of inputs must be transferred
from the production of Y to the production of X. The
27. ____________ production of Y decreases by one unit when ____________
dollars worth of inputs are taken because the MC_Y equals 2.
28. ____________ Thus, the production of Y will fall by ____________ when six
dollars worth of inputs are taken. Consequently, the rate of
product transformation equals (6/2) or 3.

The rate of product transformation increases as more
X is produced. When little X and much Y are produced, the
MC_X is low and the MC_Y is high; thus, the ratio of MCs is
29. ____________ ____________. Alternatively, when much X and little Y are
produced, the MC_X is high and the MC_Y is low; the ratio is
30. ____________ ____________. The rate of product transformation equals the
31. ____________ ____________ cost of X, how much Y that must be forgone to
produce one additional unit of X.

AN EFFICIENT MIX OF OUTPUTS

The production of an efficient mix of output requires
the rate of product transformation (RTS) to equal the
32. ____________ individual's marginal rates of ____________ (MRS). To
understand why assume that they are not equal; for
example, suppose that the RPT of oranges for apples equals

1 and that an individual's MRS equals 3. Recall that an individual's marginal rate of substitution indicates the ratio

33. ____________ in which the individual is willing to ____________ oranges for apples. Since the MRS equals 3, the individual is willing

34. ____________ to give up ____________ apples to consume one additional orange. But if the rate of product transformation equals 1, it is only necessary to reduce apple production by

35. ____________ ____________ to grow the additional orange. More oranges and fewer apples should be grown in this case. Whenever the RPT and MRSs are not equal the mix of output is

36. ____________ ____________.

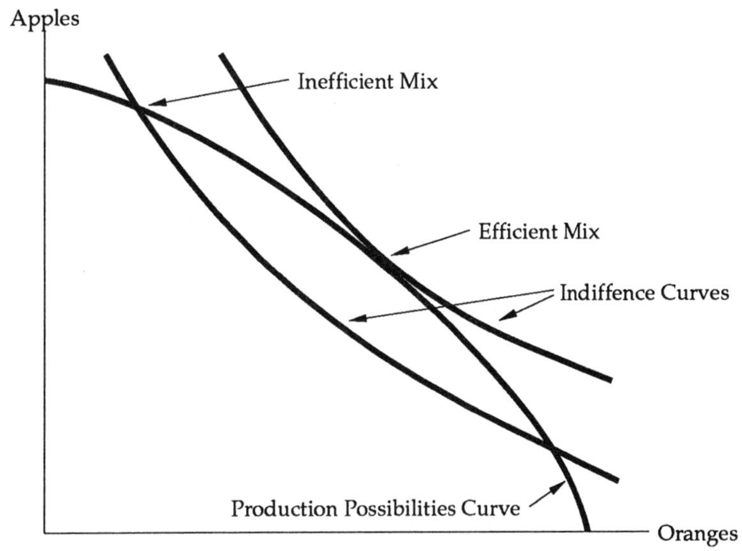

Figure 14.3: *Efficient Output Mix*

EFFICIENCY OF PERFECT COMPETITION: INPUT USE

In order to maximize profits each firm will produce its level of output with that input combination which

37. ____________ ____________ its total costs. If the input markets are perfectly competitive, the rate of technical substitution equals the wage-rental ratio at the cost minimizing input combination. Thus, with perfect competition, each firm's rate of technical substitution will equal the same wage-

38. ____________ rental ratio, ensuring ____________ input use.

EFFICIENCY OF PERFECT COMPETITION: OUTPUT MIX

In order to maximize utility each individual will consume a bundle of goods at which the individual's
39. ___________ marginal rate of ___________ equals the price ratio; that is,

$$MRS = \frac{P_X}{P_Y}$$

In order to maximize profits a firm produces the level of output at which marginal revenue equals marginal
40. ___________ ___________. In a perfectly competitive industry,
41. ___________ ___________ equals marginal revenue; therefore, price will equal marginal cost for a profit-maximizing firm in a
42. ___________ ___________ competitive industry:

$$P_X = MR_X = MC_X$$
$$P_Y = MR_Y = MC_Y$$

Thus, the marginal rate of substitution which equals the
43. ___________ price ratio also equals the ratio of marginal ___________; that is,

$$MRS = \frac{P_X}{P_Y} = \frac{MR_X}{MR_Y} = \frac{MC_X}{MC_Y}$$

Now recall that the ratio of marginal costs equals the rate of product transformation:

$$MRS = \frac{P_X}{P_Y} = \frac{MR_X}{MR_Y} = \frac{MC_X}{MC_Y} = RPT$$

The marginal rate of substitution equals the rate of product
44. ___________ transformation ensuring that an ___________ output mix will be produced.

PRICES, EFFICIENCY, AND LAISSEZ-FAIRE POLICIES

A perfectly competitive price system composed of profit-maximizing firms and utility-maximizing consumers
45. ___________ can result in an ___________ allocation of resources. Note that in justifying this conclusion we relied on the

assumption that each party will pursue his self-interest; each firm maximizes its profit and each individual maximizes his utility. What then is the role for government?

WHY MARKETS FAIL TO ACHIEVE ECONOMIC EFFICIENCY

46. ____________ ____________ competition typically leads to inefficiency. Like any firm, a firm in an imperfectly competitive industry maximizes profit by producing the level of output at which marginal revenue equals
47. ____________ ____________ cost. Price exceeds a firm's marginal revenue in an imperfectly competitive market, however.
48. ____________ Consequently, price will ____________ marginal cost; for example, if the market for good X is imperfectly competitive:

$$P_X > MR_X = MC_X$$

This of course means that the consumer's marginal rates of
49. ____________ substitution (which equal the ____________ ratio) will no longer equal the rate of product transformation (which
50. ____________ equals the ratio of marginal ____________); an inefficient output mix results.

$$MRS = \frac{P_X}{P_Y} > \frac{MR_X}{MR_Y} = \frac{MC_X}{MC_Y} = RPT$$

Inefficiency also results in the case of an externality;
51. ____________ that is, when the price system fails to capture ____________ the relationships among firms and/or consumers. For example, whenever a firm emits air pollution those individuals living nearby are hurt by the dirty air, yet the firm incurs no charge for this damage. The price system fails to capture the fact that the firm by emitting pollutants is hurting those living nearby. Consequently, the
52. ____________ ____________ costs, the costs upon which the firm bases its output decisions, are less than the true social costs of production; the ratio of private marginal costs will no longer
53. ____________ equal the rate of ____________ transformation. An inefficient output mix results because the individual's marginal rates of substitution (which equal the price ratio
54. ____________ and ratio of marginal ____________ costs) do not equal the rate of product transformation.

Public goods also cause market failure. Because it is impossible (or at least very costly) to exclude anyone from enjoying the benefits of public goods, there is an incentive for each individual to refuse to pay for them. Too few public goods are provided by the price system.

EFFICIENCY AND EQUITY

55. ____________ People ___________ on what they regard as "fair." Some Americans find the current distribution of income equitable, while others find it grossly unfair. But even if everyone agreed on what was fair, there might still be a problem in obtaining a fair outcome. There may not be a
56. ____________ ___________ to get the economy from the initial endowments to a fair outcome. For example, a system of
57. ____________ ___________ trades upon which perfect competition relies need not lead to a fair result. The government could use its power to transfer income to achieve equity. Such transfer
58. ____________ programs typically result in ___________ losses, however.

MONEY IN A PERFECTLY COMPETITIVE MODEL

Money facilitates transactions by providing a
59. ____________ medium of ___________ and acts as a store of value. Since all prices are quoted in terms of money, money serves as an accounting standard. The choice of the accounting standard
60. ____________ does not affect ___________ prices, but does affect
61. ____________ ___________ prices. If a commodity is chosen as the
62. ____________ monetary standard, the ___________ price of money is determined like any other relative price, by the forces of demand and supply. In the case of fiat money, the
63. ____________ ___________ is the sole supplier.

MULTIPLE-CHOICE QUESTIONS

64.______ The perfectly competitive model assumes that there is a
- a. large number of people purchasing each good.
- b. small number of people purchasing each good.
- c. large number of people supplying each productive input.
- d. small number of people supplying each productive input.
- e. a and c.

65.______ The perfectly competitive model assumes that there is a

a. large number of firms producing each good.
b. small number of firms producing each good.
c. large number of firms purchasing productive inputs.
d. small number of firms purchasing productive inputs.
e. a and c.

66.______ The perfectly competitive model assumes that each

a. person takes most, but not necessarily all, prices as given.
b. firm takes no prices as given.
c. firm takes most, but not necessarily all, prices as given.
d. firm takes all prices as given.
e. a and d.

67.______ The perfectly competitive model assumes that each

a. individual maximizes utility.
b. individual maximizes profit.
c. firm maximizes utility.
d. firm maximizes profit.
e. a and d.

68.______ A change in demand in one market will typically affect

a. only that market.
b. that market and at most one or two other markets.
c. that market and other markets only if the good involved is inferior.
d. that market and many other markets.
e. only markets of normal goods.

69.______ General equilibrium studies

a. each market in isolation.
b. several markets in isolation.
c. how a small number of markets interact with each other.
d. how all markets interact with each other.
e. a and c.

70.______ When the economy is technically efficient

a. additional production of one good can be achieved without reducing the production of other goods.
b. it is impossible to increase the production of any good.
c. additional production of one good can be achieved only by reducing the production of some other good.
d. the production of all goods can be increased simultaneously.
e. a and d.

71.______ The rate of technical substitution indicates how

a. a firm can substitute labor for capital while keeping production constant.
b. production of one good can be substituted for the production of another.
c. an individual is willing to substitute the consumption of one good for another.
d. an individual is willing to substitute the consumption of goods today for the consumption of goods in the future.
e. c and d.

72.______ The rate of technical substitution is indicated by the slope of

a. a firm's isoquant.
b. a firm's indifference curve.
c. the production possibility curve.
d. a consumer's isoquant curve.
e. a consumer's indifference curve.

73.______ Technical efficiency requires

a. each firm to have the same rate of technical substitution.
b. each firm to have the same marginal rate of substitution.
c. each consumer to have the same marginal rate of substitution.
d. equality of the rates of technical substitution and the marginal rates of substitution.
e. a and c.

74.______ The production possibility frontier illustrates the

a. combinations of labor and capital that a firm can use to produce a given amount output.
b. alternative outputs of two goods that can be produced with the fixed amounts of inputs available to an economy.
c. combinations of two goods that would provide a consumer with a given amount of utility.
d. combinations of labor and capital that would provide a consumer with a given level of utility.
e. b and c.

75.______ If an economy is operating at a point on its production possibility frontier

a. production efficiency is guaranteed.
b. an efficient mix of outputs is guaranteed.
c. each individual's marginal rate of substitution is equal.
d. each firm's rate of technical substitution is equal.
e. a and d.

76.______ The rate of product transformation indicates how

a. a firm can substitute labor for capital while keeping production constant.
b. production of one good can be substituted for the production of another.
c. an individual is willing to substitute the consumption of one good for another.
d. a firm can substitute the production of one good today for the production of the good in the future.
e. a and d.

77.______ The rate of product transformation is indicated by the slope of

a. a firm's isoquant.
b. a firm's indifference curve.
c. the production possibility curve.
d. a consumer's isoquant curve.
e. a consumer's indifference curve.

78.______ The rate of product transformation equals the ratio of

a. marginal utilities.
b. the rates of technical substitution.
c. marginal revenue.
d. marginal cost.
e. b and d.

79.______ The production of an efficient mix of outputs requires

a. each consumer to have the same rate of technical substitution.
b. each firm to have the same marginal rate of substitution.
c. equality of the rates of technical substitution and the marginal rates of substitution.
d. equality of the rates of technical substitution and the rate of product transformation.
e. equality of the marginal rates of substitution and the rate of product transformation.

80.______ When a firm takes prices as given and produces its level of output by using the cost-minimizing combination of labor and capital its

a. marginal revenue must equal its marginal cost.
b. marginal rate of substitution must equal the price ratio.
c. rate of technical substitution must equal the wage-rental ratio.
d. rate of product transformation must equal the wage-rental ratio.
e. a and d.

81.______ When each firm takes prices as given and produces its level of output by using the cost-minimizing combination of labor and capital

a. production efficiency is guaranteed.
b. an efficient mix of outputs is guaranteed.
c. production efficiency is guaranteed only if each firm is producing the profit maximizing level of output.
d. efficient exchange is guaranteed.
e. a and b.

82.______ When a firm takes prices as given and maximizes profits

a. the price of its output will equal its marginal revenue.
b. its marginal revenue will equal its marginal cost.
c. the price of its output will equal its marginal cost.
d. the price of its output will equal its rate of technical substitution.
e. a, b, and c.

83.______ When each firm takes prices as given and maximizes profits

a. the price ratio must equal the ratio of marginal costs.
b. the price ratio must equal the rate of product transformation.
c. an efficient mix of outputs is guaranteed.
d. a and b.
e. a, b, and c.

84.______ The marginal rate of substitution indicates

a. how a firm can substitute labor for capital while keeping production constant.
b. how production of one good can be substituted for the production of another.
c. how an individual is willing to substitute the consumption of one good for another.
d. how a firm can substitute the production of a good today with the production of that good in the future.
e. a and c.

85.______ The marginal rate of substitution is indicated by the slope of

a. a firm's isoquant.
b. a firm's indifference curve.
c. the production possibility curve.
d. a consumer's isoquant curve.
e. a consumer's indifference curve.

86.______ When each consumer takes prices as given and maximizes utility

a. the price ratio must equal the ratio of marginal costs.
b. the price ratio must equal the rates of technical substitution.
c. the price ratio must equal the marginal rates of substitution.
d. an efficient mix of output is guaranteed.
e. c and d.

87.______ When each firm takes prices as given and maximizes profit and also each consumer takes prices as given and maximizes utility

a. an efficient mix of output is guaranteed.
b. efficient exchange is guaranteed.
c. efficiency in production is guaranteed.
d. a and b.
e. a, b, and c.

88.______ Which typically leads to inefficiency in markets?

a. imperfect competition.
b. externalities.
c. public goods.
d. a, b, and c.
e. none of the above.

RUNNING GLOSSARY

Perfectly competitive price system: an economic model in
89. ____________ which individuals maximize ____________, firms maximize profits, information concerning prices is freely available,
90. ____________ and every economic actor is a price ____________.

91. ____________ ____________ efficient allocation of resources: an allocation of available resources such that producing more of one good requires producing less of some other good.

92. ____________ ____________ box diagram: a graphic device for illustrating all the possible allocations of two goods (or two inputs) that are in fixed supply.

Production possibility frontier: a figure illustrating the
93. ____________ technically efficient ____________ possibilities for an
94. ____________ economy with fixed amounts of ____________.

95. ____________
96. ____________

Rate of product transformation: the slope of the ____________ possibility frontier that shows the ____________ costs involved in producing more of one good and less of some other good.

97. ____________ Economically efficient allocation of resources: a technically efficient allocation of resources in which the ____________ combination also reflects people's preferences.

98. ____________ Imperfect competition: a market situation in which buyers or sellers have some influence on the ____________ of goods or services.

99. ____________ ____________: the effect of one party's economic activities on another party's well-being that is not taken into account by the price system.

100. ____________ Public goods: goods that provide nonexclusive benefits to everyone in a group and that can be provided to one more user at ____________ marginal cost.

101. ____________ Equity: the ____________ of the distribution of goods or utility.

102. ____________ Initial endowments: the ____________ holdings of goods from which trading begins.

ANSWERS

1. large
2. prices
3. large
4. good
5. profit
6. all
7. increases
8. increase
9. reduce
10. without
11. constant
12. equal
13. affected
14. one
15. increase
16. two
17. allocate
18. efficient
19. technical
20. both
21. inefficiently
22. on
23. reduce
24. slope
25. ratio
26. six
27. two
28. three
29. low
30. high
31. opportunity
32. substitution
33. trade
34. three
35. one
36. inefficient
37. minimizes
38. efficient
39. substitution
40. cost
41. price
42. perfectly
43. costs
44. efficient
45. efficient
46. imperfect
47. marginal
48. exceed
49. price
50. costs
51. all
52. private
53. product
54. private
55. disagree
56. mechanism
57. voluntary
58. efficiency
59. exchange
60. relative
61. absolute
62. relative
63. government
64. e
65. e
66. d
67. e
68. d
69. d
70. c
71. a
72. a
73. a
74. b
75. e
76. b
77. c
78. d
79. e
80. c
81. a
82. e
83. d
84. c
85. e
86. c
87. e
88. d
89. utility
90. taker
91. Technically
92. Edgeworth
93. output
94. input
95. production
96. opportunity
97. output
98. prices
99. Externality
100. zero
101. fairness
102. initial

CHAPTER 15

INFORMATION AND COMPETITIVE EQUILIBRIUM

WALKING TOUR SUMMARIES

ESTABLISHING COMPETITIVE EQUILIBRIUM PRICES

While we know that an equilibrium price exists in every market, we have yet to describe a process that would lead the market to that price. In some markets an auctioneer
1. ____________ serves this role. The____________ calls prices. Only when
2. ____________ the quantity demanded ____________ the quantity supplied
will the transaction actually take place.

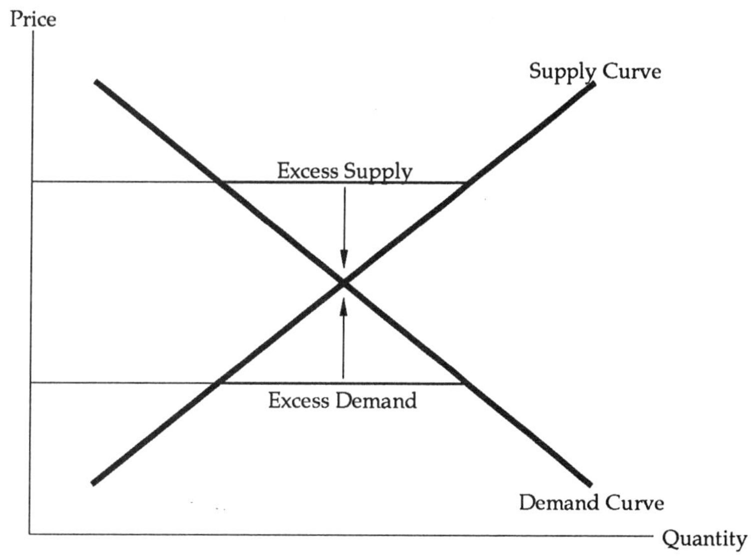

Figure 15.1: *Walrawian Price Adjustment*

Most markets do not employ actual auctioneers, however. Recontracting tries to circumvent this void.
3. ____________ Buyers and sellers enter into ____________ contracts which
4. ____________ they complete only if price proves to be the ____________
price. Otherwise, the parties negotiate new provisional contracts. After enough bargaining, the parties will achieve the equilibrium. Leon Walras proposed a second approach

5. ____________ which relies on the notion of excess ___________. Excess
demand equals the difference between the quantity
demanded and the quantity supplied. The price increases
6. ____________ whenever ___________ demand is positive and decreases
7. ____________ when excess demand is ___________.
8. ____________ While Walras views the ___________ as the
9. ____________ motivating force in the adjustment process, ___________
relies on quantity instead. When the quantity is below the
equilibrium level, individuals are willing to pay more for
the good than its marginal cost. In this case, firms produce
10. ____________ ___________. Alternatively, when the quantity exceeds the
11. ____________ equilibrium level, marginal cost ___________ what
individuals are willing to pay and the quantity decreases.
Both Walras and Marshall achieve the same equilibrium
result, but the process responsible differs.

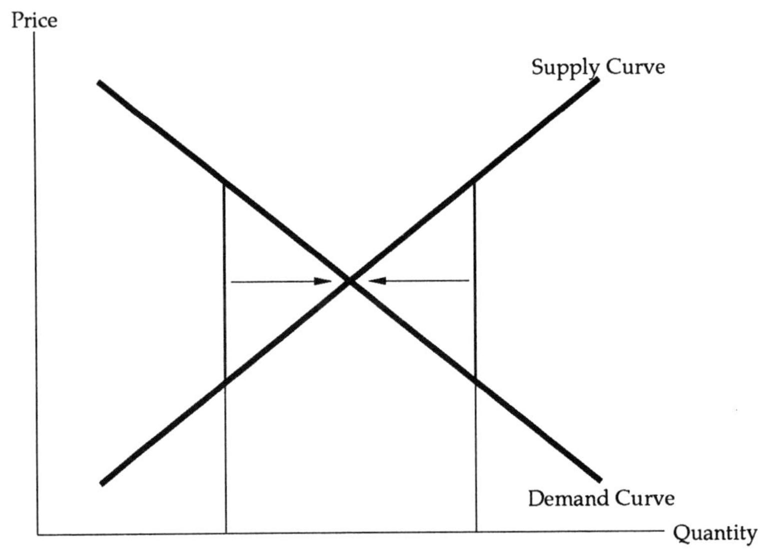

Figure 15.2: *Marshallian Price Adjustment*

Movement to an equilibrium typically involves
changes in both price and quantity. Economists explain
why demanders and sellers do not adjust instantaneously to
12. ____________ the equilibrium by recognizing that ___________ costs exist.
Demanders must discover where they can buy a particular
good and also must invest time in learning about the market
prices. Suppliers face similar costs. They must learn about
the demand for their product. Typically they react to the
short-run random nature of demand by maintaining
13. ____________ ___________. These transaction costs prevent the price and
quantity from adjusting to the equilibrium immediately.

Therefore, economists have studied the disequilibrium behavior of prices.

MODELS OF DISEQUILIBRIUM PRICING

The cobweb model of price adjustment assumes that suppliers base this period's production decisions on the
14. ___________ ___________ period's price. Suppliers expect that the current period's price will equal last period's and decide on their levels of production accordingly. After producing the good, suppliers sell the output for what the market will bear. This process can result in a stable or unstable equilibrium. In the stable case, the price moves
15. ___________ ___________ the equilibrium. In the unstable case, the
16. ___________ price moves away from the ___________. The rational expectations model recognizes that demanders and suppliers typically base their price expectations on more
17. ___________ than last period's price. With enough ___________ parties all could calculate the equilibrium price precisely. Buyers and sellers would make their decisions on the actual equilibrium price. The quantity of information required for these calculations is considerable, however. Typically buyers and sellers base their expectations on incomplete
18. ___________ ___________.

INFORMATION AND ECONOMIC EFFICIENCY

Our proof that competitive markets lead to efficiency implicitly assumed that all economic actors are
19. ___________ ___________ informed. Without full information, competitive markets can result in inefficiency. Asymmetric information on the part of the buyer and seller can lead to such a result. For example, the seller of a used car has more information about the quality of the automobile than the
20. ___________ buyer. The ___________ problem can arise. Buyers and sellers will trade fewer used cars than efficiency dictates.
21. ___________ This is an example of ___________ selection. Adverse selection occurs whenever one party has more information than others. The party possessing the most information enjoys an advantage in the marketplace. Adverse selection can occur in a wide variety of markets: insurance, labor, etc. Competitive markets provide buyers and sellers with
22. ___________ incentives to acquire ___________. The ramifications of this

are complex, however, and economists have been unable to draw many general conclusions.

MULTIPLE-CHOICE QUESTIONS

23. ______ An impartial auctioneer finds the equilibrium price by
    a. precise calculations involving demand and supply.
    b. calling out a single price.
    c. calling out successive prices until one is found at which quantity demanded equals quantity supplied.
    d. call out successive prices until one is found at which excess demand equals zero.
    e. c and d.

24. ______ Recontracting has been mentioned as a
    a. substitute for the impartial auctioneer when a market has none.
    b. way to increase the income of lawyers.
    c. way to reduce a firm's risks.
    d. way to find an equilibrium price.
    e. a and d.

25. ______ Excess demand equals the
    a. quantity demanded plus the quantity supplied.
    b. amount consumers would like to purchase if the market were in equilibrium.
    c. difference between the value consumers place on the consumption of a good and what they must pay to purchase the good.
    d. sum of consumers' surplus and profit.
    e. none of the above.

26. ______ Walras argues that an equilibrium will be achieved by
    a. an increase (decrease) in the price whenever excess demand is positive (negative).
    b. a decrease (increase) in the price whenever excess demand is positive (negative).
    c. an increase (decrease) in the quantity whenever the price exceeds marginal cost.
    d. a decrease (increase) in the quantity whenever the price exceeds (falls short of) marginal cost.
    e. a and c.

27. ______ Marshall argues that an equilibrium will be achieved by

a. an increase (decrease) in the price whenever excess demand is positive (negative).
b. a decrease (increase) in the price whenever excess demand is positive (negative).
c. an increase (decrease) in the quantity whenever the price exceeds marginal cost.
d. a decrease (increase) in the quantity whenever the price exceeds (falls short of) marginal cost.
e. b and d.

28. ______ Transaction costs explain why

a. a market must always be in disequilibrium.
b. a market must always be in equilibrium.
c. the quantity demanded equals the quantity supplied.
d. the length of time during which a market is in disequilibrium varies from market to market.
e. none of the above.

29. ______ The cobweb model assumes that

a. demanders base their consumption decisions on last period's price.
b. suppliers base their production decisions on last period's price.
c. demanders base their consumption decisions on this period's price.
d. b and c.
e. a and b.

30. ______ The cobweb model predicts that

a. all markets will be stable.
b. all markets will be unstable.
c. some markets will have a stable price, but an unstable quantity.
d. some markets will have an unstable price, but a stable quantity.
e. none of the above.

31. ______ Rational expectations argues that

a. the cobweb model is oversimplistic.
b. with complete information individuals would be able to calculate the equilibrium price.
c. all individuals know about elasticities.
d. prices should never change.
e. none of the above.

32. ______ Asymmetric information

a. explains why colleges admit some students who do not graduate.
b. explains why the "lemons" problem exists.
c. occurs whenever all individuals are not fully informed.
d. occurs only if all individuals are fully informed.
e. none of the above.

33. ______ Adverse selection

a. may occur when buyers and sellers have different information.
b. may occur when there is asymmetric information.
c. may lead to inefficiency.
d. helps those groups who have better information.
e. all of the above.

34. ______ Models attempting to capture the acquisition of information

a. yield many general and far reaching results.
b. suggest that market equilibrium is complex in this context.
c. indicate that efficiency always results if there is asymmetric information.
d. suggest that information can be acquired costlessly.
e. none of the above.

RUNNING GLOSSARY

35. ____________ ____________ demand: the extent to which quantity demanded exceeds quantity supplied at a particular price.

36. ____________ ____________ costs: costs involved in making market transactions and in gathering information with which to make those transactions.

37. ____________ Cobweb model: a model of price adjustment in which some trading takes place at ____________ prices.

38. ____________ Stable equilibrium: a situation in which market forces cause price to move ____________ its equilibrium level.

39. ___________ Unstable equilibrium: a situation in which market forces cause price to move ___________ its equilibrium level.

40. ___________ Rational expectations: basing price expectations on ___________ information about the equilibrium price determined by the interaction of supply and demand in the market.

41. ___________ Asymmetric information: a situation in which buyers and sellers have ___________ amounts of information about a market transaction.

42. ___________ ___________ selection: when buyers and sellers have different information, market outcomes may exhibit adverse selection – the quality of goods or services traded will be biased toward market participants with better information.

ANSWERS

1. auctioneer
2. equals
3. provisional
4. equilibrium
5. demand
6. excess
7. negative
8. price
9. Marshall
10. more
11. exceeds
12. transactions
13. inventories
14. previous
15. toward
16. equilibrium
17. information
18. information
19. fully
20. lemon
21. adverse
22. information
23. e
24. e
25. e
26. a
27. c
28. d
29. d
30. e
31. b
32. b
33. e
34. b
35. Excess
36. Transactions
37. nonequilibrium
38. to
39. from
40. complete
41. different
42. Adverse

PART 4

THE PERFECTLY COMPETITIVE MODEL

WALKING TOUR PROBLEMS

FIRM AND INDUSTRY REACTIONS IN THE SHORT AND LONG RUN

1. Initially a perfectly competitive market is in long-run equilibrium. Subsequently, the fixed costs of each firm increase.

   a. Initially are profits of a typical firm in the industry positive, negative, or zero?

      Since the industry is in long-run equilibrium the
      1. ____________ typical firm in the industry has ____________
      incentive to leave the industry; consequently, profits
      2. ____________ cannot be ____________. Furthermore, no firm can
      3. ____________ have an incentive to ____________ the industry;
      4. ____________ consequently, profits cannot be ____________.
      Therefore, profits must be zero.

      The answer is zero.

   b. Initially, how is the price related to the typical firm's average cost?

      Profits for the typical firm are zero; hence, total
      5. ____________ revenue ____________ total cost. Total revenue
      6. ____________ equals price times ____________; total cost equals
      7. ____________ average cost times quantity. Price must ____________
      average cost.

      The answer is price equals average cost.

   c. In the short run, after fixed costs increase what happens to the market demand curve?

8. ____________ The position of the market demand curve is ____________ by the change in fixed costs.

The answer is nothing.

d. In the short run, after fixed costs increase what happens to each firm's marginal cost curve? Each firm's individual supply curve? The market supply curve?

Marginal cost equals the change in the firm's total
9. ____________ cost as a consequence of producing ____________ additional unit of output. The increase in fixed costs
10. ____________ will ____________ affect a firm's marginal cost curve.

The answer is nothing.

11. ____________ An individual firm's supply curve is its ____________ cost curve (as long as price exceeds average variable costs). Since the change in fixed costs will not affect
12. ____________ the firm's marginal cost curves, it will ____________ affect their individual supply curves.

The answer is nothing.

13. ____________ The market supply curve is the ____________ sum of each individual firm's supply curve. Since the individual supply curves are not affected, the market
14. ____________ supply curve will ____________ be affected.

The answer is nothing.

e. In the short run, after variable costs increase what happens to the price and quantity?

In a perfectly competitive market the price and
15. ____________ quantity are determined by the market ____________ and supply curves. Neither the demand curve nor the
16. ____________ supply curve has ____________; consequently, the price and quantity are unchanged.

The answer is nothing.

f. What has happened to the typical firm's average cost curve? The typical firm's profits? Is the industry still in a long-run equilibrium? What happens in the long run?

Since fixed costs have risen the average cost curve
17. ___________ will shift ___________.

The answer is it has risen.

To determine the sign of profits compare
18. ___________ ___________ and average cost. Initially the price equals average cost. The increase in fixed costs leaves the price unchanged whereas average cost has risen; price is now less than average cost. Consequently, profits are now negative.

The answer is profits are negative.

The industry is not in long-run equilibrium because
19. ___________ the typical firm now earns ___________ profits.

The answer is no.

20. ___________ When profits are ___________ the owners of firms can earn more from their resources by using them elsewhere in the economy. Consequently, firms will exit the industry in the long run.

The answer is firms will exit.

g. In the long run, what happens to the market supply curve? The price and quantity?

The market supply curve is the horizontal sum of
21. ___________ each firm's ___________ supply curve. Since there are fewer firms in the industry, the market supply
22. ___________ curve will shift to the ___________.

The answer is it shifts to the left.

When the market supply curve shifts to the left, the
23. ___________ equilibrium price ___________ and the equilibrium quantity decreases.

The answer is the price increases and the quantity decreases.

2. Initially a perfectly competitive market is in long-run equilibrium. Subsequently, the variable costs of each firm increase raising the firm's marginal and average cost by $.10.

   a. Initially are profits of a typical firm in the industry positive, negative, or zero?

24. ____________ Since the industry is in ___________-run equilibrium the typical firm in the industry has no incentive to leave the industry; consequently, profits cannot be negative. Furthermore, no firm can have an incentive
25. ____________ to enter the industry; consequently, ___________
26. ____________ cannot be positive. Therefore, ___________ must be zero.

      The answer is zero.

   b. Initially, how is the price related to the typical firm's average cost?

27. ____________ Profits for the typical firm are ___________; hence, total revenue equals total cost. Total revenue equals
28. ____________ ___________ times quantity; total cost equals
29. ____________ ___________ cost times quantity. Price must equal
30. ____________ ___________ cost.

      The answer is price equals average cost.

   c. In the short run, after variable costs increase what happens to the market demand curve?

31. ____________ The position of the market ___________ curve is unaffected by the change in variable costs.

      The answer is nothing.

   d. In the short run, after variable costs increase what happens to each firm's marginal cost curve? Each firm's individual supply curve? The market supply curve?

      The increase in variable costs shifts each firm's marginal cost curve up by $.10.

The answer is shift up by $.10.

32. ____________ An individual firm's ___________ curve is its
marginal cost curve (as long as price exceeds average
33. ____________ ___________ costs). The change in variable costs will
shift each firm's individual supply curve up by $.10.

The answer is shift up by $.10.

The market supply curve is the horizontal sum of
34. ____________ each ___________ firm's supply curve; consequently,
35. ____________ the market supply curve will shift ___________ by
$.10.

The answer is shift up by $.10.

e. In the short run, after fixed costs increase what happens to the price and quantity?

In a perfectly competitive market the equilibrium
price and quantity are determined by the
36. ____________ ___________ demand and supply curves. Since the
demand curve has remained stationary and the
supply curve has shifted up, the quantity will
37. ____________ ___________ and the price will increase. The price
38. ____________ will rise by less than $___________, however,
because the supply curve has shifted up by only $.10.

The answer is the price increases by less than $.10 and the quantity decreases.

f. What has happened to the typical firm's average cost curve? The typical firm's profits? Is the industry still in a long-run equilibrium? What happens in the long run?

The average cost curve has shifted up by $.10.

The answer is it has risen by $.10.

To determine the sign of profits compare price and
39. ____________ average cost. The price has risen by ___________
than $.10. Since price equaled average costs initially,
40. ____________ price is now ___________ than average cost.
Consequently, profits are now negative.

The answer is negative.

41. ____________ The industry is not in long-run equilibrium because the typical firm now earns ____________ profits.

The answer is no.

42. ____________ When profits are ____________ the owners of firms can earn more from their resources by using them elsewhere in the economy. Consequently, firms will exit the industry in the long run.

The answer is firms will exit.

g. In the long run, what happens to the market supply curve? The price and quantity?

43. ____________
44. ____________

The market supply curve is the horizontal sum of each firm's ____________ supply curve. Since there are fewer firms in the industry, the market supply curve will shift to the ____________.

The answer is it shifts to the left.

45. ____________ When the market supply curve shifts to the left, the equilibrium price ____________ and the equilibrium quantity decreases.

The answer is the price increases and the quantity decreases.

3. Initially a perfectly competitive market is in long-run equilibrium. Subsequently, there is an increase in demand.

46. ____________ a. Initially are profits of a typical firm in the industry positive, negative, or zero?

47. ____________ b. Initially, how is the price related to the typical firm's average cost?

48. ____________ c. In the short run, what happens to the market demand curve?

49. ____________
50. ____________
51. ____________

d. In the short run, what happens to each firm's marginal cost curve? What happens to each firm's individual supply curve? What happens to the market supply curve?

52. ____________
53. ____________

e. In the short run, what happens to the price? What happens to the quantity?

54. ____________
55. ____________
56. ____________

f. What has happened to the typical firm's average cost curve? What happens to the profits earned by the typical firm? What happens to the profits in the long run?

57. ____________
58. ____________
59. ____________

g. In the long run, what happens to the market supply curve? In the long run, what happens to the price? In the long run what happens to the quantity?

EFFICIENCY

4. The rate of technical substitution for Firm X is 5 and that for Firm Y is 2.

a. From the information provided above can you determine if the economy is efficient from a technical, exchange, or output mix standpoint?

60. ____________
61. ____________
62. ____________

The relationship between the firm's rates of technical substitution determine whether or not the economy is ____________ efficient. The relationship between the consumer's marginal rates of substitution determine whether or not the economy is efficient from the standpoint of ____________. The relationship between the consumer's marginal rates of substitution and the rate of ______________ transformation determine whether or not the economy is producing an efficient mix of output.

The answer is from the standpoint of production.

b. What does efficiency mean in this context?

63. ____________

Technical efficiency refers to whether inputs could be reallocated between firms so as to ____________ the production of one firm without reducing the production of the other firm.

The answer is inputs can be reallocated so as to increase the production of one firm without reducing the production of other firms.

c. Is the economy efficient in this context? What change would enhance efficiency?

Since the rates of technical substitution are not equal,
64. ____________ ____________ results.

The answer is no.

Since the rate of technical substitution for Firm X is 5, Firm X could produce the same amount of output by
65. ____________ using one more unit of labor and ____________ less units of capital. Similarly, Firm Y could produce the same amount of output by using one less unit of labor
66. ____________ and ____________ more units of capital. If Firm Y gives Firm X one unit of labor in exchange for three
67. ____________ units of capital, both firms can produce ____________ output.

The answer is Firm X should give labor to Firm Y in exchange for captial.

5. The rate of product transformation is 3 and marginal rate of substitution for Smith is 5.

a. From the information provided above can you determine if the economy is efficient from a technical, exchange, or output mix standpoint?

The relationship between the firm's rates of
68. ____________ ____________ substitution determine whether or not the economy is technically efficient. The relationship between the consumer's marginal rates of
69. ____________ ____________ determine whether or not the economy is efficient from the standpoint of exchange. The relationship between the consumer's marginal rates of substitution and the rate of product transformation determine whether or not the economy is producing
70. ____________ an efficient ____________ of output.

The answer is from the standpoint of the output mix.

b. What does efficiency mean in this context?

71. ____________ An efficient mix of outputs refers to whether consumers could be made better off by the production of a different ____________ of outputs.

The answer is consumers can be made better off if a different output mix were produced.

c. Is the economy efficient in this context? What change would enhance efficiency?

72. ____________ Since the consumer's marginal rates of substitution do not equal the rate of product transformation ____________ results.

The answer is no.

73. ____________
74. ____________

Smith's marginal rate of substitution is 5; he is willing to forgo the consumption of ____________ units of good Y in order to consume one additional unit of good X. Since the rate of product transformation is 3, one additional unit of good X could be produced at the sacrifice of only ____________ units of good Y. More of good X should be produced.

The answer is produce more good X.

6. The marginal rate of substitution for Smith is 4 and that for Jones is 4 also.

75. ____________ a. From the information provided above can you determine if the economy is efficient from a technical, exchange, or output mix standpoint?

76. ____________ b. Is the economy efficient in this context?

7. The marginal rate of substitution for Smith is 3; the marginal rate of substitution for Jones is 6.

    a. From the information provided above can you determine if the economy is efficient from a technical, exchange, or output mix standpoint?

77. ____________

    b. Is the economy efficient in this context?

78. ____________

8. The rate of technical substitution for Firm X is 2; the rate of technical substitution for Firm Y is 3.

    a. From the information provided above can you determine if the economy is efficient from a technical, exchange, or output mix standpoint?

79. ____________

    b. Is the economy efficient in this context?

80. ____________

9. The marginal rate of substitution for Smith is 4; the rate of product transformation is 8.

    a. From the information provided above can you determine if the economy is efficient from a technical, exchange, or output mix standpoint?

81. ____________

    b. Is the economy efficient in this context?

82. ____________

ANSWERS

1. no
2. negative
3. enter
4. positive
5. equals
6. quantity
7. equal
8. unaffected
9. one
10. not
11. marginal
12. not
13. horizontal
14. not
15. demand
16. shifted
17. up
18. price
19. negative
20. negative
21. individual
22. left
23. increases
24. long
25. profits
26. profits
27. zero
28. price
29. average
30. average
31. demand
32. supply
33. variable
34. individual
35. up
36. market
37. decrease
38. .10
39. less
40. less
41. negative
42. negative
43. individual
44. left
45. increases
46. zero
47. equal
48. shifts right
49. nothing
50. nothing
51. nothing
52. increases
53. decreases
54. nothing
55. become positive
56. firms enter
57. shifts right
58. decreases
59. decreases
60. technically
61. exchange
62. product
63. increase
64. inefficiency
65. five
66. two
67. more
68. technical
69. substitution
70. mix
71. mix
72. inefficiency
73. five
74. two
75. exchange
76. yes
77. exchange
78. no
79. technical
80. no
81. output mix
82. no

PART 5

IMPERFECT COMPETITION

CHAPTER 16

PRICING IN MONOPOLY MARKETS

WALKING TOUR SUMMARIES

CAUSES OF MONOPOLY

Monopolies exist because other firms find it unprofitable or impossible to enter the market; barriers to
1. ___________ ___________ are the source of monopoly power. There are two types of barriers to entry: technical and legal. Technical
2. ___________ barriers to entry exist whenever there is ___________ average cost (increasing returns to scale) within the relevant range of production. In this case one firm producing at high production levels has a distinct cost advantage over small firms producing low levels of output. Because average cost
3. ___________ is ___________ for the large firm, it could charge a price which would force the small, high average cost firms out of business. Ownership of low-cost methods of production, unique resources, unique management talents, etc. may also be a source of technical barriers to entry. Legal barriers to entry can exist due to patents, exclusive franchises, etc.,
4. ___________ which grant ___________ firm unique rights.

PROFIT MAXIMIZATION

In one sense a monopoly is just like a price taking firm: the monopolist's profit-maximizing production level
5. ___________ occurs where marginal revenue ___________ marginal cost. Monopolies differ from price taking firms in the relationship
6. ___________ between marginal revenue and ___________, however.

7. ____________ Marginal revenue equals price for the price taking firm. Marginal revenue is ____________ than price for the monopolist because the monopolist faces a downward sloping demand curve. When it sells one additional unit of
8. ____________ output it must ____________ the price on all units sold. While the sale of the additional unit itself tends to increase revenues by an amount equal to the price, the firm must sell
9. ____________ all other units at the ____________ price. In net, the change in total revenues from the sale of one additional unit
10. ____________ (marginal revenue) will be ____________ than the price. Let us now summarize. For a profit-maximizing monopolist:

$$P > MR = MC$$

11. ____________ ____________ exceeds marginal cost for the profit-
12. ____________ maximizing monopolist while price ____________ marginal cost for the profit-maximizing price taking firm.

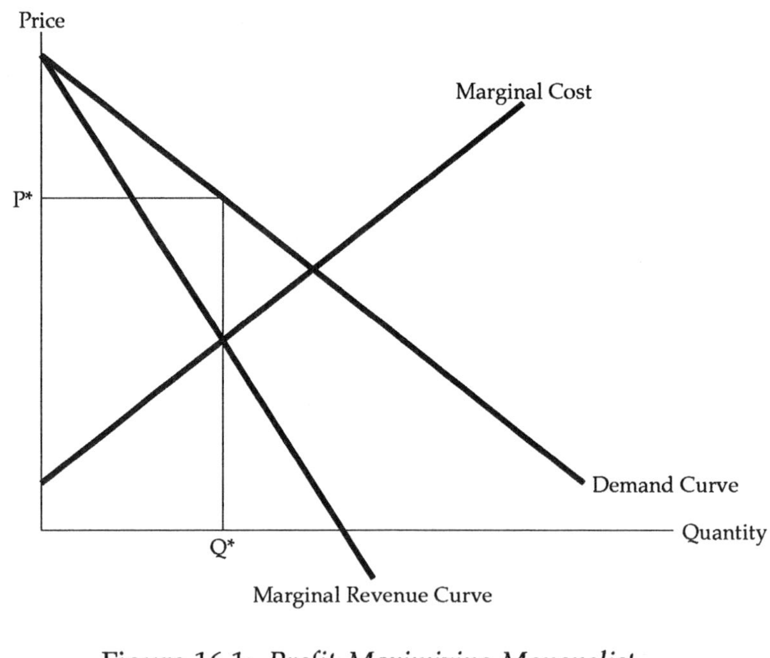

Figure 16.1: *Profit-Maximizing Monopolist*

MONOPOLY PROFITS

We calculate the profits of a monopoly just as we calculate the profits of any firm. A firm's profit equals total revenue less total cost, which in turn equals the quantity
13. ____________ times the difference between price and ____________ cost:

$$\begin{aligned} \text{Profits} &= \text{TR} - \text{TC} \\ &= (P \times Q) - (AC \times Q) \\ &= (P - AC) \times Q \end{aligned}$$

In perfect competition the existence of positive profits is a temporary phenomenon. In the long run, positive profits entice firms to enter the industry. The new firms drive
14. ____________ profits to ____________. The existence of barriers to entry in
15. ____________ a monopoly means entry ____________ occur. Accordingly, positive profits can persist in a monopoly.

WHAT'S WRONG WITH MONOPOLY PROFITS

Most people object to monopolies on distributional grounds. The owners of a monopoly (as opposed to the owners of a perfectly competitive firm) can receive
16. ____________ ____________ profits indefinitely. It is not true that these profits must be large, however. The size of profits depends
17. ____________ on the difference between price and ____________ cost. The existence of a monopoly does not guarantee that this difference will be large. In fact the difference could even equal zero, meaning that the monopoly was earning zero profits.

A more sophisticated objection to monopoly concerns the allocation of resources. A profit-maximizing monopolist
18. ____________ produces where price exceeds ____________ cost. Consider an additional unit of output. The cost of producing the
19. ____________ additional unit is ____________ than what consumers are willing to pay for it. From a social perspective, the
20. ____________ monopoly produces too ____________ of the good. Society devotes too few resources to the production of the good.

CONSUMER SURPLUS

If a monopoly could be a perfect price discriminator, it would be able to dole out the good one unit at a time. It would sell each unit to that consumer who would pay the
21. ____________ ____________ price. The perfect price discriminator could
22. ____________ collect revenues equal to the area beneath the ____________
23. ____________ curve. This area represents the ____________ value individuals place upon the consumption of the good. It is virtually impossible for a producer to practice perfect price discrimination, however; firms typically do not charge different prices to different buyers. Firms usually charge

24. __________ the __________ price to all. Most consumers buy the good
25. __________ at a price __________ that which the perfect price discriminator would charge. Economists call this bonus
26. __________ __________ surplus. Graphically, it is the area beneath
27. __________ the __________ curve which lies above the price. Consumer surplus equals the total value individuals place
28. __________ upon the consumption of the good __________ what they actually pay to purchase the good.

MONOPOLISTIC EFFECT ON ALLOCATION AND DISTRIBUTION

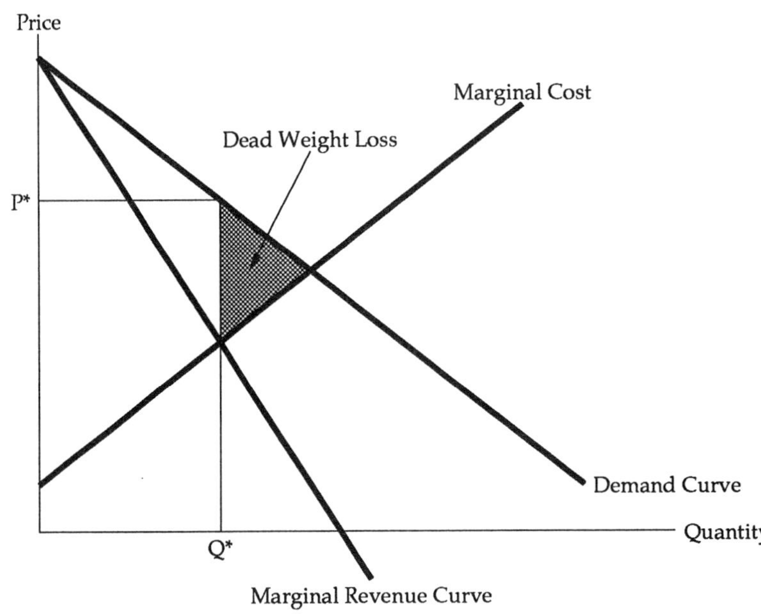

Figure 16.2: *Deadweight Loss of a Monopoly*

A monopoly restricts output below the competitive level. The restriction has two effects. Individuals have less of the "monopoly" good to consume. On the other hand,
29. __________ __________ inputs are used to produce the "monopoly" good; consequently, the inputs are used by other firms to produce "other" goods. The monopoly affects consumers in
30. __________ two ways: __________ of the "monopoly" good is
31. __________ produced, but __________ "other" goods are manufactured. The value consumers place upon the
32. __________ unproduced "monopoly" good __________ the value consumers place on the "other" goods, however. We call the
33. __________ difference the __________ loss of monopoly; it measures the distortion of resources caused by the monopoly. In

addition to the allocation distortion, there is also a distributional effect. Part of what would be consumer
34. ____________ surplus in a competitive situation becomes ___________ for the monopolist.

PRICE DISCRIMINATION

In theory a monopoly could practice perfect price discrimination, selling each unit of output for the maximum amount that buyers are willing to pay. As the market demand curve suggests, the second unit would be sold for a slightly lower price than the first, the third unit for a slightly lower price than the second, etc. Total revenue would equal the area beneath the demand curve. The perfect price discriminating monopolist would continue to produce and
35. ____________ sell output until the ___________ of the last unit sold just equaled marginal cost. Paradoxically, a perfect price discrimination scheme would be efficient; deadweight loss would equal zero.

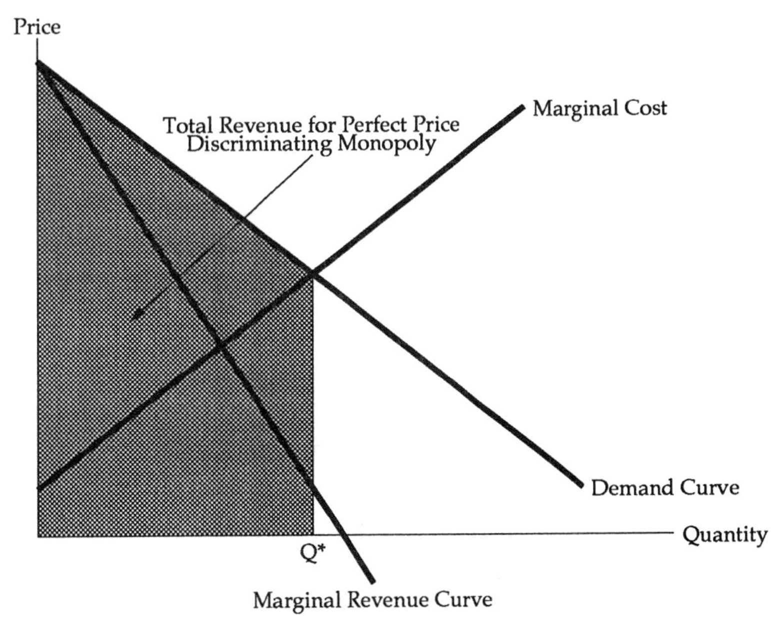

Figure 16.3: *Perfect Price Discriminating Monopolist*

In practice, it is virtually impossible for a monopolist to be a perfect price discriminator. It is sometimes possible for a monopolist to divide its customers into several different groups, however. In this case, the monopolist could increase its profits by practicing price

discrimination. That is, the monopolist could charge different groups different prices. To maximize profits the monopolist charges the groups with the more inelastic
36. ____________ demand a ___________ price.

REGULATION OF MONOPOLIES

To eliminate deadweight loss, monopolists must
37. ____________ charge a price equal to ___________ cost. Unfortunately,
38. ____________ this cannot be done when a ___________ monopoly exists. Natural monopolies occur whenever average cost
39. ____________ ___________ in the relevant region of production. Since average cost is decreasing, marginal cost must be
40. ____________ ___________ than average cost. To eliminate deadweight loss entirely the monopolist must be forced to charge a price
41. ____________ ___________ to marginal cost. Since marginal cost is less than average, forcing a natural monopoly to charge a price equal to marginal cost forces it to charge a price less than average cost. This means that the monopolist would incur a
42. ____________ ___________ and the firm would exit the industry in the
43. ____________ ___________ run. Economists have devised several approaches to resolve this dilemma, most notably
44. ____________ ___________-tier pricing and rate of return regulation.

MULTIPLE-CHOICE QUESTIONS

45. _____ Which of the following are referred to as technical barriers to entry?
    a. decreasing average cost.
    b. patents.
    c. increasing returns to scale.
    d. a and c.
    e. b and c.

46. _____ Which of the following are referred to as legal barriers to entry?
    a. decreasing average cost.
    b. patents.
    c. increasing returns to scale.
    d. a and c.
    e. b and c.

47. ______ A monopolist maximizes profits by producing the level of output at which

a. marginal revenue equals marginal cost, just like the price taking firm.
b. marginal revenue equals marginal cost, unlike the price taking firm.
c. price equals marginal cost, just like the price taking firm.
d. price equals marginal cost, unlike the price taking firm.
e. price equals average cost.

48. ______ A monopolist's marginal revenue is

a. equal to the price, just like the price taking firm.
b. less than the price, just like the price taking firm.
c. greater than the price, just like the price taking firm.
d. equal to the price, unlike the price taking firm.
e. less than the price, unlike the price taking firm.

49. ______ With a profit-maximizing monopolist, the price will be

a. equal to marginal cost, just like the price taking firm.
b. greater than marginal cost, just like the price taking firm.
c. equal to marginal cost, unlike the price taking firm.
d. less than marginal cost, unlike the price taking firm.
e. greater than marginal cost, unlike the price taking firm.

50. ______ Monopolies earn positive profits

a. in all cases.
b. only when price exceeds marginal cost.
c. only when price exceeds average cost.
d. only when there are no barriers to entry.
e. whenever price exceeds marginal cost.

51. ______ From a social perspective, a profit-maximizing monopoly typically

a. produces too much output.
b. produces too little output.
c. produces the correct amount of output.
d. uses too many resources.
e. b and d.

52. ______ The area beneath the market demand curve represents the
   a. total value individuals place upon the consumption of the good.
   b. revenues that firms actually collect from the sale of the good.
   c. expenditures that households actually make to purchase the good.
   d. revenues a perfect price discriminator could collect from the sale of the good.
   e. a and d.

53. ______ In the real world, perfect price discrimination occurs
   a. in virtually every market.
   b. in virtually every monopolistic market.
   c. in about half the monopolistic markets.
   d. very infrequently, if ever.
   e. in virtually all competitive markets.

54. ______ A monopoly usually charges
   a. the same price to all customers.
   b. a different price to each customer.
   c. different prices to men and women.
   d. different prices to those with elastic and inelastic demand.
   e. c and d.

55. ______ Consumer surplus refers to the
   a. total value individuals place upon the consumption of the good.
   b. difference between the total value individuals place upon the consumption of the good and what individuals actually pay.
   c. expenditures individuals make to purchase the good.
   d. revenues a perfect price discriminator could collect from the sale of the good.
   e. a and d.

56. ______ Graphically, consumer surplus equals the area
   a. beneath the demand curve.
   b. between the demand curve and the price.
   c. beneath the marginal revenue curve.
   d. between the marginal revenue and marginal cost curves.
   e. b and d.

57. ______ The level of output produced by a profit-maximizing monopoly

a. is below the competitive level.
b. is above the competitive level.
c. is equal to the competitive level.
d. may be below, above, or equal to the competitive level.
e. is never below the competitive level.

58. ______ The price charged by a profit-maximizing monopoly is

a. below the competitive price.
b. above the competitive price.
c. equal to the competitive price.
d. may be below, above, or equal to the competitive price.
e. equal to marginal revenue.

59. ______ The deadweight loss of monopoly refers to the

a. profits earned by the monopolist.
b. profits earned by the monopolist in excess of what would be earned in the competitive case.
c. value individuals place upon the goods that are not produced due to the monopolist's restriction of output.
d. value of the inputs that are not used due to the monopolist's restriction of output.
e. difference between c and d.

60. ______ To eliminate deadweight loss a monopoly must be forced to

a. charge a price equal to marginal cost.
b. charge a price equal to average cost.
c. charge a price equal to average variable cost.
d. reduce its level of production.
e. a and d.

61. ______ Whenever a natural monopoly is forced to charge a price equal to marginal cost, the monopoly will

a. incur a loss.
b. earn a profit.
c. cause no deadweight loss.
d. wish to exit the industry in the long run.
e. a, c, and d.

62. ______ When a profit-maximizing monopolist can divide its customers into separate groups, it will charge

   a. all groups the same price.
   b. groups with the more inelastic demand a higher price.
   c. groups with a more elastic demand a higher price.
   d. groups with unit elasticity the highest price.
   e. none of the above.

RUNNING GLOSSARY

63. ____________ ____________ to entry: factors that prevent new firms from entering a market or industry.

64. ____________ Natural monopoly: a firm that exhibits diminishing ____________ cost over a broad range of output levels.

65. ____________ Monopoly rents: the ____________ that a monopoly earns in the long run.

66. ____________ Deadweight loss: a loss of consumer ____________ that is not transferred to another economic actor.

67. ____________ Price discrimination: the practice of charging ____________ prices for a good in different markets.

ANSWERS

1. entry
2. decreasing
3. less
4. one
5. equals
6. price
7. less
8. lower
9. lower
10. less
11. Price
12. equals
13. average
14. zero
15. cannot
16. positive
17. average
18. marginal
19. less
20. little
21. highest
22. demand
23. total
24. same
25. below
26. consumer
27. demand
28. less
29. fewer
30. less
31. more
32. exceeds
33. deadweight
34. profit
35. price
36. higher
37. marginal
38. natural
39. decreases
40. less
41. equal
42. loss
43. long
44. two
45. d
46. b
47. a
48. e
49. e
50. c
51. b
52. e
53. d
54. a
55. b
56. b
57. a
58. b
59. e
60. a
61. e
62. b
63. Barriers
64. average
65. profits
66. surplus
67. different

CHAPTER 17

PRICING IN IMPERFECTLY COMPETITIVE MARKETS

WALKING TOUR SUMMARIES

PRICING OF HOMOGENEOUS GOODS

1. __________ There are __________ models which set outer limits
on how an industry composed of a small number of firms
(an oligopoly) may behave: the quasi-competitive and cartel
models. In the quasi-competitive model the firms behave
2. __________ like price __________. Each firm's marginal revenue
3. __________ equals the __________. Just as in the competitive case
4. __________ price will equal __________ cost. Furthermore, if there are
no barriers to entry, price will also equal average cost in the
5. __________ __________ run. In the cartel model, the cartel acts as a
6. __________ multiplant __________ where firms behave as different
divisions of a single large firm. As in the monopoly case,
7. __________ marginal revenue for the cartel will be __________ than
price. When the cartel maximizes profits of the industry as a
8. __________ whole, price will __________ marginal cost. While
9. __________ it is in the firms' __________ interests to act like a cartel,
three problems often limit their ability to do so. First, most
cartels are illegal. Second, the implementation of a cartel
agreement requires considerable information. Third, it is in
10. __________ the __________ interests of each firm to cheat on the cartel
agreement.

OTHER PRICING POSSIBILITIES

In addition to using the quasi-competitive and cartel
11. __________ models to illustrate the outer limits of __________
behavior, economists have developed many models which
try to predict more precisely how oligopolies act. Perhaps
the most famous two are the kinked demand and price
leadership models. The kinked demand model
hypothesizes that firms make decisions very cautiously. The
model assumes that if one particular firm were to lower its

12. ____________ price, other firms would react by ____________ prices also.
13. ____________ On the other hand, if one firm were to ____________ its price, others would not respond. The kinked demand model explains why oligopolists rarely adjust their prices to
14. ____________ changes in ____________. The price leadership model hypothesizes that the firms in an oligopolistic industry look upon one firm (or a small group of firms) as the leader. Other firms will change their prices whenever the leader does.

THE COURNOT MODEL

The Cournot model describes the behavior of an
15. ____________ industry composed of two firms, a ____________. Each firm
16. ____________ assumes that the other firm's ____________ will not change. Firm 1's reaction function describes its level of output
17. ____________ ____________ what firm 2 produces. Similarly, firm 2 has a reaction function which describes how much it will produce given firm 1's level of output. The intersection of the two
18. ____________ reaction functions graphically represents a ____________ equilibrium. At a Cournot equilibrium each firm makes an
19. ____________ ____________ assumption about how much output the other
20. ____________ is producing. The profits of the two firms is ____________ than the level of profits in the monopoly case.

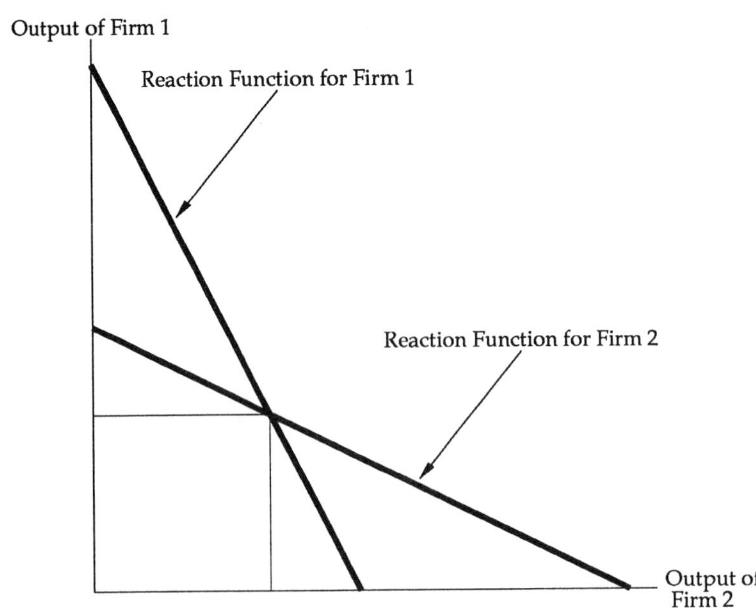

Figure 17.1: *Cournot Equilibrium*

PRODUCT DIFFERENTIATION

The firms of many industries produce goods that are not homogeneous. In fact, firms often attempt to
21. ____________ ____________ their products in the minds of potential buyers. To differentiate their products firms engage in a wide variety of strategies. The decisions one firm makes will affect the decisions made by other firms in a very complicated way. Consequently, few general conclusions can be drawn in this case. The only conclusions we can
22. ____________ make are rather obvious. Firms are ____________ price takers; furthermore, they often react to this very complex environment by using "rules of thumb."

ADVERTISING AND RESOURCE ALLOCATION

A pair of arguments suggest that our economy
23. ____________ devotes too ____________ resources to production of
24. ____________ advertising. The ____________ product argument claims that firms will produce advertising until the change in total revenue resulting from one additional message equals the cost of the additional message. The additional revenue generated reflects individuals' willingness to pay for both the good itself and the information provided by the message. This means that the value consumers place on the
25. ____________ information provided by the message must be ____________ than the cost of providing the message. The second argument makes a distinction between constructive and
26. ____________ combative advertising. Some argue that ____________ advertising, advertising designed to draw customers from competitors rather than enlarge the market, is wasteful.

ENTRY BY NEW FIRMS

If there are no barriers to entry profits must equal
27. ____________ ____________ in the long run. Positive profits will lure new firms into the industry driving the price down until price
28. ____________ ____________ average cost. In perfect competition, where all
29. ____________ firms are price takers, the price will ____________ minimum average cost. Alternatively, traditional analysis of
30. ____________ oligopolies suggests that ____________ will not equal minimum average cost when firms have some control over the price. Recently, some economists have challenged this view, however. The contestable markets hypothesis argues

that potential entry will force firms to charge a price equal to minimum average cost. Otherwise, a "hit-and-run" entrant could earn a profit by producing at minimum average cost
31. ____________ and charging a price slightly ____________ than that which prevails. Note that if the contestable market view is correct and price equals minimum average cost, price will also
32. ____________ equal ____________ cost. The average cost and marginal
33. ____________ cost curves intersect at ____________ average cost.

INDUSTRIAL ORGANIZATION THEORY

The three parts of industrial organization theory are market structure, firm conduct, and economic performance. Market structure describes the industry by using various statistics: the number of firms, size of firms, technology used, etc. The most frequently cited market structure
34. ____________ statistics are the ____________ ratios. These ratios report on the percent of total domestic shipments produced by the 4, 8, 20, and 50 largest firms. Firm conduct describes how the firms interact with each other. Is there a price leader, do firms enter explicit or tacit agreements, are rules-of-thumb used, do firms try to differentiate their products from competitors, etc.? Industry performance describes how efficiently the industry operates. Static efficiency estimates
35. ____________ how close the price is to ____________ cost. Dynamic efficiency is concerned with industry growth, productivity improvements, etc.

MULTIPLE-CHOICE QUESTIONS

36. ______ Which of the following models sets outer limits on how an oligopoly producing homogeneous goods will behave?
   a. quasi-competitive model.
   b. price leadership model.
   c. cartel model.
   d. a and c.
   e. b and c.

37. ______ In the quasi-competitive model

a. each firm behaves like a price taker.
b. the firms behave like a multiplant monopoly where each firm acts like a separate division of a single monopolistic firm.
c. the firms follow a price leader.
d. each firm observes a kinked demand curve.
e. c and d.

38. ______ In the quasi-competitive model the price will

a. equal marginal cost, just as in the perfectly competitive case.
b. exceed marginal cost, just as in the perfectly competitive case.
c. equal marginal cost, just as in the monopoly case.
d. exceed marginal cost, just as in the monopoly case.
e. equal average variable cost.

39. ______ In the cartel model

a. each firm behaves like a price taker.
b. the firms behave like a multiplant monopoly where each firm acts like a separate division of a single monopolistic firm.
c. the firms follow a price leader.
d. each firm observes a kinked demand curve.
e. c and d.

40. ______ In the cartel model the price will

a. equal marginal cost, just as in the perfectly competitive case.
b. exceed marginal cost, just as in the perfectly competitive case.
c. equal marginal cost, just as in the monopoly case.
d. exceed marginal cost, just as in the monopoly case.
e. equal average cost always.

41. ______ Cartel agreements

a. are often illegal.
b. require little information to implement.
c. are in the collective interests of cartel members.
d. are inherently unstable because it is in the individual interest of each member to cheat on the agreement.
e. a, c, and d.

42. ______ The price leadership model assumes that

a. each firm acts independently.
b. each firm acts like a single plant in a monopoly.
c. all the firms follow the price set by a leader.
d. all firms are price takers.
e. a and d.

43. ______ The kinked demand model hypothesizes that each firm believes that other firms will

a. follow when it increases its price.
b. follow when it decreases its price.
c. not follow when it increases its price.
d. not follow when it decreases its price.
e. b and c.

44. ______ In the Cournot model each firm assumes that

a. the other firm's price will not change.
b. the other firm's quantity will not change.
c. the other firm's price and quantity will not change.
d. the other firm's quantity may change.
e. none of the above.

45. ______ A reaction function describes how one firm's

a. price will change as the other firm's price changes.
b. price will change as the other firm's quantity changes.
c. quantity will change as the other firm's price changes.
d. quantity will change as the other firm's quantity changes.
e. profits will change as the other firm's profits change.

46. ______ At a Cournot equilibrium the profits of the total industry are

a. more than the monopoly case.
b. less than the monopoly case.
c. more than the competitive case.
d. less than the competitive case.
e. b and c.

47. ______ When oligopolies do not produce homogeneous goods

a. the industry will always act like a cartel.
b. the industry will always act like a perfectly competitive industry.
c. the decisions of one firm will not affect other firms in the industry.
d. few general conclusions can be drawn.
e. c and d.

48. ______ A firm engaging in constructive advertising is attempting to
   a. draw customers away from competitors.
   b. enlarge the market of the entire industry.
   c. drive competitors out of business.
   d. a and b.
   e. a, b, and c.

49. ______ In the long run, if there are no barriers to entry, economic profits
   a. must equal zero.
   b. must be positive.
   c. must be negative.
   d. may be positive, negative, or zero.
   e. must equal one.

50. ______ In contestable markets the price must
   a. equal minimum average cost.
   b. equal marginal cost.
   c. equal average variable cost.
   d. exceed average cost.
   e. a and b.

51. ______ Which of the following are considered parts of industrial organization theory?
   a. market structure.
   b. firm conduct.
   c. economic performance.
   d. Giffen's paradox.
   e. a, b, and c.

52. ______ Market structure is concerned with
   a. a description of the industry.
   b. how firms interact with each other.
   c. how close the price is to marginal cost.
   d. the growth of the industry.
   e. c and d.

53. ______ Firm conduct is concerned with
   a. a description of the industry.
   b. how firms interact with each other.
   c. how close the price is to marginal cost.
   d. the growth of the industry.
   e. c and d.

54. _____ Industry performance is concerned with

a. a description of the industry.
b. how firms interact with each other.
c. how close the price is to marginal cost.
d. the growth of the industry.
e. c and d.

RUNNING GLOSSARY

55. ___________ Quasi-competitive model: a model of oligopoly pricing in which each firm acts as a price ___________.

56. ___________ ___________ model: a model of oligopoly pricing in which firms coordinate their decisions to act as a multiplant monopoly.

57. ___________
58. ___________ Kinked demand curve model: a model in which firms believe that price ___________ result in a very elastic demand while price decreases result in an ___________ demand for their products.

59. ___________ Price ___________ model: a model in which one dominant firm takes reactions of all other firms into account in its output and pricing decisions.

60. ___________ Competitive fringe: a group of firms that act as price ___________ in a market dominated by a price leader.

61. ___________ Cournot model: a model of duopoly in which each firm assumes the other firm's ___________ will not change if it changes its own output level.

62. ___________ Reaction function: in the ___________ model a function or graph that shows how much one firm will produce given what the other firm produces.

63. ___________ Cournot equilibrium: a solution to the Cournot model in which each firm makes the ___________ assumption about what the other firm will produce.

64. ____________ Product group: set of ____________ products that are highly substitutable for one another.

65. ____________ ____________ products: the inseparable combination of two goods in production, such as advertising, which is paid for by the consumer as part of the good being advertised.

66. ____________ Monopolistic competition: market in which each firm faces a negatively sloped demand curve and there are ____________ barriers to entry.

67. ____________ Contestable market: market in which entry and exit are ____________.

ANSWERS

1. two
2. takers
3. price
4. marginal
5. long
6. monopoly
7. less
8. exceed
9. collective
10. individual
11. oligopolistic
12. lowering
13. raise
14. costs
15. duopoly
16. output
17. given
18. Cournot
19. accurate
20. less
21. differentiate
22. not
23. many
24. joint
25. less
26. combative
27. zero
28. equals
29. equal
30. price
31. less
32. marginal
33. minimum
34. concentration
35. marginal
36. d
37. a
38. a
39. b
40. d
41. e
42. c
43. e
44. b
45. d
46. e
47. d
48. b
49. a
50. e
51. e
52. a
53. b
54. e
55. taker
56. Cartel
57. increases
58. inelastic
59. leadership
60. takers
61. output
62. Cournot
63. correct
64. differentiated
65. Joint
66. no
67. costless

CHAPTER 18

STRATEGY AND GAME THEORY

WALKING TOUR SUMMARY

BASIC CONCEPTS

Economists try to capture the strategic relationships
1. ____________ by using ____________ theory. In a game each player
2. ____________ chooses a course of action, a ____________. Each player's payoff not only depends on his strategy, but also on the
3. ____________ strategies that ____________ employ. The payoff matrix describes what a player's payoff will be depending on the strategies that he and others use. In a zero-sum game what
4. ____________ one player wins, the other player ____________. Most market situations are not zero sum, however.

EQUILIBRIUM CONCEPTS

The Nash equilibrium is the most frequently used equilibrium notion in game theory. At a Nash equilibrium,
5. ____________ no player has an incentive to ____________ his strategy assuming that the other players do not alter their strategies. Not all games have an equilibrium. Economists call such games nonequilibrium games. A particular strategy is
6. ____________ ____________ for a player if that player is always better off by choosing the strategy regardless of what his opponent does.

THE PRISONER'S DILEMMA

In the prisoner's dilemma, there are two players. Each player's prison sentence depends on whether or not he confesses and also whether or not the other player confesses.
7. ____________ The equilibrium occurs when both players ____________. This outcome is second best, however, since each player could receive a lighter sentence if neither confessed.
8. ____________ Unfortunately, this cooperative situation is ____________. Each player has an incentive to cheat and confess if he believes that the other player will not confess. The behavior

of a duopoly can be viewed as a prisoner's dilemma. The cooperative outcome in which industry profits are maximized is unstable because each firm has an incentive to

9. ____________ ____________.

Communication can help the players cooperate in order to avoid the second-best outcome. Also, if the game is played repeatedly, the prospect of cooperation is

10. ____________ ____________.

MANY PERIOD GAMES

Many period games better reflect real-world markets

11. ____________ ____________ than single period games. A player can try to influence his opponent's strategy by issuing threats. A

12. ____________ threat is ____________ only if the player actually has an incentive to follow through on it should the situation arise. Consequently, players can eliminate strategies that involve noncreditable threats in deciding their best course of action. A perfect equilibrium is a Nash equilibrium in which the

13. ____________ strategy choices of each player do not involve ____________

14. ____________ threats. No strategy in a ____________ equilibrium requires a player to pursue an action that is not in his best interest at the time.

MODELS OF PRICING BEHAVIOR

At a Betrand equilibrium the firms share the market

15. ____________ ____________ for the homogeneous good. Each firm faces

16. ____________ the ____________ costs and charge a price equal to marginal cost. A Betrand equilibrium is a Nash equilibrium. If the Betrand assumptions regarding the homogeneity of the good and the firms' costs is not met, a Betrand equilibrium may not exist. In these situations, a

17. ____________ ____________ stage game may be played. The first stage involves decision to entry and/or investment. The second

18. ____________ stage involves ____________ competition. The Cournot equilibrium illustrates such a two stage game in which firms

19. ____________ first choose the quantity and then the ____________. The welfare implications of Betrand and Cournot equilibria

20. ____________ ____________ dramatically. Since price equals marginal

21. ____________ cost at a Betrand equilibrium, ____________ results. A Cournot equilibrium produce monopoly-like inefficiencies

22. ____________ because price ____________ marginal cost.

When one adds the possibility of playing a Betrand game repeatedly, the welfare implications depend on the
23. ________ time horizon of the players. If the horizon is ________,
efficiency results; price will equal marginal cost, just as in the single period case. On the other hand, price may
24. ________ ________ marginal cost in the infinite time horizon
case resulting in inefficiency.

ENTRY, EXIT, AND STRATEGY

When a firm contemplates entering a market, it must predict how its entry will affect the price in subsequent periods. To do so, it must consider how firms now in the
25. ________ industry will respond. A firm incurs ________ costs
when it invest in capital that cannot be shifted to other uses
26. ________ easily. Sunk costs provide ________ movers with an
advantage. By incurring sunk costs, a first mover stakes a claim to a market by making a commitment. This
27. ________ commitment may deter potential rivals from ________
the industry. In particular, when production exhibits
28. ________ ________ returns to scale, the first mover may be able
to deter the entry of others by investing in a large scale operation.

The effectiveness of limit pricing as a method of entry
29. ________ deterrence must be questioned if ________ to entry are
not present. Incomplete information, however, could deter entry. If potential entrants do not have as much information
30. ________ as the incumbent, entry could be deterred. ________
pricing refers to the deliberate use of low prices to drive competitors out of business. While similar to limit pricing, predatory pricing models stress the importance of asymmetric information.

n-PLAYER GAME THEORY

n-player games are more complicated than two-player games because the number of potential coalitions is larger and complexity of the payoff matrix expand rapidly
31. ________ as the number of players ________. The likelihood of
32. ________ successful coalitions depends upon ________ costs,
costs associated with the information required to determine coalition strategies and the enforcement mechanism required to ensure that the chosen strategy is followed. When incentives to cheat are great, enforcement costs can be

33. ___________ ___________. If these costs are too high, successful coalitions will not be established.

MULTIPLE-CHOICE QUESTIONS

34. _____ A payoff matrix describes the
    a. salaries earned by a firm's workers.
    b. bribes collected by corrupt politicians.
    c. what a player's rewards will be in a game.
    d. the rewards of a college education.
    e. none of the above.

35. _____ A Nash equilibrium
    a. is a generalization of the Cournot equilibrium.
    b. exists in all games.
    c. exists in all zero-sum games.
    d. occurs when no player has an incentive to change when all strategies are unknown.
    e. none of the above.

36. _____ In a zero-sum game
    a. what one player wins never equals what other players lose.
    b. what one player wins always equals what other players lose.
    c. at least one of the players never loses.
    d. each player must win nothing.
    e. none of the above.

37. _____ In a non-zero-sum game
    a. one player wins twice as much as the other.
    b. what one player wins always equals what other players lose.
    c. at least one of the players never loses.
    d. each player must win nothing.
    e. none of the above.

38. _____ The prisoner's dilemma
    a. has no equilibrium.
    b. has a single equilibrium.
    c. illustrates the incentive players have to cheat.
    d. a and c.
    e. b and c.

39. ______ A Betrand model assumes that firms

a. are public spirited.
b. face the same costs.
c. act as a cartel.
d. share the market equally if they charge the same price.
e. b and d.

40. ______ At a Betrand equilibrium

a. price equals marginal cost.
b. price exceeds marginal cost.
c price is less than marginal cost.
d. inefficiency results.
e. b and d.

41. ______ At a Cournot equilibrium

a. price equals marginal cost.
b. price exceeds marginal cost.
c price is less than marginal cost.
d. inefficiency results.
e. b and d.

42. ______ Sunk costs refer to

a. all fixed costs.
b. all variable costs.
c. all investment in capital
d. all investment in capital which cannot be shifted to other uses easily.
e. total costs.

RUNNING GLOSSARY

44. ____________ Game: a simple representation of a strategic situation in which the outcome depends on what ____________ player in the game does.

45. ____________ ____________: a participant in a game. May be an individual, a firm, or groups of individuals and firms.

45. ____________ ________: the various courses of action open to the players of a game.

46. ____________ Payoffs: the outcomes of a game for each player. Payoffs depend on what ____________ have been chosen.

47. ____________ ____________ equilibrium: a choice of strategies by the players of a game such that once all the strategies are known, no player has an incentive to choose a different strategy.

48. ____________ Zero-sum game: a game in which the amount one player loses the other player ____________.

49. ____________ ____________ dilemma: a game in which the players' most desirable outcome is unstable because each player has an incentive to cheat in the strategy actually chosen.

50. ____________ Creditable threats: threats which the player has an incentive to ____________ out if the situation arises.

51. ____________ ____________ equilibrium: a Nash equilibrium in which the strategy chooses of the players do not involve noncreditable threats.

52. ____________ ____________ costs: the costs incurred by a firm when it invests in capital that cannot be shifted to other uses easily.

53. ____________ Predatory pricing: the deliberate use of ____________ prices to drive competitors out of business.

ANSWERS

1. game
2. strategy
3. others
4. loses
5. change
6. dominant
7. confess
8. unstable
9. cheat
10. enhanced
11. better
12. creditable
13. noncreditable
14. perfect
15. equally
16. same
17. two
18. price
19. price
20. differ
21. efficiency
22. exceeds
23. finite
24. exceeds
25. sunk
26. first
27. entering
28. increasing
29. barriers
30. Predatory
31. increases
32. organization
33. high
34. c
35. a
36. b
37. e
38. e
39. e
40. a
41. e
42. d
43. each
44. Player
45. Strategies
46. strategies
47. Nash
48. wins
49. Prisoner's
50. carry
51. Perfect
52. Sunk
53. low

PART 6

PRICING OF FACTORS OF PRODUCTION

CHAPTER 19

THE DEMAND FOR FACTORS OF PRODUCTION

WALKING TOUR SUMMARIES

DERIVED DEMAND

A firm's demand for an input is derived from the
1. ____________ firm's desire to produce ____________. A firm's demand
2. ____________ curve for an input is ____________ sloping for two reasons.
Whenever the price of an input falls, a firm can produce the
3. ____________ same amount of output more cheaply by using ____________
of that input. Second, if the firm chooses to produce more
4. ____________ output, the firm typically will use ____________ of all
inputs.

ECONOMIC RENT

Economic rent is the difference between the actual
5. ____________ payments to an input and the ____________ amount
required to keep the input in its present use. The market
supply curve illustrates the quantity of input supplied at
6. ____________ each ____________. The height of the supply curve
represents the amount of payment necessary to draw each
successive unit of input into service. If firms could perfectly
discriminate among input suppliers by hiring one unit at a
time, the total payments to the input would equal the area
7. ____________ beneath the ____________ curve. Of course, perfect
discrimination rarely (if ever) occurs in practice. Usually
8. ____________ each unit of input receives the ____________ price.

9. ____________ Consequently, the area above the supply curve which lies below the ____________ equals the economic rent.

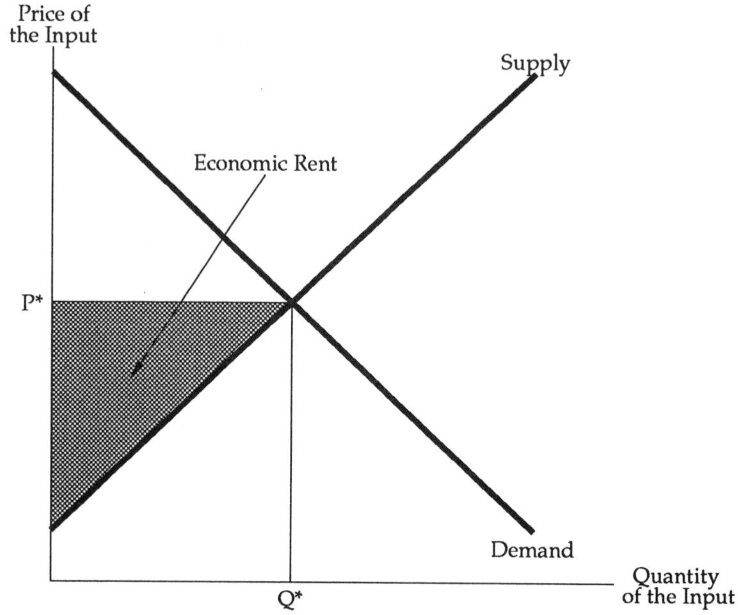

Figure 19.1: *Economic Rent*

The magnitude of economic rent depends on the
10. ____________ elasticity of ____________. The more inelastic, the larger the area between the supply curve and the price, which results in more economic rent. The elasticity of supply in turn
11. ____________ depends on ____________ cost. An input that has few alternative uses has a low opportunity cost and a very
12. ____________ ____________ supply curve. Such an input earns much economic rent. With a fixed supply of land, the supply
13. ____________ curve is completely ____________; the entire payment to land is economic rent.

If all the units of an input are not equally productive, Ricardian rent exists. For example, Ricardian rent exists for farmland when the productivity varies from acre to acre.
14. ____________ The most fertile land earns the ____________ Ricardian
15. ____________ rents. As the land becomes less fertile, it earns ____________ rents.

MARGINAL PRODUCTIVITY THEORY OF FACTOR DEMAND

A profit-maximizing firm will hire an input until the
16. ____________ marginal revenue product ____________ the marginal expense. The marginal revenue product of labor (MR_L) equals the change in total revenue resulting from the use of
17. ____________ one additional unit of ____________. The marginal expense
18. ____________ of labor (ME_L) equals the change in total ____________ resulting from the employment of one additional unit of labor.

MARGINAL REVENUE PRODUCT OF LABOR

The marginal revenue product of labor equals
19. ____________ marginal physical product (MR_L) ____________ marginal revenue (MR):

$$MR_L = MP_L \times MR$$

20. ____________ Marginal physical product of labor equals the change in total ____________ resulting from the use of one additional unit of labor. Marginal revenue equals the change in total revenue resulting from the sale of one additional unit of
21. ____________ ____________. When a firm hires one additional unit of
22. ____________ labor, total ____________ increases by MP_L units. When sold, each additional unit of output increases total
23. ____________ ____________ by MR dollars. Consequently, MP_L additional
24. ____________ units of output will increase total ____________ by $MR_L \times MR$.

MARGINAL EXPENSE OF LABOR

If a firm is a price taker in the labor market, the
25. ____________ marginal expense of labor ____________ the wage rate:

$$ME_L = w$$

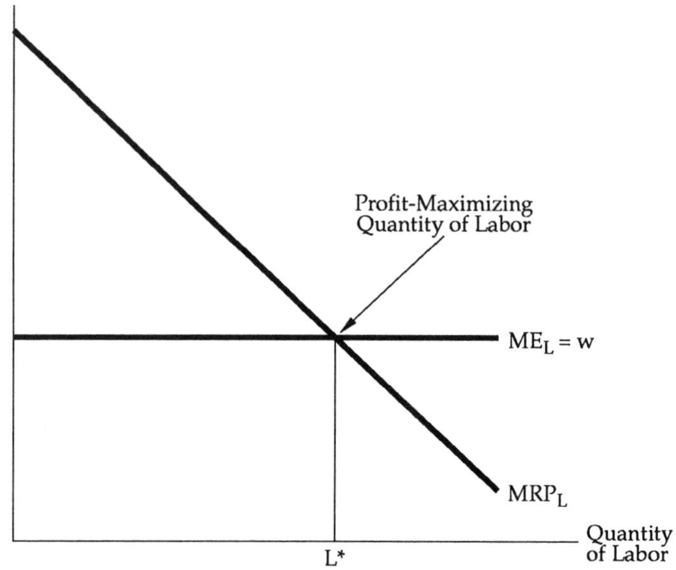

Figure 19.2: *Profit Maximizing in a Competitive Labor Market*

To summarize, a profit-maximizing firm which is a price taker in the labor market will hire labor until

$$w = ME_L = MR_L = MP_L \times MR$$

A SPECIAL CASE: MARGINAL VALUE PRODUCT

The marginal value product of labor (MVP_L) equals the value of the additional output that a firm produces when
26. ____________ it hires one additional unit of ____________. Marginal value product equals marginal physical product times the
27. ____________ ____________ of output:

$$MVP_L = MP_L \times P$$

If the firm is selling its output in a competitive market, then
28. ____________ marginal revenue product ____________ marginal value
29. ____________ product because marginal revenue equals ____________:

$$MVP_L = MP_L \times P = MP_L \times MR = MR_L$$

RESPONSES TO CHANGES IN INPUT PRICES

30. ____________ In the single input case, a fall in the wage rate reduces the marginal ____________ of labor because the marginal expense of labor equals the wage rate. The firm

31. ____________ reacts by hiring ____________ labor.

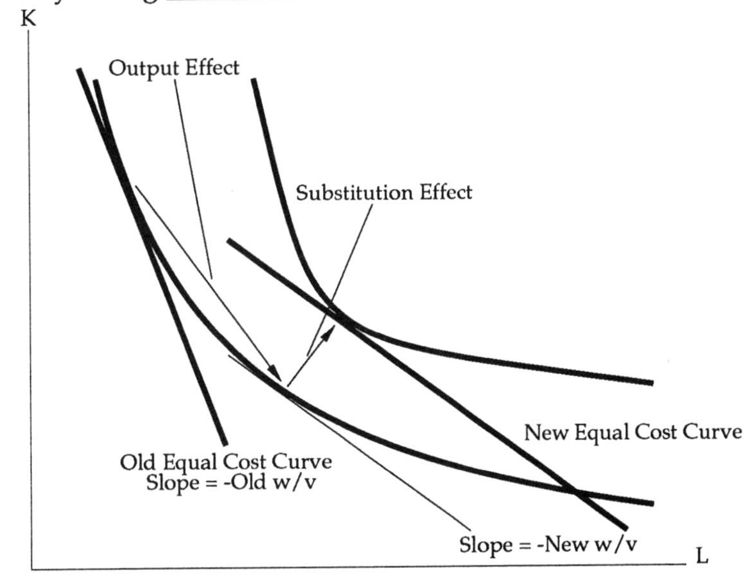

Figure 19.3: *Decrease in the Wage Rate*

In the two input case, a fall in the wage rate leads to two effects, a substitution effect and an output effect. The

32. ____________ ____________ in the wage rate reduces the ratio of the wage rate to the rental rate of capital. Thus, at a constant level of output the cost minimizing combination of labor and capital

33. ____________ changes. As a result of the ____________ effect, the firm substitutes the now cheaper labor for capital and thereby uses more labor and less capital. Of course we would not expect the firm's level of output to remain constant when the wage rate falls. A change in the wage rate typically shifts the firm's cost curves. A downward shift in the firm's

34. ____________ ____________ cost curve would increase the profit-maximizing level of production. To produce more the firm would move along its expansion path. Assuming that labor

35. ____________ is not an ____________ input, the firm would use more labor

36. ____________ as a result of the ____________ effect.

MONOPSONY

There are situations in which a firm is not a price taker for the inputs that it hires. A monopsony (a single buyer) is the polar case of such a situation. Because the monopsonist is the sole purchaser, he is aware of the
37. __________ __________ curve. The monopsonist realizes that when he
38. __________ hires more of the input, he must offer a __________ price. Otherwise, the quantity supplied will not change.

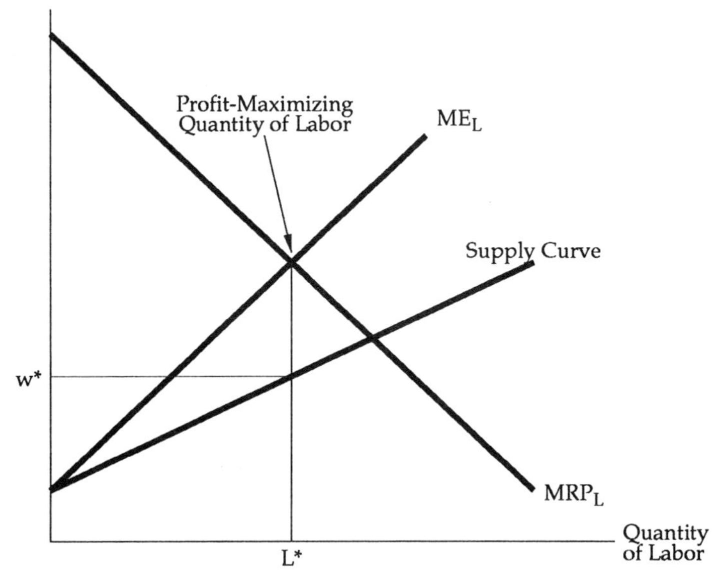

Figure 19.4: *Profit Maximizing Monopolist*

In this case the marginal expense of the input will
39. __________ __________ the input's price. To explain why recall the definition of the marginal expense of labor. The marginal expense of labor equals the change in firm's total costs when it hires one additional unit of labor. Unlike a price taker, the
40. __________ monopsonist must offer a __________ wage to hire the additional unit of labor. This has two effects on total costs. As a result of the additional unit of labor itself, total costs
41. __________ rise by an amount equal to the __________. The firm, however, must also pay the higher wage to all other workers. Labor costs for the other workers will
42. __________ __________. Total costs will rise by an amount greater
43. __________ than the __________. When the monopsonist maximizes profits, its marginal revenue product of labor will
44. __________ __________ the wage:

$$w < ME_L = MR_L$$

The most frequently cited examples of monopsonies are company towns, towns in which there is only a single employer. In an geographically isolated town with a single employer, workers have little choice. They have only
45. ____________ ____________ potential source of employment. Similarly, specialized employment skills can also limit a worker's sources of possible employment. If a profit-maximizing firm has a monopsony in two input markets, it often has an incentive to discriminate between the groups. Typically, it
46. ____________ will pay the groups different ____________ even though the groups may be equally productive.

MULTIPLE-CHOICE QUESTIONS

47. ______ Derived demand refers to
   a. an individual's demand for a good from which he derives utility.
   b. an individual's demand for an input from which he derives utility.
   c. a firm's demand for a good from which it derives utility.
   d. a firm's demand for a input for the purpose of producing output.
   e. a and d.

48. ______ A firm's demand curve for an input is downward sloping because a lower input price will
   a. decrease demand for the firm's output.
   b. enable the firm to produce any given level of output more cheaply by using more of that input.
   c. typically cause the firm to use more of every input if the firm chooses to expand production.
   d. enable the firm to produce any given level of output more cheaply by using less of that input.
   e. b and c.

49. ______ Economic rent equals

a. the actual payment made to an input.
b. the minimum amount required to keep the input in its present use.
c. the sum of the actual payment made to an input and the minimum amount required to keep the input in its present use.
d. the difference between the actual payment made to an input and the minimum amount required to keep the input in its present use.
e. the payments a tenant makes to his landlord.

50. ______ Graphically economic rent can be illustrated by the area

a. beneath the input's supply curve.
b. beneath the input's demand curve.
c. between the input's supply curve and its price.
d. between the input's demand curve and its price.
e. a and b.

51. ______ The magnitude of an input's economic rent depends on the

a. demand elasticity of the good being produced.
b. cross price elasticity of demand of the good being produced.
c. demand elasticity of the input itself.
d. supply elasticity of the input itself.
e. a and b.

52. ______ As supply for an input becomes more inelastic economic rent

a. increases.
b. decreases.
c. remains the same.
d. may increase, decrease, or remain the same.
e. never increases.

53. ______ When the entire payment to an input is economic rent its supply is

a. elastic.
b. unit elastic.
c. inelastic, but not completely inelastic.
d. completely inelastic.
e. perfectly elastic.

54. ______ A firm's marginal revenue is defined as the

a. change in the firm's total revenue resulting from the production of one additional unit of output.
b. ratio of the firm's total revenue to output.
c. change in the firm's total revenue resulting from the employment of one additional unit of the input.
d. ratio of the firm's total revenue to the amount of input used.
e. value of the additional output produced resulting from the employment of one additional unit of the input.

55. ______ A firm's marginal revenue product of an input is defined as the

a. change in the firm's total revenue resulting from the production of one additional unit of output.
b. ratio of the firm's total revenue to output.
c. change in the firm's total revenue resulting from the employment of one additional unit of the input.
d. ratio of the firm's total revenue to the amount of input used.
e. value of the additional output produced resulting from the employment of one additional unit of the input.

56. ______ A firm's marginal revenue product of an input equals

a. the firm's marginal revenue times the price of the input.
b. the firm's marginal revenue times the input's marginal physical product.
c. the price of the output times the input's marginal expense.
d. the price of the input times the input's marginal physical product.
e. b and c.

57. ______ A firm's marginal cost equals the

a. change in the firm's total cost resulting from the production of one additional unit of output.
b. ratio of the firm's total cost to output.
c. change in the firm's total cost resulting from the employment of one additional unit of the input.
d. ratio of the firm's total cost to the amount of input used.
e. b and d.

58. ______ A firm's marginal expense of an input equals the
   a. change in the firm's total cost resulting from the production of one additional unit of output.
   b. ratio of the firm's total cost to output.
   c. change in the firm's total cost resulting from the employment of one additional unit of the input.
   d. ratio of the firm's total cost to the amount of input used.
   e. b and d.

59. ______ A profit-maximizing firm will hire an input until marginal revenue
   a. equals the input's marginal expense.
   b. product of the input equals the input's marginal expense.
   c. product of the input equals marginal cost.
   d. equals marginal cost.
   e. a and b.

60. ______ If a firm is a price taker in the input market the input's marginal expense
   a. will be greater than the input's price.
   b. will be less than the input's price.
   c. will equal the input's price.
   d. may be greater than, less than, or equal to the input's price.
   e. will be less than marginal revenue.

61. ______ A firm's marginal value product of an input is defined as the
   a. change in the firm's total revenue resulting from the production of one additional unit of output.
   b. ratio of the firm's total revenue to output.
   c. change in the firm's total revenue resulting from the employment of one additional unit of the input.
   d. ratio of the firm's total revenue to the amount of input used.
   e. value of the additional output produced resulting from the employment of one additional unit of the input.

62. ______ firm's marginal value product of an input equals
   a. the firm's marginal revenue times the price of the input.
   b. the firm's marginal revenue times the input's marginal expense.
   c. the price of the output times the input's marginal physical product.
   d. the price of the input times the input's marginal physical product.
   e. b and d.

63. ______ If a firm is a price taker in the output market its marginal value product

a. will be greater than its marginal revenue product.
b. will be less than its marginal revenue product.
c. will equal its marginal revenue product.
d. may be greater than, less than, or equal to its marginal revenue product.
e. will equal marginal revenue.

64. ______ A decrease in the price of an input leads to

a. a substitution effect only.
b. an income effect only.
c. both a substitution and income effect.
d. an output effect only.
e. both a substitution and output effect.

65. ______ As a consequence of the substitution effect, a decrease in an input's price will cause a firm to use

a. more of the input always.
b. less of the input always.
c. the same amount of the input always.
d. less of the input, if the input is not inferior.
e. the same amount of the input, if the input is not inferior.

66. ______ As a consequence of the output effect, a decrease in an input's price which leads to a downward shift of a firm's cost curves will cause the firm to use

a. more of the input always.
b. less of the input always.
c. the same amount of the input always.
d. more of the input, if the input is not inferior.
e. less of the input, if the input is not inferior.

67. ______ If a firm is a monopsonist in an input market, the firm is

a. the only supplier of the input.
b. the only supplier of the output.
c. the only demander of the input.
d. the only demander of the output.
e. a and d.

68. _____ If a firm is a monopsonist in an input market, the input's marginal expense
   a. will be greater than the input's price.
   b. will be less than the input's price.
   c. will equal the input's price.
   d. may be greater than, less than, or equal to the input's price.
   e. is never greater than the input's price.

RUNNING GLOSSARY

69. ____________ ___________ demand: demand for a factor of production that is determined by the demand for the good it produces.

70. ____________ Economic rent: the amount by which payments of a factor ___________ the minimal amount required to retain it in its present use.

71. ____________ Marginal revenue product: the extra revenue obtained from selling the output produced by hiring an ___________ worker or machine.

72. ____________ Marginal value product: a special case of marginal revenue product in which the firm is a price taker for its ___________.

73. ____________ Substitution effect: in the theory of production, the substitution of one input for another while holding output ___________ in response to a change in the input's price.

74. ____________ Output effect: the change in the amount of an input that the firm hires that results from a change in ___________ level. Output changes because the change in an input's price affects the firm's costs.

75. ____________ ___________: a firm that is the only hirer in a particular input market.

76. ____________ Marginal expense: the cost of hiring one more unit of the ___________. Will exceed the price of the input if the firm faces an upward sloping supply curve for the input.

ANSWERS

1. output
2. downward
3. more
4. more
5. minimal
6. price
7. supply
8. same
9. price
10. supply
11. opportunity
12. inelastic
13. inelastic
14. high
15. lower
16. equals
17. labor
18. cost
19. times
20. output
21. output
22. output
23. revenues
24. revenues
25. equals
26. labor
27. price
28. equals
29. price
30. expense
31. more
32. fall
33. substitution
34. marginal
35. inferior
36. output
37. supply
38. higher
39. exceed
40. higher
41. wage
42. increase
43. wage
44. exceed
45. one
46. wages
47. d
48. e
49. d
50. c
51. d
52. a
53. d
54. a
55. c
56. b
57. a
58. c
59. b
60. c
61. e
62. c
63. c
64. e
65. a
66. d
67. c
68. a
69. Derived
70. exceed
71. extra
72. output
73. constant
74. output
75. Monopsony
76. input

CHAPTER 20

PRICING OF LABOR

WALKING TOUR SUMMARIES

ALLOCATION OF TIME

To purchase consumption goods, individuals must
1 ____________ first earn ____________. The more hours worked, the more income one earns. On the other hand, the more hours one
2. ____________ works, the fewer hours of ____________ one has to enjoy. Every individual faces a budget constraint which illustrates his tradeoff between consumption goods and leisure.

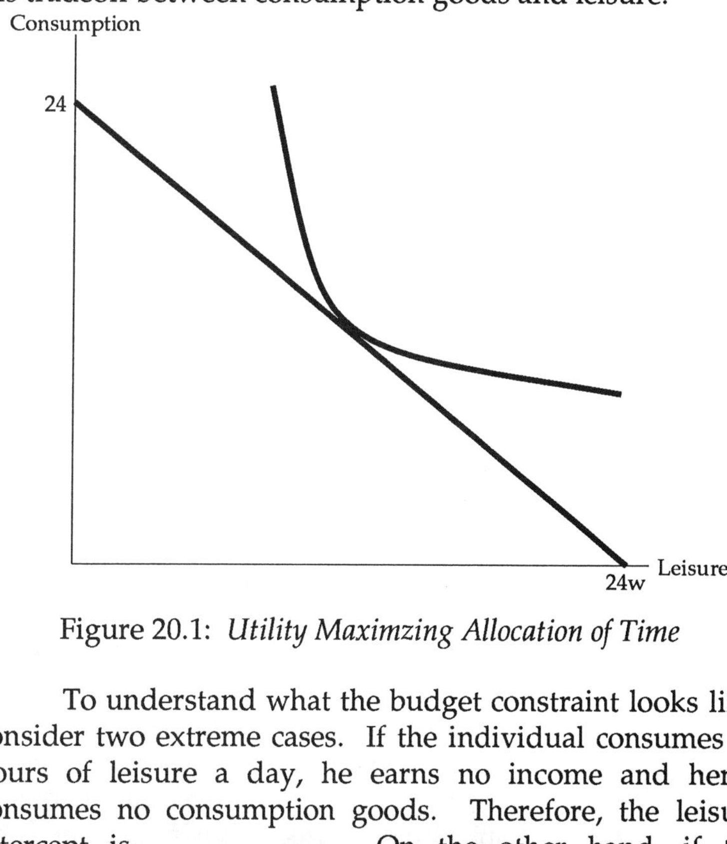

Figure 20.1: *Utility Maximzing Allocation of Time*

To understand what the budget constraint looks like, consider two extreme cases. If the individual consumes 24 hours of leisure a day, he earns no income and hence consumes no consumption goods. Therefore, the leisure
3. ____________ intercept is ____________. On the other hand, if the individual consumes no leisure, he would be working 24 hours a day. In this case, he can buy 24 × w dollars of consumption goods. Therefore, the

4. ____________ ____________ intercept is $24 \times w$. 24 and $24 \times w$ are the two intercepts of the budget constraint. Graphing leisure on the horizontal axis and consumption goods on the vertical axis,
5. ____________ the ____________ of the budget constraint equals w. The individual will choose that bundle of consumption goods
6. ____________ and leisure on his budget constraint which ____________ his utility. The indifference curve passing through the individual's utility maximizing bundle must be
7. ____________ ____________ to his budget constraint. Thus, his marginal
8. ____________ rate of ____________ will equal the wage rate.

INCOME AND SUBSTITUTION EFFECTS OF A CHANGE IN THE REAL WAGE RATE

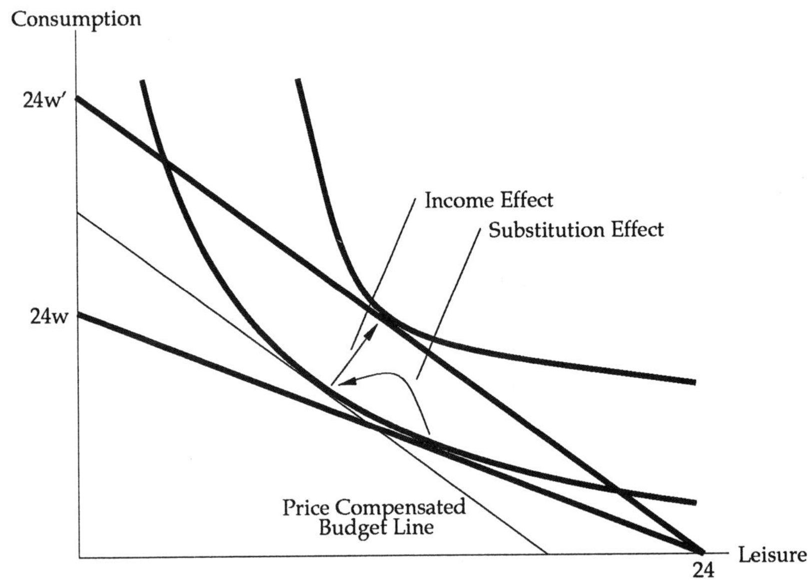

Figure 20.2: *Allocation of Time – Increase in the Wage*

If the wage rate increases, the budget constraint shifts
9. ____________ out by rotating about the 24 hour point on the ____________
10. ____________ axis; the consumption good intercept ____________ while the leisure intercept remains the same. Obviously, the individual can now achieve a higher level of utility. We can use income and substitution effects to describe what happens to his utility maximizing bundle. As a result of the
11. ____________ substitution effect, the individual consumes ____________ leisure. The income effect leads to the consumption of more
12. ____________ leisure, however, because leisure is a ____________ good. The net effect on leisure depends on the relative magnitudes of the two effects. If the substitution effect dominates,

13. ____________ higher wages lead to ___________ leisure and consequently
14. ____________ ___________ work. The individual's supply curve for labor
15. ____________ will be ___________ sloping. On the other hand, if the income effect dominates, the individual's labor supply curve
16. ____________ would be ___________ sloping. We can construct the market labor supply curve by adding each individual's
17. ____________ curve ___________.

OCCUPATIONAL CHOICE AND COMPENSATING WAGE DIFFERENTIALS

Wage differences can occur for many reasons. Differences in the skill levels of workers lead to wage differentials; workers with higher marginal productivity
18. ____________ receive ___________ wages. If workers can restrict the
19. ____________ ___________ of labor to a particular job, that job's wage will be higher. If the market demand curves for two jobs are identical, but workers perceive one job to be less attractive than the other, the jobs would offer different wages. The
20. ____________ less attractive job will offer a ___________ wage to compensate the workers for the job's undesirable characteristics. Economists call such a difference in wages a compensating wage differential.

LABOR UNIONS

If a union is strong, it will have an effective
21. ____________ ___________ on the supply of labor. The union would face
22. ____________ a ___________ sloping demand curve for labor. It can exert its monopoly power to select a wage and a quantity of labor
23. ____________ that lies on the ___________ curve. In this situation the union can pursue various goals. It could maximize the total wage bill, that is, the total income received by its members. To illustrate this case, draw the marginal revenue curve associated with the labor demand curve. By supplying the quantity of labor at which marginal revenue equals
24. ____________ ___________, the union would be maximizing its members' income. Alternatively, the union could maximize the total economic rent of its members. It could choose to supply the quantity at which the marginal revenue curve intersects the
25. ____________ ___________ curve. One last possibility is to maximize the employment of its members. This would be where the
26. ____________ ___________ and supply curves intersect, the competitive solution.

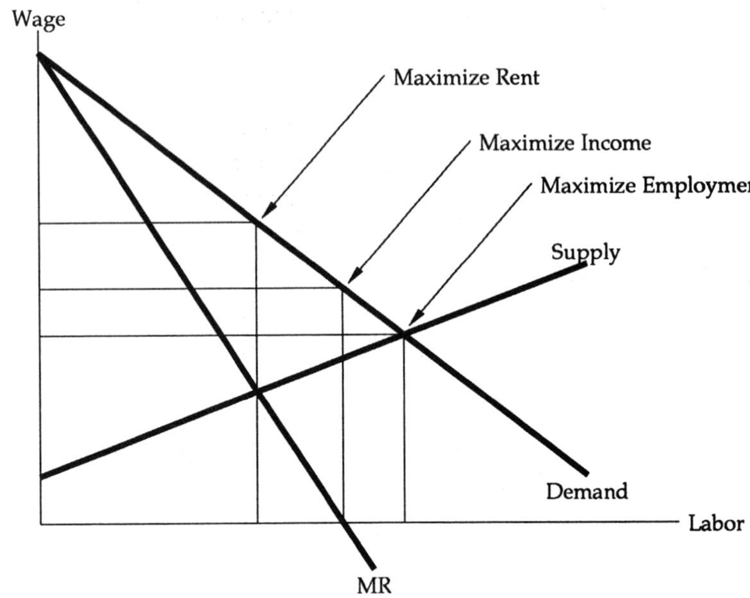

Figure 20.3: *Goals of Unions*

MULTIPLE-CHOICE QUESTIONS

27. ______ The more hours an individual works
   a. the more income he earns.
   b. the more consumption goods he can purchase.
   c. the more leisure he can enjoy.
   d. the less his wage rate becomes.
   e. a and b.

28. ______ An individual's "time use" budget constraint illustrates
   a. all the bundles of work and leisure that the individual can consume.
   b. all the bundles of consumption goods and leisure that the individual can consume.
   c. all the bundles of work and leisure that will keep the individual just as well off.
   d. all the bundles of consumption goods and leisure that keep the individual just as well off.
   e. c and d.

29. ______ For a given day, the leisure intercept of an individual's "time use" budget constraint is

a. 24 hours.
b. 24 times the individual's hourly wage.
c. 24 divided by the individual's hourly wage.
d. 356 times the individual's hourly wage.
e. none of the above.

30. ______ For a given day, the consumption good intercept of an individual's "time use" budget constraint is

a. 24 hours.
b. the amount of consumption goods the individual could purchase with 24 times his wage rate of income.
c. the amount of consumption goods the individual could purchase with 24 divided by his wage rate of income.
d. the amount of consumption goods the individual could purchase with 365 times his wage rate of income.
e. none of the above.

31. ______ For a given day with consumption goods on the vertical axis and leisure on the horizontal axis, the slope of an individual's "time use" budget constraint is the negative of

a. his hourly wage rate.
b. 1 divided by his hourly wage rate.
c. 24 times his hourly wage rate.
d. 24 divided by his hourly wage rate.
e. b and d.

32. ______ An individual's "time use" indifference curve illustrates

a. all the bundles of work and leisure that the individual can consume.
b. all the bundles of consumption goods and leisure that the individual can consume.
c. all the bundles of work and leisure that keep the individual just as well off.
d. all the bundles of consumption goods and leisure that keep the individual just as well off.
e. a and b.

33. ______ When an individual maximizes his utility

a. the indifference curve passing through his bundle must be tangent to the budget constraint.
b. his marginal rate of substitution equals the wage.
c. his marginal rate of substitution must equal the slope of the utility function.
d. all bundles that he prefers must lie above the budget constraint.
e. a, b, and d.

34. ______ Whenever the wage rate increases, the "time use" budget constraint shifts

a. outward in a parallel fashion.
b. inward in a parallel fashion.
c. outward by rotating about the leisure intercept.
d. outward by rotating about the consumption goods intercept.
e. inward by rotating about the consumption goods intercept.

35. ______ An increase in the wage rate leads to

a. an income effect only.
b. a substitution effect only.
c. both an income and a substitution effect.
d. neither an income nor a substitution effect.
e. an output effect.

36. ______ As a consequence of the substitution effect an increase in the wage will lead to

a. an increase in leisure.
b. a decrease in leisure.
c. an increase in consumption goods.
d. a decrease in consumption goods.
e. b and c.

37. ______ As a consequence of the income effect an increase in the wage will lead to

a. an increase in leisure always.
b. a decrease in leisure always.
c. an increase in leisure, if leisure is a normal good.
d. a decrease in leisure, if leisure is an normal good.
e. none of the above.

38. ______ If leisure were an inferior good, an increase in the wage will lead to
   a. an increase in leisure always.
   b. a decrease in leisure always.
   c. an increase in leisure only if the substitution effect dominates the income effect.
   d. an increase in leisure only if the income effect dominates the substitution effect.
   e. none of the above.

39. ______ If leisure is a normal good, an increase in the wage will lead to
   a. an increase in leisure always.
   b. a decrease in leisure always.
   c. an increase in leisure only if the substitution effect dominates the income effect.
   d. an increase in leisure only if the income effect dominates the substitution effect.
   e. none of the above.

40. ______ If leisure is a normal good, an increase in the wage will lead to
   a. an increase in hours worked always.
   b. a decrease in hours worked always.
   c. an increase in hours worked only if the substitution effect dominates the income effect.
   d. an increase in hours worked only if the income effect dominates the substitution effect.
   e. none of the above.

41. ______ Wage differentials among different workers can be explained by
   a. differences in work productivity.
   b. restriction of labor supply in some occupations.
   c. differences in the attractiveness of jobs.
   d. none of the above.
   e. a, b, and c.

42. ______ The goal of U. S. labor unions is typically to
   a. champion a political ideology.
   b. exert monopoly power in order to maximize its members' total income.
   c. exert monopoly power in order to maximize its members' total economic rent.
   d. maximize its members' employment.
   e. b, c, or d.

RUNNING GLOSSARY

43. ____________ ____________: time spent in any activity other than market work.

Substitution effect of a change in the wage: movement

44. ____________ ____________ an indifference curve in response to a change in the real wage. A rise in the wage causes an individual to

45. ____________ work ____________.

Income effect of a change in the wage: movement to a higher

46. ____________ indifference curve in response to a ____________ in the real wage. If leisure is a normal good, a rise in the wage causes

47. ____________ an individual to work ____________.

48. ____________ ____________ wage differentials: differences in wages caused by differing job characteristics.

ANSWERS

1. income
2. leisure
3. 24
4. consumption
5. slope
6. maximizes
7. tangent
8. substitution
9. leisure
10. increases
11. less
12. normal
13. less
14. more
15. upward
16. downward
17. horizontally
18. higher
19. supply
20. higher
21. monopoly
22. downward
23. demand
24. zero
25. supply
26. demand
27. e
28. b
29. a
30. b
31. a
32. d
33. e
34. c
35. c
36. e
37. c
38. b
39. d
40. c
41. e
42. e
43. Leisure
44. along
45. more
46. rise
47. less
48. Compensating

CHAPTER 21

PRICING OF CAPITAL

WALKING TOUR SUMMARIES

DEFINITION OF CAPITAL

Capital refers to the machines, buildings, and other man-made, nonlabor resources that exist at a particular point in time. Capital accumulation consists of withholding
1. ___________ some ___________ from current consumption,
2. ___________ ___________ that output in equipment, and using the
equipment to produce output in the future.

RATE OF RETURN

The rate of return indicates how we transfer present day output into future output. It measures how much
3. ___________ additional consumption will result in the ___________
whenever we withhold output from consumption today.

DETERMINATION OF THE RATE OF RETURN

Consider the market for future goods by graphing the demand and supply curves for future goods. The horizontal axis measures the quantity of goods demanded and supplied in the future (future goods). The vertical axis measures the price of future goods. The price reflects how
4. ___________ many ___________ goods must be forgone now to obtain
one unit of future goods. The demand curve for future goods is downward sloping. As future goods become more expensive, consumers are not willing to buy as many. The
5. ___________ supply curve is ___________ sloping. As the price
increases, firms are willing to produce more. In equilibrium
6. ___________ the quantity demanded ___________ the quantity supplied.
Economists believe that the equilibrium price of future
7. ___________ goods (P_F^*) will be ___________ than one. One unit of
future goods should "cost" less than one unit of
8. ___________ ___________ goods. The equilibrium rate of return (r) can
be calculated from the following equation:

$$P_F = \frac{1}{1+r}$$

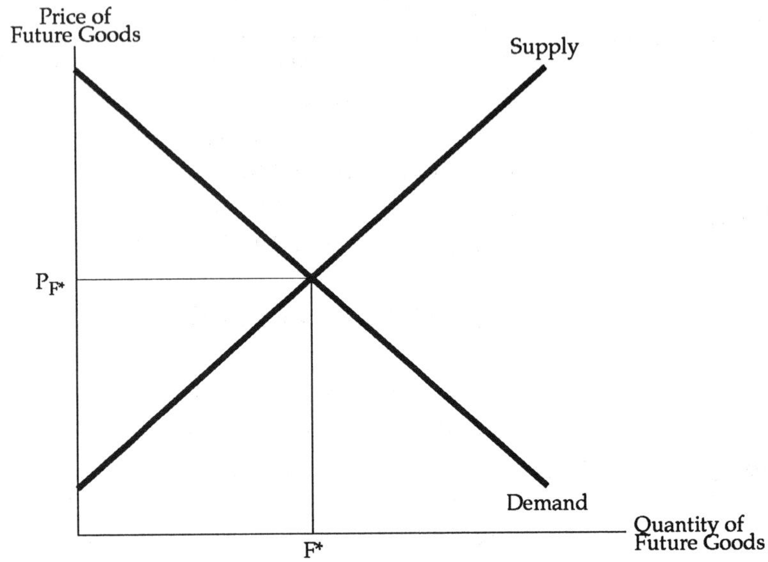

Figure 21.1: *Market for Future Goods*

RENTAL RATE ON MACHINES AND THE THEORY OF INVESTMENT

A firm in the business of renting capital to others experiences two types of costs over the course of a year:
9. __________ depreciation and opportunity costs. __________ costs refer to the "wear and tear" that the machine has
10. __________ experienced during the year. __________ cost refers to what the firm forgoes during the year by having its funds tied up in the machine. Depreciation costs depend on the rate of depreciation, d. Opportunity costs depend on the
11. __________ rate of return on other investments (the __________ rate), r. If the market value of the machine is P, the yearly costs equal:

$$dP + rP = P(r + d)$$

In equilibrium the yearly rental rate for the machine, v, must
12. __________ __________ the yearly costs:

$$v = P(r + d)$$

OWNERSHIP OF EQUIPMENT

In practice firms usually own the capital that they use
13. __________ rather than __________ it. Whether the firm owns or rents
its capital is irrelevant when explaining its use of inputs,
however. If the firm rents the machine it incurs an
14. __________ __________ cost of v, the rental rate of the machine. On
the other hand if the firm owns the machine, it experiences
15. __________ an __________ cost of P(r + d). Since v = P(r + d), it does
not matter who actually owns the machine.

THEORY OF INVESTMENT

Whenever r – the rate of return on alternative
investments (the interest rate) – falls, the rental rate of
16. __________ capital __________. It becomes cheaper to use capital
regardless of whether the firm rents or owns the machines it
uses. When it becomes cheaper to use capital, firms respond
by purchasing new equipment directly or renting it from
17. __________ others. In either case investment __________.

PRESENT DISCOUNTED VALUE AND INVESTMENT

The use of present discounted value is an alternative
way to explain the theory of investment. It makes a
18. __________ distinction between the capital stock and the __________
provided by the capital stock. The word stock refers to
19. __________ something which we measured at __________ point in
time. The capital stock refers to all machines, equipment,
etc. that exist at one particular moment in one particular
day. The word flow refers to something that occurs over a
20. __________ __________ of time. Capital services refer to the number
of machine hours that a firm uses over the course of a year.
The price of capital equals what a firm must pay to acquire
the ownership of a particular type of capital (machine). P
21. __________ denotes the price of capital. The __________ rate of capital
equals what it costs a firm to use a machine over the course
22. __________ of a year. v denotes the cost of capital __________.

Present discounted value focuses on the demand for
23. __________ capital __________ rather than the demand for capital
services. When a firm purchases a machine, the machine
generates a stream of income over its lifetime. It generates
R_1 dollars next year, R_2 dollars in the year after that, etc.
The present discounted value (PDV) equals what would be

required at the present time to generate the stream of income:

$$PDV = \frac{R_1}{(1+r)} + \frac{R_2}{(1+r)^2} + \frac{R_3}{(1+r)^3} + \ . \ . \ .$$

$R_1/(1 + r)$ dollars at the present time would generate R_1
24. ____________ dollars ____________ year. $R_2/(1 + r)^2$ dollars at the present time would generate R_2 dollars in the year after next. The firm will purchase the machine whenever the present discounted value of the stream of income from a machine
25. ____________ ____________ the current price of the machine, P. Of course, as the firm purchases more and more machines, diminishing
26. ____________ marginal productivity will ____________ the income generated by each additional machine. Eventually, the price of a machine will equal its present discounted value which
27. ____________ establishes an ____________. We can show that this equilibrium condition $P = PDV$ is equivalent to $v = P(r + d)$.

HUMAN CAPITAL

People can invest in themselves by acquiring human capital. We can enroll in college, learn new skills, accept apprenticeships, etc. Like a firm investing in new machines,
28. ____________ all these activities involve some sacrifice at the ____________ time in the hope of future gain. While investing in human capital is similar to investing in physical capital, one important difference exists. Physical capital can be
29. ____________ ____________ from one firm to another; that is, firms can buy and sell machines. We cannot transfer human capital,
30. ____________ however. If one person acquires a skill, he ____________ sell that skill to another individual.

PRICING OF FINITE NATURAL RESOURCES

Production of an exhaustible resource today reduces
31. ____________ the amount that will be available in the ____________. Thus, when a firm produces an exhaustible resource now, it will
32. ____________ not be able to sell as much in the ____________. Economists
33. ____________ call this opportunity cost a ____________ cost. The magnitude of the scarcity cost depends on the expectation of future prices. If we believe that the price will rise rapidly, then the sale of the resource today will lead to a large
34. ____________ ____________ in future revenues. The scarcity cost would be

35. ____________ ____________. On the other hand, if we believe that the price will rise very slowly, the scarcity cost would be small.

We estimate scarcity costs by comparing the price to

36. ____________ ____________ production costs. In a perfectly competitive industry, the price fully reflects all costs. Therefore, the scarcity costs would equal the difference between the price and marginal production costs.

MULTIPLE-CHOICE QUESTIONS

37. ______ Economists use the word capital to refer to
   - a. man-made nonlabor resources.
   - b. corporate stocks.
   - c. corporate bonds.
   - d. U. S. government bonds.
   - e. b, c, and d.

38. ______ Capital is
   - a. the stock of man-made nonlabor resources which exists at one point in time.
   - b. the flow of man-made nonlabor resources which exists at one point in time.
   - c. the stock of man-made nonlabor resources which is produced over a period of time.
   - d. the flow of man-made nonlabor resources which is produced over a period of time.
   - e. a and c.

39. ______ Investment is
   - a. the stock of man-made nonlabor resources which exists at one point in time.
   - b. the flow of man-made nonlabor resources which exists at one point in time.
   - c. the stock of man-made nonlabor resources which is produced over a period of time.
   - d. the flow of man-made nonlabor resources which is produced over a period of time.
   - e. a and c.

40. ______ Capital accumulation involves
   a. withdrawing some output from current consumption.
   b. investing output in man-made nonlabor resources.
   c. the purchase of stocks and bonds.
   d. using man-made nonlabor resources to produce output in the future.
   e. a, b, and d.

41. ______ The rate of return indicates the rate at which
   a. future output withdrawn from consumption can be converted into present output.
   b. present output withdrawn from consumption can be converted into future output.
   c. banks can borrow from the Federal Reserve Board.
   d. capital depreciates.
   e. b and d.

42. ______ The rental rate of a machine equals
   a. the initial purchase price of the machine.
   b. the yearly opportunity costs of using the machine.
   c. the yearly depreciation costs of using the machine.
   d. the sum of the yearly opportunity and depreciation costs.
   e. a and d.

43. ______ The yearly opportunity cost of using a machine equals the price of the machine times the
   a. interest rate.
   b. depreciation rate.
   c. sum of the interest rate and the depreciation rate.
   d. difference between the interest rate and the depreciation rate.
   e. none of the above.

44. ______ The yearly depreciation cost of using a machine equals the price of the machine times the
   a. interest rate.
   b. depreciation rate.
   c. sum of the interest rate and the depreciation rate.
   d. difference between the interest rate and the depreciation rate.
   e. none of the above.

45. ______ The rental rate of a machine equals the price of the machine times the

a. interest rate.
b. depreciation rate.
c. sum of the interest rate and the depreciation rate.
d. difference between the interest rate and the depreciation rate.
e. none of the above.

46. ______ The rental rate associated with owning a machine

a. is less than the rental rate associated with renting the machine.
b. is greater than the rental rate associated with renting the machine.
c. is equal to the rental rate associated with renting the machine.
d. may be less than, greater than, or equal to the rental rate associated with renting the machine.
e. is always negative.

47. ______ Which of the following will not affect a firm's decision to invest?

a. whether the firm plans to own or rent the machines.
b. an increase in the interest rate.
c. a decrease in the interest rate.
d. an increase in the depreciation allowed by the tax laws.
e. a and d.

48. ______ An increase in the interest rate

a. increases the rental rate of a machine.
b. decreases the rental rate of a machine.
c. does not change the rental rate of a machine.
d. typically decreases investment.
e. a and d.

49. ______ The present discounted value of a stream of payments is

a. calculated by summing each year's payment together.
b. calculated by summing the product of each year's payment times the interest rate.
c. calculated by summing the difference between each year's payment and the interest.
d. that which is required at the present time to generate the stream of payments.
e. that which would be produced by the stream of payments in the future if all payments were saved.

50. ______ When comparing next year's dollars with this year's dollars one must keep in mind that next year's dollars

a. are worth more.
b. are worth less.
c. are worth precisely the same.
d. may be worth more, less, or the same.
e. are worth nothing.

51. ______ When an individual acquires a skill, he is described as investing in

a. physical capital.
b. a nonlabor resource.
c. human capital.
d. a corporation.
e. a and c.

52. ______ The production of an exhaustible resource at the present time

a. increases the amount that can be produced in the future.
b. decreases the amount that can be produced in the future.
c. has no effect on the amount that can be produced in the future.
d. may increase, decrease, or have no effect on the amount that can be produced in the future.
e. decreases the amount that can be produced in the future only if the input is inferior.

53. ______ The scarcity cost is

a. the out-of-pocket cost a firm incurs when producing an exhaustible resource at the present time.
b. the accounting cost a firm incurs when producing an exhaustible resource at the present time.
c. the opportunity cost a firm incurs when producing an exhaustible resource at the present time.
d. the sum of the accounting and opportunity costs a firm incurs when producing an exhaustible resource at the present time.
e. a and b.

54. ______ If a firm believes that the price of an exhaustible resource will rise rapidly in the future, scarcity cost

a. will be low.
b. will be high.
c. will be unaffected.
d. may be high, low, or unaffected.
e. will be negative.

RUNNING GLOSSARY

55. ____________ Capital stock: the total amount of machines, buildings, and all other man-made ____________ resources in an economy.

56. ____________ Rate of return: the increase in future output made possible by investing one unit of ____________ output in capital accumulation.

57. ____________ ____________ goods: goods that are purchased today by investing some present output as capital whose output is then consumed in the future.

58. ____________ Investment: the purchase of ____________ capital.

59. ____________ Present discounted value: the present value of funds payable in the future after taking account of the opportunity cost of ____________ foregone.

60. ____________ ____________ capital: capital in the form of learned abilities acquired through training, education, or experience.

61. ____________ Yield: the interest rate at which the present discounted value of the returns from an investment are exactly equal to the investment's current ____________.

62. ____________ ____________ costs: the opportunity costs of forgone future production that cannot be made because of current production that uses exhaustible resources.

63. ____________ ____________: payment for the current use of funds.

64. ____________ Compound interest: interest paid on prior ____________ earned.

65. ____________ Perpetuity: a promise of a certain number of dollars each year, ____________.

ANSWERS

1. output
2. investing
3. future
4. present
5. upward
6. equals
7. less
8. present
9. Depreciation
10. Opportunity
11. interest
12. equal
13. rent
14. explicit
15. implicit
16. decreases
17. increases
18. services
19. one
20. period
21. rental
22. services
23. stock
24. next
25. exceeds
26. reduce
27. equilibrium
28. present
29. transferred
30. cannot
31. future
32. future
33. scarcity
34. decrease
35. high
36. current
37. a
38. a
39. d
40. e
41. b
42. d
43. a
44. b
45. c
46. c
47. a
48. a
49. d
50. b
51. c
52. b
53. c
54. b
55. nonlabor
56. current
57. Future
58. new
59. interest
60. Human
61. cost
62. Scarcity
63. Interest
64. interest
65. forever

PART 6

PRICING OF FACTORS OF PRODUCTION

WALKING TOUR PROBLEMS

SUBSTITUTION AND OUTPUT EFFECTS

1. Initially, the wage rate of labor is \$5.00 and the rental rate of capital is \$10.00. The firm is producing 1000 units of output. The wage rate increases from \$5.00 to \$7.50. Labor and capital are normal inputs.

   a. What happens to the slope of the firm's equal cost curve?

   The slope of the firm's equal cost curve is determined by the wage-rental ratio; it is the negative of the wage rate divided by the rental rate. Since the wage rate has risen, the equal costs curve has become

1. ____________ ____________ steeply sloped.

   The answer is it becomes more steeply sloped.

   b. As a consequence of the substitution effect, what has happened to the cost minimizing combination of labor and capital?

   The substitution effect indicates how the firm's choice of inputs would be affected, if it were to keep the level of output constant. Because labor has become

2. ____________ more ____________ relative to capital, the firm would substitute capital for labor if it wanted to produce the same level of output.

   The answer is there is less labor and more capital.

   c. Typically what happens to the firm's marginal cost curve? To its profit-maximizing level of output?

Since the cost of an input has increased, the marginal
3. ____________ cost curve typically shifts ____________.

The answer is it shifts up.

Since the marginal cost curve has shifted up, the
4. ____________ profit-maximizing level of output ____________.

The answer is it decreases.

d. As a consequence of the output effect what happens to the cost minimizing combination of capital and labor?

The output effect indicates how the firm's choice of
5. ____________ inputs are affected by the ____________ in the level of
6. ____________ production. The level of output has ____________. If
an input is normal when the level of output
7. ____________ decreases, the firm uses ____________; on the other
8. ____________ hand if an input is ____________ when the level of
output decreases, the firm uses more. Since both
labor and capital are normal, the usage of each will
9. ____________ ____________ as a consequence of the output effect.

The answer is both decrease.

e. Accounting for both the substitution and output effects, what happens to the usage of labor and capital?

For labor the substitution and output effects work in
the same direction causing the amount of labor used
10. ____________ to ____________ unambiguously. With capital the
substitution effect leads to more usage, but the output
effect leads to less; the total effect is uncertain.

The answer is less labor is used and there is an ambiguous effect on capital.

2. Initially, the wage rate of labor is $5.00 and the rental rate of capital is $10.00. The firm is producing 1000 units of output. The wage rate increases from $5.00 to $7.50. Labor is a normal input; capital is inferior.

a. What happens to the slope of the firm's equal cost curve?

The slope of the firm's equal cost curve is determined
11. ___________ by the wage-rental ratio; it is the ___________ of the wage rate divided by the rental rate. Since the wage rate has risen, the equal costs curve has become
12. ___________ ___________ steeply sloped.

The answer is it becomes more steeply sloped.

b. As a consequence of the substitution effect, what has happened to the cost minimizing combination of labor and capital?

The substitution effect indicates how the firm's choice of inputs would be affected, if it were to keep the
13. ___________ level of output ___________. Because labor has become more expensive relative to capital, the firm
14. ___________ would substitute ___________ for labor if it wanted to produce the same level of output.

The answer is there is less labor and more capital.

c. Typically what happens to the firm's marginal cost curve? To its profit-maximizing level of output?

Since the cost of an input has increased, the marginal costs curve typically shifts up.

The answer is it shifts up.

Since the marginal cost curve has shifted
15. ___________ ___________, the profit- maximizing level of output has decreased.

The answer is it decreases.

d. As a consequence of the output effect what happens to the cost minimizing combination of capital and labor?

The output effect indicates how the firm's choice of
16. ___________ inputs is affected by the ___________ in the level of production. The level of output has decreased. If an

17. ____________ input is ____________ when the level of output decreases, the firm uses less; on the other hand if an input is inferior when the level of output decreases,
18. ____________ the firm uses ____________. Since labor is normal, less labor is used as a consequence of the output effect;
19. ____________ since capital is inferior, ____________ capital is used.

The answer is labor decreases and capital increases.

e. Accounting for both the substitution and output effects, what happens to the usage of labor and capital?

For labor the substitution and output effects work in
20. ____________ the ____________ direction causing the amount of labor used to decrease. For capital the substitution and output effects work in the same direction also
21. ____________ causing the amount used to ____________.

The answer is less labor used and more capital used.

3. Initially, the wage rate of labor is \$5.00 and the rental rate of capital is \$10.00. The firm is producing 1000 units of output. The rental rate decreases from \$10.00 to \$8.00. Labor is a normal input; capital is inferior.

a. What happens to the slope of the firm's equal cost
22. ____________ curve?

b. As a consequence of the substitution effect, what has happened to the cost minimizing combination of
23. ____________ labor and capital?

c. Typically what happens to the firm's marginal cost
24. ____________ curve? What happens to its profit-maximizing level
25. ____________ of output?

d. As a consequence of the output effect what happens to the cost minimizing combination of capital and
26. ____________ labor?

e. Accounting for both the substitution and output effects, what happens to the usage of labor and
27. ____________ capital?

4. Initially, the wage rate of labor is \$5.00 and the rental rate of capital is \$10.00. The firm is producing 1000 units of output. The wage rate decreases from \$5.00 to \$3.50. Labor and capital are normal inputs.

   a. What happens to the slope of the firm's equal cost curve?

28. ____________

   b. As a consequence of the substitution effect, what has happened to the cost minimizing combination of labor and capital?

29. ____________

   c. Typically what happens to the firm's marginal cost curve? What happens to its profit-maximizing level of output?

30. ____________
31. ____________

   d. As a consequence of the output effect what happens to the cost minimizing combination of capital and labor?

32. ____________

   e. Accounting for both the substitution and output effects, what happens to the usage of labor and capital?

33. ____________

5. Initially, the wage rate of labor is \$5.00 and the rental rate of capital is \$10.00. The firm is producing 1000 units of output. The wage rate increases from \$5.00 to \$7.50. Labor is an inferior input; capital is normal.

   a. What happens to the slope of the firm's equal cost curve?

34. ____________

   b. As a consequence of the substitution effect, what has happened to the cost minimizing combination of labor and capital?

35. ____________

   c. Typically what happens to the firm's marginal cost curve? What happens to its profit-maximizing level of output?

36. ____________
37. ____________

   d. As a consequence of the output effect what happens to the cost minimizing combination of capital and labor?

38. ____________

e. Accounting for both the substitution and output effects, what happens to the usage of labor and
39. ___________ capital?

PRICING OF LABOR

1. The labor market is competitive and the market for the good produced is competitive also. The price of the good produced has increased.

   a. What happens to the marginal physical product of labor curve?

   Nothing, the increase in the price of the good will
40. ___________ ___________ affect the marginal productivity of labor.

   The answer is nothing.

   b. What happens to the marginal revenue product of labor curve?

   The marginal revenue product of labor equals the change in the firm's total revenues resulting from the
41. ___________ employment of one additional unit of ___________.
When one additional unit of labor is hired, total output increases by an amount equal to the marginal
42. ___________ ___________ product of labor. Each additional unit of output increases total revenue by an amount equal
43. ___________ to marginal ___________. Consequently, marginal revenue product of labor equals marginal physical
44. ___________ product of labor ___________ marginal revenue. Since the market for the good being produced is competitive, marginal revenue will equal the
45. ___________ ___________ of the good. The higher price of the
46. ___________ good will ___________ marginal revenue causing the marginal revenue product of labor curve to shift
47. ___________ ___________ and to the right.

   The answer is it shifts up and to the right.

   c. What happens to each individual firm's demand curve for labor? To the market demand curve for labor?

Each individual firm's demand curve for labor is its
48. ____________ marginal ____________ product of labor curve. Since each firm's marginal revenue product curve has shifted up and to the right, each firm's individual demand curve for labor will shift to the
49. ____________ ____________.

The answer is it shifts to the right.

The market demand curve for labor is the
50. ____________ ____________ sum of each firm's individual demand curve. Since each firm's individual demand curve shifts to the right, the market demand curve will shift
51. ____________ to the ____________ also.

The answer is it shifts to the right.

d. What happens to the supply curve for labor?

The increase in the price of the good being produced has no effect on the supply curve for labor.

The answer is nothing.

e. What happens to the equilibrium wage rate and quantity of labor?

The equilibrium wage rate and quantity of labor in a competitive labor market is determined by the
52. ____________ ____________ demand and supply curves for labor. The demand curve has shifted to the right and the supply curve is unchanged. The equilibrium wage
53. ____________ rate and quantity will ____________.

The answer is both increase.

2. The labor market is competitive and the market for the good produced is competitive also. Labor becomes more productive.

a. What happens to the marginal physical product of
54. ____________ labor curve?

55. ____________ b. What happens to the marginal revenue product of labor curve?

56. ____________
57. ____________ c. What happens to each individual firm's demand curve for labor? The market demand curve for labor?

58. ____________ d. What happens to the supply curve for labor?

59. ____________ e. What happens to the equilibrium wage rate and quantity of labor?

3. The labor market is competitive and the market for the good produced is competitive also. The supply of labor decreases.

60. ____________ a. What happens to the marginal physical product of labor curve?

61. ____________ b. What happens to the marginal revenue product of labor curve?

62. ____________
63. ____________ c. What happens to each individual firm's demand curve for labor? The market demand curve for labor?

64. ____________ d. What happens to the supply curve for labor?

65. ____________ e. What happens to the equilibrium wage rate and quantity of labor?

4. The labor market is competitive and the market for the good produced is a monopoly. The monopolist's fixed costs increase.

66. ____________ a. What happens to the marginal physical product of labor curve?

67. ____________ b. What happens to the marginal revenue product of labor curve?

68. ____________
69. ____________ c. What happens to each individual firm's demand curve for labor? The market demand curve for labor?

70. ____________ d. What happens to the supply curve for labor?

71. ____________ e. What happens to the equilibrium wage rate and quantity of labor?

5. The labor market is competitive and the market for the good produced is a monopoly. The monopolist's marginal revenues increase.

72. ____________ a. What happens to the marginal physical product of labor curve?

73. ____________ b. What happens to the marginal revenue product of labor curve?

74. ____________
75. ____________ c. What happens to each individual firm's demand curve for labor? The market demand curve for labor?

76. ____________ d. What happens to the supply curve for labor?

77. ____________ e. What happens to the equilibrium wage rate and quantity of labor?

ANSWERS

1. more
2. expensive
3. up
4. decreases
5. change
6. decreased
7. less
8. inferior
9. decrease
10. decrease
11. negative
12. more
13. constant
14. capital
15. up
16. change
17. normal
18. more
19. more
20. same
21. increase
22. more steeply sloped
23. less L, more K
24. shifts down
25. increases
26. more L, less K
27. both ambiguous
28. less steeply sloped
29. more L, less K
30. shifts up
31. decreases
32. more L, more K
33. More L, K ambiguous
34. more steeply sloped
35. less L, more K
36. shifts down
37. increases
38. more L, less K
39. both ambiguous
40. not
41. labor
42. physical
43. revenue
44. times
45. price
46. increase
47. up
48. revenue
49. right
50. horizontal
51. right
52. market
53. increase
54. shifts up and right
55. shifts up and right
56. shifts right
57. shifts right
58. nothing
59. both increase
60. nothing
61. nothing
62. nothing
63. nothing
64. shifts left
65. wage up, quanity down
66. nothing
67. nothing
68. nothing
69. nothing
70. nothing
71. nothing
72. nothing
73. shift up and right
74. shifts right
75. shifts right
76. nothing
77. both increase

PART 7

LIMITS OF THE MARKET

CHAPTER 22

EXTERNALITIES AND PROPERTY RIGHTS

WALKING TOUR SUMMARIES

DEFINITION

An externality occurs whenever the price system does not account for an action undertaken by one economic actor
1. ____________ which directly affects the well-being of ____________ actor.

EXTERNALITIES, MARKETS, AND ALLOCATIONAL EFFICIENCY

Consider two firms, one producing eyeglasses and one charcoal. The charcoal firm pollutes the atmosphere whenever it produces charcoal. These pollutants damage the grinding instruments used by the eyeglass firm. Of course the production of eyeglasses depends on the inputs hired by the eyeglass firm. Eyeglass production also depends on the charcoal firm's level of production, however. When the charcoal firm increases production, it emits more pollutants causing more damage to the eyeglass firm. The
2. ____________ pollution represents an ____________. The price system does not account for the harm which the charcoal firm inflicts upon the eyeglass firm. Inefficiency results because
3. ____________ the charcoal firm's ____________ costs are not equal to its social costs. The charcoal firm does not account for the damages done by its pollution; its private marginal cost
4. ____________ curve lies ____________ its social marginal cost curve. The difference in height represents the damage done by the

pollutants. Since efficiency requires production to occur
5. ___________ where price equals marginal ___________ cost, the charcoal
firm produces too much charcoal.

TRADITIONAL WAYS OF COPING WITH EXTERNALITIES

First, economists have long advocated the use of taxes to deal with externalities. The government could impose an excise tax on the charcoal firm. If the tax equaled the
6. ___________ difference between the private and ___________ marginal
costs, the charcoal firm would reduce production to the efficient level. Second, the two firms could merge. The single firm would recognize the detrimental effect that charcoal production has on its glass grinding equipment. The firm would include this injurious effect in its marginal private cost curve of charcoal production. Consequently, the
7. ___________ single firm would ___________ the production of charcoal.
8. ___________ Both taxes and mergers are traditional way to ___________
the externality.

PROPERTY RIGHTS, ALLOCATION, AND EQUITY

Property rights refer to the legal specification of who owns a good. Furthermore, property rights may restrict the types of trades that the owner is allowed to make with others. Society at large owns ___________ property.
9. ___________ Therefore anyone can use it. Specific individuals own
10. ___________ ___________ property. Private property may be
exchangeable or nonexchangeable.

If bargaining were costless in our charcoal-eyeglass externality example and if the air were made exchangeable
11. ___________ private property, bargaining would lead to ___________.
The efficient outcome would occur regardless of which firm received the property right. If the charcoal firm received the right, the eyeglass firm would bribe the charcoal firm to reduce air pollutants. On the other hand, if the eyeglass firm received the right, the charcoal firm would pay for the right to pollute the air. While the assignment of
12. ___________ ___________ rights will not affect the allocation of
13. ___________ resources, it will have a ___________ impact. If the
charcoal firm receives the property right, it would receive a payment (from the eyeglass firm). Alternatively, if the

eyeglass firm receives the right, the charcoal firm would make a payment (to the eyeglass firm).

14. __________ If bargaining were not costless, __________ would typically result, however. Environmental externalities
15. __________ usually involve __________ bargaining costs. For example, air pollution in an urban area affects the well-
16. __________ being of __________ individuals. It is frequently difficult, if not impossible, to organize these individuals into an effective bargaining unit. Furthermore, how can the affected parties calculate the monetary value of the losses suffered.
17. __________ When bargaining costs are __________, the assignment of property rights does affect the allocation of resources.

THE EVOLUTION OF PROPERTY RIGHTS

Some economists argue that legal institutions evolve
18. __________ over time toward economically __________ outcomes. They contend that society assigns private property rights whenever the benefits exceed the costs. That is, property rights evolve whenever the benefits of using property rights
19. __________ to cope with an __________ exceed the costs of enforcing private property rights.

COMMON PROPERTY

20. __________ All members of society can use __________ property without a direct charge. This frequently results in overuse, however. For example, ocean fisheries are, in most cases, common property. Each fisherman considers his
21. __________ __________ costs of catching fish. Each ignores the externality, however. Whenever one fisherman catches more fish, the stock is depleting. This makes it more costly
22. __________ for __________ to catch fish not only in the current year, but also in the future.

MULTIPLE-CHOICE QUESTIONS

23. ______ An externality causes competitive markets to be inefficient because
    a. one economic actor's well-being is affected by another in a way that is not taken into account by the normal operations of the market system.
    b. the market system does not make an economic actor aware of the full social consequences of his actions.
    c. consumers are public spirited.
    d. a and b.
    e. a and c.

24. ______ Which of the following are traditional solutions to the externality problem?
    a. forcing the firm producing the externality to shut down.
    b. placing a tax on the economic activity that produces the externality.
    c. prohibiting the activity associated with the externality.
    d. a, b, and c.
    e. a and b.

25. ______ Property rights
    a. specify who owns a good.
    b. can never be bought and/or sold.
    c. for a particular good are always owned by a single person.
    d. specify the types of trades the owner of a good can make with others.
    e. a and d.

26. ______ Private property
    a. is owned by society at large.
    b. must be exchangeable.
    c. must by nonexchangeable.
    d. is owned by one specific person or group.
    e. c and d.

27. ______ If bargaining were costless the assignment of private exchangeable property rights for an externality would
    a. guarantee efficiency.
    b. guarantee inefficiency.
    c. always have no effect.
    d. none of the above.
    e. b and c.

28. ______ If bargaining were costless exactly who received the property rights for an externality would

a. influence the allocation of resources.
b. not influence the allocation of resources.
c. not have a distributional impact.
d. a and c.
e. b and c.

29. ______ If bargaining were costly exactly who received the property rights for an externality would

a. influence the allocation of resources.
b. not influence the allocation of resources.
c. have a distributional impact.
d. not have a distributional impact.
e. a and c.

30. ______ Common property

a. is owned by society at large.
b. can be used by anyone with a direct charge.
c. is owned by a small group of individuals.
d. is owned by one specific group of people.
e. a and b.

RUNNING GLOSSARY

31. ____________ Externality: the effect of one party's economic activities on ____________ party that is not taken into account by the price system.

32. ____________ ____________ costs: costs of production that include both input costs and costs of the externalities that production may cause.

33. ____________ Pigovian tax: a tax or subsidy on an externality that brings about an equality of private and ____________ marginal costs.

34. ____________ ____________ of an externality: incorporation of the social marginal costs of an externality into an economic actor's decision (as through taxation or merger).

35. ____________ Property rights: the legal specification of who owns a good and the trades the ___________ is allowed to make with it.

36. ____________ Common property: property that may be used by __________ without cost.

37. ____________ __________ property: property that is owned by specific people who may prevent others from using it.

38. ____________ Coase theorem: if bargaining is ___________, the social cost of an externality will be taken into account by the parties, and the allocation of resources will be the same no matter how property rights are assigned.

ANSWERS

1. another
2. externality
3. private
4. below
5. social
6. social
7. reduce
8. internalize
9. common
10. private
11. efficiency
12. property
13. distributional
14. inefficiency
15. high
16. many
17. high
18. efficient
19. externality
20. common
21. private
22. others
23. d
24. b
25. e
26. d
27. a
28. b
29. e
30. a
31. another
32. Social
33. social
34. internalization
35. owner
36. anyone
37. Private
38. costless

CHAPTER 23

PUBLIC GOODS AND PUBLIC CHOICE

WALKING TOUR SUMMARIES

PUBLIC GOODS

The most common definition of public goods stresses
two aspects: non-exclusivity and non-rivalry. Exclusivity
1. ___________ refers to whether an individual can be ___________ from
the benefits of a good, once the good is produced. A
hamburger is exclusive, whereas national defense is not.
Rivalry refers to the costs of extending the benefits to an
2. ___________ ___________ individual. A hamburger is rival, whereas a
bridge at an off-peak hour is not.

Private markets tend to produce an inefficiently
3. ___________ ___________ level of public goods. Each consumer in
making his decision about whether or not to purchase a
good only considers the benefits that will accrue to him
individually. In the case of public goods this means that the
potential buyer will not take into account the benefits that
4. ___________ others enjoy. Since each consumer ___________ the full
social benefits involved, too little of a public good will be
produced in a private market.

5. ___________ As Lindahl demonstrates ___________ provision of a
public good requires information regarding each
individual's demand for the good. As a consequence of
6. ___________ nonexclusivity, however, a ___________ rider problem
arises whenever one attempts to collect this information.
Each individual has an incentive to misrepresent his true
7. ___________ preference regarding the ___________ good.

LOCAL PUBLIC GOODS

Some economists suggest that a market-like
mechanism exists for providing those public goods whose
8. ___________ benefits are confined to a ___________ rather than national
level. Just as individuals "vote with their dollars" to express
their preferences in a market for private goods, individuals

may "vote with their feet" to express their preferences by choosing their community of residence.

DIRECT VOTING AND RESOURCE ALLOCATION

If preferences are single-peaked, majority rule will
9. ___________ result in the adoption of the ___________ voter's most
favored choice. Unfortunately, since many issues of public choice are multidimensional, preferences are typically not single peaked. In such cases, a voting equilibrium need not exist; every proposal may be defeated by some other proposal.

ANALYSIS OF REPRESENTATIVE GOVERNMENT

10. ___________ ___________ argues that parties in a representative
democracy will behave in ways similar to firms in an
11. ___________ economy. A party will seek to ___________ its political
support; it will pursue policies up to the point at which the marginal gain in votes from those individuals who benefit
12. ___________ from the policy ___________ the marginal loss in votes
from those who are hurt.

13. ___________ ___________ describes the process of representative
democracy quite differently by focusing on the role played
14. ___________ by special interest groups. ___________ contends that in a
pluralistic society a systematic bias exists concerning the kinds of pressure groups that will develop. He contends that only those groups that represent narrow special interests will arise. In these close-knit groups each member
15. ___________ recognizes the benefits of ___________ action. Groups
representing the broad public interest (that is the interests of a large number of individuals) will not develop as a
16. ___________ consequence of the ___________ rider problem, however.

These two views of representative democracy can be
17. ___________ combined by recognizing the ___________ constraint.
Special interest groups no doubt play a major role in the process, but politicians still must be concerned with
18. ___________ pursuing policies that obtain the support of a ___________
of their electorate.

MULTIPLE-CHOICE QUESTIONS

19. ______ The exclusive aspect of a good indicates
    a. how much it costs to extend the benefits of the good to an additional person.
    b. whether an individual can be excluded from consuming the benefits of a good once the good has been produced.
    c. whether the good is produced in a competitive industry.
    d. whether the good is sold by exclusive shops.
    e. a and b.

20. ______ The rivalry aspect of a good indicates
    a. how much it costs to extend the benefits of the good to an additional person.
    b. whether an individual can be excluded from consuming the benefits of a good once the good has been produced.
    c. whether the good is produced in a competitive industry.
    d. whether the good is sold by exclusive shops.
    e. b and c.

21. ______ Pure public goods are
    a. rival.
    b. nonrival.
    c. nonexclusive.
    d. a and c.
    e. b and c.

22. ______ Private markets produce
    a. an efficient level of pure public goods always.
    b. an inefficiently low level of pure public goods always.
    c. an inefficiently high level of pure public goods always.
    d. a level of pure public goods that may be greater than, less than, or equal to the efficient level.
    e. an efficient level of pure public goods when they are normal goods.

23. ______ Private markets produce an inefficiently low level of pure public goods because each individual in making his decision to purchase the good considers the benefits accruing to
    a. all society.
    b. the entire community.
    c. himself.
    d. the entire state.
    e. b and d.

24. ______ With a pure public good the free rider problem arises because
   a. of the good's nonexclusivity.
   b. of the good's nonrivalry.
   c. each individual has an incentive to misrepresent his preferences for the good.
   d. of the good's rivalry.
   e. a and c.

25. ______ If voter preferences are single peaked, majority rule results in
   a. no clear cut choice.
   b. the choice of the average voter.
   c. the choice of the median voter.
   d. a deadlock.
   e. a and d.

26. ______ Downs argues that in a representative democracy political parties will
   a. seek to maximize their political support.
   b. pursue policies up to the point at which the marginal gain in votes from individuals who benefit from the policy equals the marginal loss from those who are hurt.
   c. represent the broad public interest.
   d. represent the interests of narrow special concerns.
   e. a and b.

27. ______ Olson argues that in a representative democracy the special interest groups which develop will
   a. seek to maximize their political support.
   b. pursue policies up to the point at which the marginal gain in votes from individuals who benefit from the policy equals the marginal loss from those who are hurt.
   c. represent the broad public interest.
   d. represent the interests of narrow special concerns.
   e. a and c.

RUNNING GLOSSARY

28. ____________ ____________ goods: goods that provide benefits that no one can be excluded from enjoying.

29. ____________ Nonrival goods: goods that additional consumers may use at ____________ marginal costs.

30. ____________ ____________ goods: goods that are both nonexclusive and nonrival.

31. ____________ Lindahl equilibrium: balance between people's demand for public goods and the ____________ shares that each must pay for them.

32. ____________ Free rider: a consumer of a nonexclusive good who does not pay for it in the hope that ____________ consumers will.

33. ____________ ____________ voter: a voter whose preferences for a public good represent the middle point of all voters' preferences for the good.

34. ____________ Rent-seeking behavior: firms or individuals influencing ____________ policy to increase their own welfare.

ANSWERS

1. excluded
2. additional
3. low
4. underestimates
5. efficient
6. free
7. public
8. local
9. median
10. Downs
11. maximize
12. equals
13. Pluralism
14. Olson
15. collective
16. free
17. reelection
18. majority
19. b
20. a
21. e
22. b
23. c
24. e
25. c
26. e
27. d
28. Nonexclusive
29. zero
30. Public
31. tax
32. other
33. Median
34. government